THE DILEMMAS
OF
INDIVIDUALISM

THE DILEMMAS OF INDIVIDUALISM

Status, Liberty, and American Constitutional Law

Michael J. Phillips

Contributions in American Studies, Number 67

Greenwood Press
Westport, Connecticut • London, England

Library of Congress Cataloging in Publication Data

Phillips, Michael Joseph.
    The dilemmas of individualism.

    (Contributions in American studies, ISSN 0084-9227 ;
no. 67).
    Bibliography: p.
    Includes index.
    1. Liberty.   2. Status (Law)—United States.
3. United States—Constitutional law.   I. Title.
II. Series.
KF4749.P46   1983   342.73'085   82-15580
ISBN 0-313-23690-9 (lib. bdg.) 347.30285

Library of Congress Catalog Card Number: 82-15580
ISBN: 0-313-23690-9
ISSN: 0084-9227

First published in 1983

Greenwood Press
A division of Congressional Information Service, Inc.
88 Post Road West
Westport, Connecticut 06881

Printed in the United States of America

10 9 8 7 6 5 4 3 2 1

Contents

Preface

The 1960s and 1970s saw any number of books attributing the industrialized world's increasing problems to the liberalism it has so wholeheartedly embraced. These books have had little to do with the recent triumphs of conservative politicians and policies. Indeed, although the label may mislead, their authors are probably best classed as people of the Left. The body of ideas they attacked went beyond the competing but overlapping liberalisms of figures like Franklin D. Roosevelt, John F. Kennedy, Henry Jackson and George McGovern. To such critics, liberalism is a body of ideas dominating the entire American political spectrum. This liberalism had its origins in the seventeenth century, but only in recent decades has it clearly overcome lingering premodern values and institutions. Its ruling ideas are very familiar, so much so that they now comprise a set of givens for many Americans. Central to this liberalism is a highly individualistic idea of freedom. Other elements of the syndrome are: an emphasis on least-common-denominator values like material plenty, physical security, and the satisfaction of hedonistic impulses; an egoistic, exploitive attitude toward nature; and a general disregard for traditional forms of ordering and conceptions of virtue. From time to time, the counterculture of the 1960s showed some disposition to reject this syndrome of attitudes, although its liberal aspects won out in the end. Disaffection with this syndrome also helped fuel the environmental movement of the 1970s. These movements,

however, and the general critique they reflected, hardly went
all the way in their rejection of liberal ideas. Left virtually un-
touched by both was liberalism's indeterminate view of freedom. This book is an attempt to remedy this deficiency.

Formally, this book examines the themes of status and freedom as they manifest themselves in American constitutional
law. Chapter 1 develops the conceptual apparatus used throughout the book. This involves three contrasting ideas of freedom
and their different relations with two general forms of status.
Chapters 2 through 4 classify different constitutional statuses
in terms of these various relations. Chapter 2 discusses a lengthy
array of statuses in which the defining feature of the status is a
diminution of constitutional rights for an affected group. It
also chronicles the overall demise of these statuses throughout
the twentieth century. Chapter 3 abandons the realm of the
formally constitutional to examine the status-freedom relations
obtaining in modern organizations. Chapter 4 returns to expressly legal concerns by exploring the status features of recent efforts to assist racial minorities. Here, unlike chapter 2, a status
attribute can confer a practical legal benefit. Chapters 5 and 6
explore the implications of the different status-freedom relationships described in chapters 2 through 4. It is here that the
critique of liberalism's idea of freedom assumes importance.
Chapter 5 tries to render coherent these different relations by
employing a few very general assumptions about liberal freedom.
Chapter 6 employs these assumptions to take a speculative look
at the future. Its principal argument is that the need for control
will be the overriding concern of coming decades.

The chief actor in this book is something I call the liberal
individualist advance. This term refers to the longstanding historical movement toward a situation in which human behavior
reflects the choices of an unfettered ego, "I," or self. The vo-
luminous celebratory literature on this movement tends to
regard it as a virtually unqualified Good Thing. This book is
not an addition to that literature. It does not applaud the un-
folding of liberty from the Magna Carta through the Glorious
Revolution of 1688, the Declaration of Independence, the
Declaration of the Rights of Man, the Emancipation Proclama-
tion, the civil rights movement, and finally,perhaps, the libera-

tion of animals. Obviously, there are good reasons to treat this
movement in a favorable light, and if these are not given enough
emphasis here, it is because they have been repeated so often.
Instead, this book examines liberalism's version of freedom in
a no less one-sided fashion: as above all else a problem. Specifically, it argues that this idea of freedom is not personally or
socially viable without determinate restraints of one sort or
another, restraints it tends to erode as it continues its advance.
In their different ways, the status-freedom relationships of
chapters 2 and 3 display such restraints in action.

In making this argument, I adopt a more or less descriptive
posture. In saying this, I wish to skirt the well-known difficulties surrounding the relation between facts and values, as well
as related problems of social science methodology. Although
this book deals with value-related phenomena, it is not an
openly moralistic, hortatory endeavor. There is an obvious
rough-and-ready difference between writing that ethically evalu-
ates all that it touches and writing that merely attempts to
relate what is "there." This book, I hope, is largely of the latter
sort. It is mainly concerned with describing the problems and
contradictions generated by a particular conception of freedom
in as clinical a fashion as possible. No doubt its formally objective analysis is affected by my own values. To speak of freedom
as a problem, for instance, seems to imply an ethical standpoint.
In this connection, I can only state that although my enthusi-
asm for liberal individualism's current manifestations is well
under control, the available alternatives do not strike me as too
compelling either. In any event, I present no coherent system
of alternative moral possibilities because I have no such scheme
to offer.

By way of conclusion, a few additional qualifiers and caveats
seem appropriate. The final portions of this book are explora-
tory and fairly abstract. Although they are stated rather dog-
matically for stylistic reasons, they should be understood as
subject to numerous implicit qualifiers. My choice of formal
constitutional materials throughout the book is selective. I dis-
claim any specialized expertise about the intraorganizational
matters discussed in chapters 3 and 5, although I doubt that this
has much bearing on the validity of the conclusions I reach

there. While this book tends toward a view of historical causation in which ideas or forms of consciousness are the dominant forces, it does not explicitly advance any particular view of social change. At points within, the liberal individualist movement may appear personified, as a sort of Idea of which concrete social phenomena are merely reflections. For all that I know, this may be so. My intent, however, has been to start with the phenomena and to utilize the term *liberal individualist advance* as an abstraction helping to explain and order them, not as their progenitor. My use of this term parallels common catch phrases like the "rise of capitalism," "the movement toward equality" and so forth.

I would like to express my special thanks to Arthur Selwyn Miller, professor emeritus of law at the National Law Center of the George Washington University. Without his active encouragement, this book would never have been written. Thanks are also due to Professor Louis H. Mayo of the National Law Center; to Professor John D. Donnell of Indiana University's School of Business, who helped provide needed inducements at crucial times; and to Professor Robert H. Walker of George Washington University, for his many helpful suggestions. Thanks are finally due to Roberta Aubin, Amber Shacklett, and Nita Gay Rogers, who typed the manuscript. This book was completed in February of 1982, and, with a few minor exceptions, does not consider events occurring after that time.

THE DILEMMAS
OF
INDIVIDUALISM

CHAPTER 1

Freedom, Status, and Their Interrelations

For Americans, one would think, definition of the words *freedom* or *liberty* should pose few problems. Yet these terms have lent themselves to many different interpretations. In fact, abstract definitions of freedom abound, and the typology employed throughout this book hardly exhausts the subject. Central to almost all conceptions of liberty, however, is the requirement that human behavior issue from the true desires of an ego, "I," or self. One way of distinguishing different ideas of freedom is to identify the drives and desires each associates with the true self.[1]

Negative Freedom

The basic,"negative" conception of freedom is the simple absence of external obstacles.[2] To Thomas Hobbes, for instance, "By LIBERTY, is understood . . . the absence of external impediments."[3] This idea of freedom has probably found its most important expression in the natural rights tradition. Historically, as with Hobbes and Locke, its exponents often conceived society as the product of an actual or hypothetical contract of rights-bearing individuals in a state of nature.[4] Since in this view individuals are basically asocial, the principal means of maintaining order within the social compact is positive law in the form of external sovereign command—not group ties, internal restraints, and other such social or psychological checks.[5] However, although the opposition between the individual and the formal

political order is often the main concern of those defining freedom in negative terms, external social impediments can also
restrict freedom so conceived.

Positive Freedom

In its negative conception, freedom can be restricted only by
impediments external to the individual. In this case, the true
desires of the self would seem to include the full range of internal drives and motivations.[6] For these reasons, the negative
definition of liberty has been severely criticized. Internal checks
as well as external impediments can hamper the practical ability
to utilize a grant of negative liberty. A catatonic sitting unimpeded in the middle of an open field, for instance, may be free
in the negative sense, but only with difficulty can this freedom
be squared with our ordinary sense of liberty's meaning. This
point can easily be extended to cover heroin addicts, alcoholics,
those suffering from various personality disorders, those subject
to severe social and economic deprivation, and so forth. As the
late nineteenth-century British idealist philosopher Thomas Hill
Green put it in a well-known statement:

> [T]he mere removal of compulsion, the mere enabling a
> man to do as he likes, is in itself no contribution to true
> freedom. In one sense no man is so well able to do as he
> likes as the wandering savage. He has no master. There is
> no one to say him nay. Yet we do not count him really
> free, because the freedom of savagery is not strength, but
> weakness. The actual powers of the noblest savage do not
> admit of comparison with those of the humblest citizen
> of a law-abiding state. He is not the slave of man, but he
> is the slave of nature. Of compulsion by natural necessity
> he has plenty of experience, though of restraint by socie-
> ty none at all. Nor can he deliver himself from that com-
> pulsion except by submitting himself to this restraint. So
> to submit is the first step in true freedom, because the
> first step towards the full exercise of the faculties with
> which man is endowed.[7]

This true freedom, usually called positive freedom, was described by Green as follows:

When we speak of freedom as something to be so highly prized, we mean a positive power or capacity of doing or enjoying something worth doing or enjoying, and that, too, something we do or enjoy in common with others. We mean by it a power which each man exercises through the help or security given him by his fellowmen, and which he in turn helps to secure for them. When we measure the progress of a society by its growth in freedom, we measure it by the increasing development and exercise on the whole of those powers of contributing to social good with which we believe the members of society to be endowed; in short, by the greater power on the part of the citizens as a body to make the most and best of themselves.[8]

The notion of capacity is central to this positive conception of liberty, but this idea is hardly without ambiguities. Capacity may be viewed in authoritarian terms: as possessing some determinate content reflecting desirable forms of human life and the appropriate disposition of human energies. Here, freedom is often identified with the claims of the rational self.[9] Green seems to have been of this view ("something worth doing or enjoying"), and he saw Saint Paul, the Stoics, Kant, and Hegel as being of much the same opinion.[10] As Green read Hegel, for instance, "the man who is determined by the objects which the well ordered state presents to him is determined by that which is the perfect expression of his reason, and is thus free."[11] This view of freedom probably had its roots in the ethics of Plato and Aristotle, with their conception of human behavior as potentially tending toward some determinate ideal state. As developed by Hegel and the English neo-Hegelians, however, it tended to involve substantial concessions to modern individualism.[12] With similar concessions, it also appears in the work of certain contemporary thinkers. Richard Goodwin, for instance, has written:

... Capacity also contains a conception of purpose. It is capacity *for*. Thus, we cannot know the full dimensions of those "material conditions and capacity" which enter into the definition of freedom until we also understand what is meant by the "fulfillment of our humanity."

D. H. Lawrence writes, "Men are not free when they are doing just what they like. . . .Men are only free when they are doing what the deepest self likes. And there is getting down to the deepest self! It takes some digging."[13]

Exponents of negative freedom and many liberals generally regard this conception of liberty as a perversion of the term and a rationalization for quasi-totalitarian exercises in domination.[14] Although this point is in a sense well taken—it is difficult to be too suspicious of political movements prating about "true freedom" or the needs of one's "real self"—the accusation that the authoritarian position necessarily leads to the imposition of virtue by political means is rather wide of the mark. Hegel and the British idealists, for instance, tended to envision an order embodying a substantial identity of interests between the individual, intermediate groups, and the political state.[15] Given such a unity of purpose, outright coercion might play a relatively minor role in the process of social ordering. Also, the key assumption animating this broad view—the idea that human behavior displays an implicit striving toward some determinate state of virtue—is not self-evidently false. If the assumption actually is true, a society organized to facilitate such ends does not impose values but rather offers an opportunity for the ends of the true self to flower.

The other, liberal, conception of positive freedom is perhaps more of an inchoate tendency than a rigorously formulated doctrine, but it is no less important for that reason. Generally, it sees the idea of capacity in an open-ended or value-free sense, as expressing what is often called autonomy. According to this view, the perfectly free individual would possess the ability to recognize, appreciate, and choose among a theoretically infinite number of options, irrespective of their nature. In order for that to happen, the "I" or self might effectively have to detach itself from all the contents of consciousness and all subconscious drives, picking and choosing among them as it wills but not being determined by them.[16] This sort of freedom is, one assumes, not a completely attainable goal.[17] Nor is it likely that anyone adheres to it with complete consistency, since it is difficult to exclude all notions of desirable human behavior from the conception of freedom.

Despite its usual lack of explicit formulation, adherence to this form of positive liberty seems to be fairly widespread. Ronald Dworkin, for instance, has recently advocated something quite like it.

> [T]here are certain things we all want government to do. We want government, for example, to select methods of education, to sponsor culture, and to do much else that looks, on the surface, like endorsing one set of personal values against another and therefore contradicting liberalism. It is very important for liberals to develop a theory that would make a distinction here between enriching the choices available to people and enforcing a choice upon people. The crucial idea, it seems to me, is the idea of imagination. The liberal is concerned to expand imagination without imposing any particular choice upon imagination.[18]

This open-ended idea of capacity also seems to be implicit in much current discourse—as for example in 1970s-style statements about the desirability of "self-realization," the need to "maintain options," and the effort to "define one's self."[19]

This liberal version of positive freedom might appear to represent little more than an extension of negative freedom, the removal of external restraints being complemented by the eradication of internal constraints on the choices of the self. In fact, it is fairly common to see freedom defined as involving a mix of negative and positive elements.[20] But the conceptual distinction between these two ideas should be clear: negative freedom is typically concerned only with external restraints on the activity of the person, while the libertarian version of positive freedom involves the removal of internal restraints and promotion of a capacity for self-definition. Also, exponents of negative freedom and liberal positive freedom often have different views on the relationship between the individual and the political state. The former tend to emphasize traditional laissez-faire, while the latter usually see promotion of the conditions of effective individuality as an affirmative governmental responsibility.[21]

Status

A status can be defined as a social position characterized by a particular collection of rights and duties.[22] Theoretically, status differences might rest on a huge variety of personal traits, conditions, or affiliations.[23] Here, however, our concern is with statuses of considerable social incidence and significance. With that qualification in mind, a constitutional status can be defined as a special constitutional position involving legal rights or powers that differentiate those occupying it from the populace at large.[24]

Throughout this book, attention will focus on two distinct types of statuses: ascribed (or ascriptive) and achieved.[25] Ascribed status is based on what an individual is; achieved status is based on what the person does.[26] More precisely, ascriptive status reflects personal characteristics over which the individual has no control—for example, birth, sex, age, and race. In its extreme form, it presents itself as the caste. An achieved status, on the other hand, is based on voluntary personal performance. Here, the position one obtains usually is determined with reference to some abstract standard of merit. Occupational statuses within large public and private organizations are obvious examples. In theory, at least, status differentiations now tend to reflect achievement criteria. As Talcott Parsons once stated, Americans "determine status very largely on the basis of achievement within an occupational system which is in turn organized primarily in terms of universalistic criteria of performance and status within functionally specialized fields."[27]

Status and Negative Liberty

Typically, an ascribed status will involve extra restrictions on those occupying the status. The array of restraints placed upon women in the nineteenth-century United States is an example. Here, the concepts of status and negative freedom plainly conflict because the status is defined precisely by the set of external restrictions it places on some ascriptive group.[28] This is especially true if the status is embodied in the legal system, which imposes its own special external checks on behavior. Laws helping to maintain the system of social restraints involved with black slavery, for instance, obviously restricted the negative freedom of blacks. There is, however, no necessary conflict between the concepts of status and negative freedom.[29] A favored status group may be accorded greater negative liberties than the rest of the population.[30] The position of men vis-à-vis women in nineteenth-century America illustrates the point.[31]

The relationship between negative liberty and achieved status is a bit more ambiguous, since this type of status is voluntary. In this case, the individual is not subjected to a particular set of rights and duties because of factors over which he or she has no control but instead can choose which status to achieve. This ability to choose is often fairly illusory, however. More importantly, once someone has attained a particular achieved status position, he or she is often subjected to the array of social restraints accompanying that status, restraints he or she might not have chosen to accept but for the benefits the status offers.[32] The conditions of life in modern bureaucracies, public and private, illustrate the point. Thus, achieved statuses typically do put some determinate external limits on what the individual can do and thus restrict negative freedom to some extent. Certain achieved statuses may also increase negative liberty in some areas of life. The president of General Motors, for instance, presumably would have easier access to prestigious country clubs than would a GM assembly line worker.

Status and Positive Freedom

Authoritarian Positive Freedom

The customary view of the relationship between status and freedom just presented does not exhaust the subject. On another view of the matter, freedom and status are not opposed but conjoined. Here, freedom *is* status. More precisely, freedom as concretely manifested in society[33] is identified with the duties and privileges attaching to a particular social position. This conception of the relationship between status and freedom is associated with the authoritarian version of positive liberty. It seems to be rooted in the classical conception of society as a collaborative enterprise in which individuals simultaneously realize their true natures and serve social purposes by performing distinct status-based functions.[34] Later, with some conces-

sions to modernity, it was expounded by Hegel and British
neo-Hegelians like Green, F. H. Bradley and Bernard Bosanquet.
As George Sabine once said of Hegel, for instance:

> Freedom, he believed, must be understood as a social
> phenomenon, a property of the social system which
> arises through the moral development of the community.
> It is less an individual endowment than a status which is
> imparted to the individual through legal and ethical insti-
> tutions that the community supports. In consequence it
> cannot be equated with self-will or the following of pri-
> vate inclinations. Freedom consists rather in the adjust-
> ment of inclination and individual capacity to the perfor-
> mance of socially significant work; or, as F. H. Bradley
> put it, in finding "my station and its duties."[35]

In one version of this status-positive freedom fusion, ascribed
statuses are very significant.[36] Here, the inferior statuses traditionally occupied by, say, women and slaves were seen as reflecting their true natures and the social tasks for which they were
best fitted. According to this view, the fact that these statuses
restrict negative freedom is largely beside the point. Later exponents of this position, however, tended to be more liberal.[37]
To them, freedom was generally identified with the rights, powers, and duties that are the incidents of one's group affiliation.[38]
Perhaps most illustrative here is Bosanquet's *Philosophical
Theory of the State*.[39] Bosanquet clearly recognizes the value
of negative liberty and regards it as one element in his view of
freedom.[40] However, he does not treat it as some abstract right
possessed by man as man but sees it as bound up with the concrete conditions of European social life. In fact, when viewed
as a tangible social phenomenon, it is a status, "the position of
a freeman as opposed to a slave."[41]

To Bosanquet, this negative conception of liberty is inadequate. It does properly focus on the fact that freedom is always
in some sense self-determination.[42] But while "[t]he claim to
obey only yourself is a claim essential to humanity," "the further significance of it rests upon what you mean by 'yourself.' "[43]

And "in order to obey yourself as you want to be, you must
obey something very different from yourself as you are."[44]
Genuine freedom, needless to say, consists in following the true
self, and this demands acquiescing to certain psychological
drives and avoiding others.[45] More concretely, sluggards, drunk-
ards, and cowards never describe themselves as resisting their
energy, overcoming their sobriety, and conquering their cour-
age.[46]

Evidently Bosanquet tends toward the authoritarian variant
of positive freedom; that is, he sees liberty as inhering in certain
determinate states of mind and types of behavior and not in
others. To him, liberty involves not only the power to do
what one likes without constraint, but the nature of that
which he likes to do.[47] In addition, he clearly rejects the
open-ended idea of capacity inhering in the liberal notion of
positive liberty.[48]

For the most part, *The Philosophical Theory of the State*
does not provide a detailed list of moral do's and don'ts representing the claims of the true self. Instead, Bosanquet, no
doubt influenced by Hegel,[49] asserts that freedom finds its
most complete realization in the state.[50] However, he plainly
does not equate freedom with simple political coercion. For
one thing, he takes considerable care to define the proper role
for political action directly affecting the individual,[51] generally
concluding that such action is legitimate only when "hindering"
"hindrances" to the common good.[52] Thus it would seem that
the union of state and individual constituting the realization of
freedom must involve the individual's unforced identification
with state purposes that are expressive of general social aims.
For another thing, the state with which the individual is spon-
taneously to identify is not merely the formal political machinery. Instead, it is an organic whole encompassing most social
institutions and expressing some collective idea of the good life.

> The State . . . is not merely the political fabric. . . . [I]t in-
> cludes the entire hierarchy of institutions by which life
> is determined, from the family to the trade, and from the
> trade to the Church and the University. In includes all of
> them, not as the mere collection of the growths of the

country, but as the structure which gives life and meaning to the political whole.[53]

Most individuals have a more or less definite place within this
organized and differentiated totality and come to see the social
order from that vantage point.

> What comes first . . . is the position, the place or places,
> function or functions, determined by the nature of the
> best life as displayed in a certain community, and the
> capacity of the individual self for a unique contribution
> to that best life. Such places and functions are imperative;
> they are the fuller self in the particular person, and make
> up the particular person as he passes into the fuller self.
> His hold on this *is* his true will, in other words, his appre-
> hension of the general will.[54]

And anyone who understands what his social position demands
from him has "a working insight" into the purposes of the
state.[55]

If freedom is identified with state purposes and if the individual apprehends these from her or his particular social position,
status and freedom must be linked or fused. As Bosanquet puts
it: "My place or position . . . and its incidents . . . constitute
my rights."[56] From the point of view of the state as a whole,
the system of rights expresses the outward conditions necessary
to the existence and perfection of humanity.[57] From the point
of view of the individual, rights are "primarily the external incidents . . . of a person's position in the world of his community,"[58] and in no way are they to be seen as claims made by
the individual as individual.[59] These rights involve corresponding duties on the part of others occupying different positions,[60]
and to some extent they involve duties on the part of the individual right holder.[61] Bosanquet, however, does not usually tie
an individual's status, and his corresponding set of rights and
duties, to particular ascriptive traits. Instead, he maintains that
basing social class on birth (or even on private property) can
effect undesirable "denials of free adjustment, of the career
open to talents."[62]

Liberal Positive Freedom

Depending on the type of capacity envisioned, the authoritarian conception of positive freedom seems compatible with both ascribed and achieved status systems. At first glance, this would not appear to be true of positive freedom's liberal variant, with its open-ended idea of capacity. Restrictive ascribed statuses like those once binding black slaves, for instance, were hardly appropriate social settings for developing a wide range of interests and abilities. There is also no dearth of testimonies to the deadening effects of modern organizational life and the achieved statuses it supports. Much of this book, however, will be devoted to the argument that a fusion of status and something resembling liberal positive freedom best describes the American organizational milieu today. Residence within comtemporary occupational structures, for example, certainly develops abilities, although it is often difficult to assign to these any precise content.[63] One of the purposes behind the array of legal status relationships created by the various types of reverse discrimination is to promote the rather diffuse set of abilities required for long-term organizational success.[64]

Notes

1. *See, e.g.,* F. Bergmann, On Being Free ch. 2 (paperback ed. 1977).

2. Employing this term is, for example, I. Berlin, Four Essays on Liberty 122-31 (Oxford paperback ed. 1969).

3. Hobbes, Leviathan 103 (Collier paperback ed., M. Oakeshott, tr. 1962).

4. *See, e.g.,* Locke, The Second Treatise of Civil Government chs. 2-3, 8-9.

5. The Hobbesian *Leviathan* is the clearest example.

6. *See* F. Bergmann, *supra* note 1, at 31-35.

7. T. H. Green, *Lecture on Liberal Legislation and Freedom of Contract*, in 3 Works of Thomas Hill Green 365, 371 (R. Nettleship ed. 1900).

8. *Id.*

9. *See, e.g.,* F. Bergmann, *supra* note 1, at 22-31.

10. T. H. Green, *On the Different Senses of "Freedom" as Applied to the Will and to the Moral Progress of Man*, in Lectures on the Principles of Political Obligation 9 (Ann Arbor paperback ed. 1967).

11. *Id.* at 6.

12. This is discussed at various points below.

13. R. Goodwin, The American Condition 26 (1974).

14. *See, e.g.,* I. Berlin, *supra* note 2, at 133.

15. This is discussed at various points below.

16. This is discussed at the beginning of chapter 5.

17. Indeed, as will be argued in chapter 5, it may be a quite destructive goal.

18. Dworkin, *Three Concepts of Liberalism,* New Republic, April 14, 1979, at 41, 48.

19. *See, e.g.,* the histories of the "Strong Formers" in D. Yankelovich, New Rules (1981).

20. *See, e.g.,* H. Muller, Issues of Freedom 5-20 (1960).

21. Actually, activist twentieth-century government often advances both forms of liberty. By eliminating race-based employment discrimination, for example, it promotes negative freedom by removing an external impediment to minority advance. This should give the black person who already possesses the relevant employment-related abilities a chance "to show what he is made of." But access to employment may also enhance the capacities of minority members exposed to it, as well as the abilities of subsequent generations of minorities. These points are treated at length in chapter 4.

22. R. Linton, The Study of Man 113 (1936).

23. For some examples, *see* T. Parsons, Essays in Sociological Theory 75-76 (rev. ed. 1954).

24. The clearest example of a constitutional status is a situation where a court expressly declares that a certain group will receive constitutional protections different from those applying to the general population. Sometimes, however, such an inequality will not be explicitly stated; instead it will be the practical consequence of a decision or pattern of decisions affecting a group. Sometimes, too, status differentiations created by legislatures, common law, or administrative bodies will be regarded as constitutional in nature, partly because of their importance and partly because of the indirect constitutional sanction they can be said to possess.

25. On this distinction, *see id.* at 76-78; R. Linton, *supra* note 22, at 115-31; M. Bierstedt, The Social Order 265-66 (2d ed. 1967).

26. Of course, some bases of status do not neatly fit either classification. How, for instance, does one classify status based on a "good family" with "old money" obtained by achievement in past generations? *See also* the case of homosexuality discussed in chapter 2.

27. T. Parsons, *supra* note 24, at 78-79.

28. The social conditioning accompanying a status being what it usually

is, this conflict, practically speaking, often may not arise. For instance, it is probably safe to say that most women were not inclined to challenge the status position they once occupied, and to some degree this is still true today. In such cases, though, the check on the ability to pursue other options is internal as well as external. That is, it involves the absence of certain capacities, as well as external impediments.

29. This is so because a status was merely defined as any differential social position.

30. Chapter 4 will provide some examples in the area of reverse discrimination.

31. This would, I suppose, suggest that for every status group whose negative liberty is diminished, one can define a corresponding status group with greater negative liberties. That is, for each group X with reduced negative freedom, there is necessarily a non-X group with greater negative freedom. Such situations will be of little or no concern in this book.

32. One can theoretically avoid these restrictions by removing oneself from the status position, but this possibility is often merely theoretical.

33. What follows is not necessarily the abstract definition of freedom given by thinkers subscribing to this status-freedom relationship. Rather, it is the way in which this concept manifests itself as a concrete social phenomenon. *See, e.g.*, R. Schacht, *Hegel on Freedom*, in A. MacIntyre (ed.), Hegel: A Collection of Critical Essays (1972).

34. *See, e.g.*, Plato, Republic 370, 415a-415c, 420d-421a, 433-34.

35. G. Sabine, A History of Political Theory 655 (3d ed. 1961).

36. *Cf., e.g.*, Plato, Republic 415a-415c (the fable of the men of gold, silver, iron, and brass), 451c-457 (the role of women). In these passages, Plato is more meritocratic than might be expected. *See also id.* 423d.

37. *See, e.g.*, Hegel's Philosophy of Right (T. M. Knox tr.) § § 185 (Remark), 206 (Remark), 299 (Remark) (where Hegel contrasts Plato's *Republic*). *See generally* J. Shklar, Freedom and Independence (1976); R. Plant, Hegel (1973); C. Taylor, Hegel (1975).

38. For Hegel, the individual realizes his freedom in the state. Philosophy of Right, *supra* note 37, § § 257, 258, 260. Hegel sees the state as involving not just formal governmental machinery but also the totality of the social groupings and institutions with which this official structure is intimately bound up. *See* Z. Pelczynski, *The Hegelian Conception of the State*, in Z. Pelczynski (ed.), Hegel's Political Philosophy: Problems and Perspectives 1-29, esp. 13-14 (Cambridge paperback ed. 1971). Moreover, the individual is linked to the formal political machinery through membership in such groupings and finds freedom thereby. *See* Philosophy of Right, *supra* note 37, § § 264-65, 302, 308 (Remark). Thus, although Hegel seems not to say so explicitly, the individual's substantive freedom

is essentially determined by his group membership or class position—that
is, by his status, broadly conceived. This freedom is clearly regarded as
more or less synonymous with duty, and not with the arbitrary individual
will. *Id.* § § 149, 155.

To T. H. Green, rights are powers possessed by individuals for the realization of their moral capacities. T. H. Green, Lecture on the Principles of
Political Obligation § § 21, 25, 29 (Ann Arbor paperback ed. 1967). And
they clearly are determined by one's position in the organic totality which
is the state.

> Now for the member of a state to say that his rights are derived
> from his social relations, and to say that they are derived from his
> position as member of a state, are the same thing. The state is for
> him the complex of those social relations out of which rights arise.
> . . . The other forms of community which precede and are indepen-
> dent of the formation of the state, do not continue to exist outside
> it, nor yet are they superseded by it. They are carried on into it.
> They become its organic members, supporting its life and in turn
> maintained by it in a new harmony with each other. *Id.* § 141.

Although Green did not always equate rights with duties, *e.g., id.* § 21,
the thrust of his thought was in this direction. As he put it in another
context: "[E]ach has primarily to fulfill the duties of his station." T. H.
Green, Prolegomena to Ethics § 183 (Apollo paperback ed. 1969). Moreover, the incidents of particular stations clearly were to differ from each
other. *E.g., id.* § 191.

Bradley wrote little, if any, political philosophy as such. *But see* F.H.
Bradley, Ethical Studies (2d Oxford paperback ed. 1962), Essay V ("My
Station and its Duties").

39. B. Bosanquet, The Philosophical Theory of the State (4th ed., 1925).
40. *Id.* at 125-26.
41. *Id.* at 126.
42. *Id.* at 133.
43. *Id.* at 134.
44. *Id.*
45. *Id.* at 131-32.
46. *Id.* at 130.
47. *Id.* at 129.
48. *See id.* at 128, 133.
49. *See supra* note 38.
50. B. Bosanquet, *supra* note 39, at 139-40.
51. *See generally id.* ch. 8.

52. *Id.*at 178-80.
53. *Id.*at 140-41.
54. *Id.*at 191.
55. *Id.*at 141.
56. *Id.*at 192.
57. *Id.*at 189.
58. *Id.*at 190.
59. *Id.*at 198.
60. *See id.* at 192-94.
61. *See id.* at 193, 194-95.
62. *Id.* at 293-94.
63. This argument will be developed in chapter 3.
64. This will be discussed in chapter 4.

CHAPTER 2

The Inferior Constitutional Statuses and Their Twentieth-Century Demise

"The movement of progressive societies," Sir Henry Maine declared in 1861, "has hitherto been a movement from *Status to Contract*."[1] In thus summarizing the gradual disintegration of feudal structures and the rise of modern, post-seventeenth-century, individualism, Maine was highlighting a phenomenon that might be termed the "liberal individualist advance."[2] Its essence, according to Robert Nisbet, is a

> . . . temper of mind that found the essence of society to lie in the solid fact of the discrete individual—autonomous, self-sufficing, and stable—and the essence of history to lie in the progressive emancipation of the individual from the tyrannous and irrational statuses handed down from the past. Competition, individuation, dislocation of status and custom, impersonality, and moral anonymity were hailed by the rationalist because these were the forces that would be most instrumental in emancipating man from the dead hand of the past and because through them the naturally stable and rational individual would be given an environment in which he could develop illimitably his inherent potentialities.[3]

This liberal individualist movement displays the antagonism between status and the negative conception of freedom. Traditional status constraints obviously imposed external limits on

certain individuals' ability to act, and the elimination of these
impediments has just as obviously opened a new field for their
activity.

This longstanding movement is plainly apparent in American
constitutional law, which has always been marked by status
differentiations of all sorts. Characterizing the nineteenth and
early twentieth centuries were a variety of traditionalistic, "inferior" constitutional statuses affording decreased[4] constitutional protection[5] to those falling within the status group [6]
they define. Because reduced constitutional rights create the
potential for increased legal restrictions, these statuses involve
limitations on freedom negatively conceived. Some of them,
however, can also be characterized as displaying another status-
freedom relationship—the fusion of status and some positive
conception of liberty. These statuses have gradually been dis-
appearing throughout the twentieth century, although in some
cases their demise is not complete.

Many of the statuses discussed in this chapter are based on a
personal or behavioral characteristic; of these, most are ascriptive in nature. Some, however, involve particular institutional
affiliations, and these statuses are most often achieved. The
account of these statuses proceeds in rough order of decreasing
ascriptiveness. No doubt other constitutional status groups can
be identified. As Justice Rehnquist once noted in a somewhat
different context: "It would hardly take extraordinary ingenu-
ity for a lawyer to find 'insular and discrete' minorities at every
turn in the road."[7]

Women

Women occupied an inferior legal position throughout the
nineteenth century.[8] During that time, for instance, the real
and personal property of a married woman was largely in the
control of her husband. Married women were usually unable
to contract or make deeds, or to make a will or sue, without
the husband's consent. Single women were generally not subject to such private law disabilities, but they were often denied
the rights to vote, to hold public office, to testify in court, and
to sit on a jury. So well entrenched were such restrictions that
they occasioned relatively little constitutional challenge and

easily survived on the infrequent occasions when they were attacked. Missouri's denial of the vote to women was upheld by the Supreme Court in an 1874 case,[9] and in two other nineteenth-century decisions[10] the Court upheld a state's limitation of legal practice to men. The special legal status occupied by women had benefits as well as burdens. Women were usually not, for example, subject to suit in their own name, to criminal prosecution for crimes committed under the command of the husband, or to compulsory military service.

This inferior legal status clearly displays the conflict between the concepts of status and negative liberty—that is, the differential legal treatment creating the status involved additional external restrictions on the actions of women. This status, however, can also be viewed in positive freedom terms because it was based on definite notions about the nature of women and the social positions in which they could best utilize their presumably unique abilities. Consider the following statement by Justice Joseph Bradley in an 1872 case:

> . . . the civil law, as well as nature herself, has always recognized a wide difference in the respective spheres and destinies of man and woman. Man is, or should be, woman's protector and defender. The natural and proper timidity and delicacy which belongs to the female sex evidently unfits it for many of the occupations of civil life. The constitution of the family organization, which is founded in the divine ordinance, as well as in the nature of things, indicates the domestic sphere as that which properly belongs to the domain and functions of womanhood. The harmony, not to say identity, of interests and views which belong, or should belong, to the family institution is repugnant to the idea of a woman adopting a distinct and independent career apart from that of her husband. . . .
>
> It is true that many women are unmarried . . . but these are exceptions to the general rule. The paramount destiny and mission of woman are to fulfill the noble and benign offices of wife and mother. This is the law of the Creator. And the rules of civil society must be adapted to the general constitution of things, and cannot be based upon exceptional cases.[11]

Such views, it is probably safe to say, then enjoyed widespread acceptance, even among women. Because of the way that these views fuse definite notions about the true nature of women with an ascriptive legal and social status, they approximate the status-freedom relationship characterizing the authoritarian form of private freedom.

The social consensus on which the inferior legal status of women was based began to erode in the late nineteenth and early twentieth centuries. The married woman's acts enacted in most states by the year 1900, for instance, substantially increased the power of married women over their property and earnings,[12] and the passage of the Nineteenth Amendment to the Constitution in 1920 guaranteed women the right to vote. Yet during this period the Supreme Court often upheld protective state legislation in the area of female employment.[13] Sometimes such legislation was justified on more or less traditional grounds. For instance, in an unsuccessful 1912 challenge to a state statute partially exempting women from payment of a fee to engage in the laundry business, Justice Holmes declared that: "[i]f Montana deems it advisable to put a lighter burden upon women than upon men with regard to an employment that our people commonly regard as more appropriate for the former, the Fourteenth Amendment does not interfere by creating a fictitious equality where there is a real difference."[14] Sometimes, however, the Court began to reflect newly emergent attitudes by emphasizing the way protective legislation could help to equalize substantive life chances as between men and women. In a 1908 case sustaining an Oregon law limiting female employment in factories or laundries to no more than ten hours a day, it stated that

> . . . history discloses the fact that woman has always been dependent upon man. He established his control at the outset by superior physical strength, and this control in various forms, with diminishing intensity, has continued to the present. As minors, though not to the same extent, she has been looked upon in the courts as needing especial care that her rights may be preserved. Education was long denied her, and while now the doors of the school room

are opened and her opportunities for acquiring knowledge
are great, yet even with that and the consequent increases
of capacity for business affairs it is still true that in the
struggle for subsistence she is not an equal competitor
with her brother. Though limitations upon personal and
contractual rights may be removed by legislation, there is
that in her disposition and habits of life which will operate against a full assertion of those rights. She will still be
where some legislation to protect her seems necessary to
secure a real equality of right. Doubtless there are individual exceptions, and there are many respects in which she
has an advantage over him; but looking at it from the
viewpoint of the effort to maintain an independent position in life, she is not upon an equality. Differentiated by
these matters from the other sex, she is properly placed
in a class by herself, and legislation designed for her protection may be sustained, even when like legislation is not
necessary for men and could not be sustained.[15]

Legal status differentiations based on traditional conceptions
of the female role continued to find Supreme Court support
in the first half of the twentieth century. For example, in a
1948 decision it sustained a Michigan statute prohibiting a woman
from being a bartender unless she was the wife or daughter of
the male owner of a licensed liquor establishment.[16]
Also, a state limitation on female jury service was upheld in a
1961 decision.[17]
   In fact, it was not until the 1970s that the inferior legal status traditionally occupied by women was subjected to aggressive constitutional attack. The device through which this
occurred was equal protection strict scrutiny, which generally
means that certain governmental classifications are constitutional only if they are "necessary," or "substantially" related
to the furtherance of some "compelling" or "important"
governmental purpose.[18] Gender-based governmental classifications disadvantaging women are now subjected to an intermediate degree of strict scrutiny. Such classifications, as a
significant 1976 case put it, now must "serve important governmental objectives and . . . be substantially related to achieve-

ment of those objectives."[19] This new judicial posture represents a decided rejection of traditional ideas regarding woman's
appropriate role. As Justice William Brennan declared in a 1973
decision:

> . . . since sex, like race and national origin, is an immutable
> characteristic determined solely by the accident of birth,
> the imposition of special disabilities upon the members
> of a particular sex because of their sex would seem to
> violate "the basic concept of our system that legal bur-
> dens should bear some relationship to individual respon-
> sibility." . . . And what differentiates sex from such
> nonsuspect statuses as intelligence or physical disability,
> and aligns it with the recognized suspect criteria, is that
> the sex characteristic frequently bears no relation to abili-
> ty to perform or contribute to society.[20]

Practically speaking, it is now fairly difficult for governmental
classifications burdening women to survive constitutional attack.[21] For this reason, passage of the equal rights amendment
is perhaps less significant than commonly believed.

Children

Traditionally children have occupied a social and legal status
quite distinct from that of adults. Legally, this status has manifested itself in age-based restrictions on voting, holding office,
marrying, drinking alcoholic beverages, driving automobiles,
being bound to contracts, consenting to sexual acts, and so
forth. This is also evident in the deference given to parental
control in directing the activities of children and in shaping
their character, attitudes, and life chances. In both cases, the
negative liberty of children is limited by imposing legal or social restraints on their actions. Thus, youth can readily be regarded as a special position marked by a conflict between the
concepts of status and negative freedom. In a recent decision,
the Supreme Court justified this differential status on three
grounds: the vulnerability of children, their relative inability
to make crucial decisions in a rational, mature fashion, and the
importance of the parental role in their socialization.[22] How-

ever, the special position traditionally occupied by children
lends itself to another status-freedom characterization: a fusion of status and positive liberty. That is, the various restraints
imposed on youth can be viewed as essential to the development of certain long-run capacities. These abilities cannot
readily be classed as authoritarian or liberal; rather, the aim
seems to be promotion of those individual traits necessary for
proper functioning within and contribution to a liberal-demo-
cratic political order. To quote the Court again:

> Properly understood, . . . the tradition of parental author-
> ity is not inconsistent with our tradition of individual
> liberty; rather, the former is one of the basic presupposi-
> tions of the latter. Legal restrictions on minors, especially
> those supportive of the parental role, may be important
> to the child's chances for the full growth and maturity
> that make eventual participation in a free society meaning-
> ful and rewarding.[23]

Or as the Court put the matter nearly forty years ago, a "democratic society rests, for its continuance, upon the healthy, well-
rounded growth of young people into full maturity as citizens,
with all that implies . . . [and] may secure this against impeding
restraints and dangers within a broad range of selection."[24] A
tentative movement away from this traditional orientation is
taking place, however.

The Constitution places minimum age requirements on service in the Presidency, the Senate, and the House[25] but otherwise is silent as to the status of minors, and such matters did
not much occupy the Supreme Court until the twentieth century. Early in this century, state restriction of child employment and regulation of minor working conditions were generally
upheld in the face of due process and equal protection attacks.[26]
Such legislation obviously restricted the negative liberty of affected youth by imposing external limits on their ability to
contract for employment, but this was easily justified by its
protective purposes and by the way their furtherance could
assist the long-term development of youth. In addition, the
well-known cases of *Meyer v. Nebraska*[27] and *Pierce v. Society*

of Sisters[28] developed the concept of a parental right to control the rearing of children, resting it in the liberty protected by the due process clause of the Fourteenth Amendment. The doctrines of state protection and parental control occasionally clashed. One instance of this was the 1944 case of *Prince v. Massachusetts*,[29] where the parental control right was subordinated to the state's interest in regulating youth employment. *Prince* involved the conviction of a Jehovah's Witness under a state statute banning on-street solicitation by children. There the Court restricted the negative liberty of the parent by upholding the conviction despite an assertion of the due process control right. It did so in positive freedom terms, justifying this utilization of the police power as an effort to develop the child's capacity for eventual adult participation in the larger society. "It is the interest of youth itself, and of the whole community," it declared, "that children be both safeguarded from abuses and given opportunities for growth into free and independent well-developed men and citizens."[30]

Supreme Court decisions since the 1960s have somewhat eroded the legal status long occupied by the young. This obviously can be related to the growing preoccupation with children's rights during that period.[31] But this liberalizing movement is only a tendency at best, and traditional themes still abound in the opinions of the justices. The Court remains emphatic in the view that constitutional guarantees assume a special meaning in the case of minors.[32] In *Ginsberg v. New York*,[33] for instance, it upheld a state criminal obscenity statute setting different standards for minors than for adults, where the magazines at issue in the case would have received First Amendment protection had they been sold to adults. Also, the doctrine of parental control was relied upon to some degree in *Wisconsin v. Yoder*,[34] in which the Court held compulsory state education laws unconstitutional as applied to Amish children required to be educated beyond the eighth grade. In a 1979 case,[35] the Court rejected a due process challenge to Georgia procedures governing the commitment of children to mental institutions, procedures that allowed substantial parental discretion regarding the decision to commit.

Other decisions of the 1960s and 1970s, however, display a tendency toward equalizing the constitutional position of children and adults. During this time, various procedural due process protections have been extended to juvenile criminal proceedings.[36] There has also been a rash of successful litigation asserting various student rights.[37] The principal manifestation of the Supreme Court's new direction has been in the area of sexual freedom for minors, especially the right to obtain an abortion.[38] In *Planned Parenthood of Central Missouri v. Danforth*,[39] a 1976 case, it struck down a state statute requiring parental consent for a minor girl's abortion. One year later, it struck down another state law making it a crime to sell contraceptives to anyone under the age of sixteen.[40] In 1979, it invalidated a state statute requiring parental consent for certain abortions on minors but allowing the abortion to be obtained by judicial order for "good cause shown" if one or both parents refused consent.[41] In 1981, however, the Court did uphold a measure requiring the physician performing an abortion to notify the parents of a dependent, unmarried minor girl before the abortion could take place.[42]

Perhaps we can obtain some perspective on these developments by considering certain idealized alternative possibilities for the social and legal treatment of children. First, imagine a hypothetical libertarian regime in which negative freedom would be maximized to the fullest practicable extent in all areas of life. (Actually, the presocial state of nature might serve this illustrative purpose even better.) Here, there presumably would be no legal distinctions between children and adults and no legal duties owed uniquely to the young. All would be equal, autonomous units subject to no external authority other than the minimal commands of a neutral rule-of-law "umpire state." In the absence of normal human benevolence or some sort of contractual arrangement, this hypothetical regime could not guarantee the survival of children or prevent many forms of adult coercion without issuing legal commands to the populace—that is, without restricting negative liberty to some extent. (For instance, free sexual relations between children and adults, to take one current example,[43] could not be proscribed without restricting the rights of child and adult alike.) Perhaps more importantly, such a regime could not guarantee the education of children and their incorporation into family structures or other developmental programs without limiting the negative

freedom of the children themselves. As a result, to the extent
that the regime is truly free, personal capacities would most
likely be very imperfectly realized under it. This conclusion
might be avoided by assuming that development of personal
abilities is primarily an asocial, individual process, but this is
unlikely for most people. It might also be avoided by asserting
natural human inclinations toward sociability, mutual depen-
dency, parental love, and so forth. But although such assertions
are no doubt plausible by and large, protective inclinations will
fail in some cases absent legal backing. Also, it is possible that
the laissez-faire political institutions might be complemented
by extreme libertarian popular sentiments. If this is so, there
is less reason to expect that protective inclinations will prevail,
since these often entail restrictions on the ability to pursue
other options.[44]

By way of contrast, imagine an extreme positive freedom-
type regime devoted to the maximization of individual capacity,
whatever its nature. Such a regime would almost certainly be
required to eliminate the family structure and to undertake a
program of state-sponsored child rearing and education. As the
Court noted in *Meyer v. Nebraska*, Plato's *Republic* establishes
just such a program:

> For the welfare of his Ideal Commonwealth, Plato sug-
> gested a law which should provide: "That the views of
> our guardians are to be common, and their children are
> to be common, and no parent is to know his own child,
> nor any child his parent. . . . The proper officers will take
> the offspring of the good parents to the pen or fold, and
> there they will deposit them with certain nurses who
> dwell in a separate quarter; but the offspring of the infer-
> ior, or of the better when they chance to be deformed,
> will be put away in some mysterious, unknown place, as
> they should be." In order to submerge the individual and
> develop ideal citizens, Sparta assembled the males at
> seven into barracks and intrusted their subsequent educa-
> tion and training to official guardians.[45]

Here we have the authoritarian version of positive freedom,
whose end is the production of determinate character types

reflecting the individual's true nature and the requirements of socially useful work. The traditional family structure would be ill suited to this task given the diversity in the attitudes and abilities of parents. The randomization created by the dispersion of nuclear families could best be avoided by standardizing the child-rearing process under political auspices.

Such an enhanced state role, however, would also be necessary in a regime devoted to the liberal variant of positive freedom, where the goal is a maximized capacity for choice among a wide range of options. This is so because of the way family structures inevitably limit the capacities of those raised within their confines. As Justice Douglas put it while dissenting in *Yoder*:

> It is the future of the student, not the future of the parents, that is imperilled by today's decision. If a parent keeps his child out of school beyond the grade school, then the child will be forever barred from entry into the new and amazing world of diversity that we have today. The child may decide that that is the preferred course, or he may rebel. It is the student's judgement, not his parents', that is essential if we are to give full meaning to what we have said about the Bill of Rights and of the right of students to be masters of their own destiny. If he is harnessed to the Amish way of life by those in authority over him and if his education is truncated, his entire life may be stunted and deformed.[46]

In this statement, Douglas seems to assume that the development of personal capacity, though aided by education, is primarily an individual matter. If the arguments I made in the preceding paragraphs are at all correct, however, this is unlikely. Thus, in order to further the goal of open-ended capacity, the state would be required to avoid the constrictive implications of family life by adopting a program of child raising and education best suited to *its* ends. It is difficult to imagine what form such a hypothetical program might take, even assuming that it is a real possibility. Perhaps the image of society as a "Great Books Club" might be some indication. But as with the authoritarian version of positive liberty, the need to supersede the effects of undirected parental control is a necessary, though not sufficient, condition for success.

The American tradition has not embraced any of these hypothetical extremes, although the tensions each suggests are apparent in the decisions discussed earlier. Rather, the preferred course has coupled a recognition of youthful incapacity for free citizenship with a maximization of negatively free parental control. That is, the family has been employed as the device by which the young develop capacity for effectively utilizing the negative liberty accorded adults. During youth, then, positive freedom and status are linked, and negative liberty is severely limited. This emphasis is plainly apparent both in the decisions announcing diminished constitutional protection for children and in the doctrine of parental control. The recent emphasis on children's rights represents a gain in negative liberty for the young, but the continued vitality of the parental control right suggests a possible conflict between these two negative liberties, one the Court has only begun to confront. Seemingly lost in the current preoccupation with these two conflicting freedoms, however, is the Court's traditional concern about the character types best suited for life in a liberal democracy and relative roles of state and family in producing such character types. Judicial attention to the means for producing "free and independent well-developed men and citizens" with "full maturity" now seems conspicuous by its absence.[47] Too often, it appears, the prevailing tacit assumption is that this will ensue more or less naturally as the negative liberties of children are increased.

Blacks

Although no longer operative,[48] certain provisions of the Constitution once treated black slaves in a fashion quite distinct from white citizens despite speaking in racially neutral terms.[49] Article I, section 2 differentiated whites from blacks for purposes of representation: "Representatives and direct Taxes shall be apportioned among the several States . . . , according to their respective Numbers, which shall be determined by adding to the whole Number of free Persons . . . , three fifths of all other persons." Article I, section 9 ensured that the move-

ment of slaves into existing states would be legal until 1808:
"The Migration or Importation of such Persons as any of the
States now existing shall think proper to admit, shall not be
prohibited by the Congress prior to the Year one thousand
eight hundred and eight." Finally, Article IV, section 2 dealt
with fugitive slaves: "No Person held to Service or Labour in
one State, under the Laws thereof, escaping into another, shall,
in Consequence of any Law or Regulation therein, be discharged from such Service or Labour, but shall be delivered up
on Claim of the Party to whom such Service or Labor may be
due."

Some Supreme Court decisions prior to the Civil War, however, took less care to be circumspect about the way race could
determine one's legal and constitutional status. In the famous
(or infamous) *Dred Scott*[50] decision, for instance, the Supreme
Court held descendants of imported African slaves not to be
United States citizens capable of utilizing the federal courts.
In addition, the *Dred Scott* Court stated that the legislation
embodying the Missouri Compromise was unconstitutional, in
part because it constituted a taking of property (slaves) without due process of law.[51] In consonance with this characterization of slaves as property, not persons, were certain Supreme
Court decisions upholding federal and state fugitive slave acts.[52]
In addition, it was commonly said that each state had the power to determine the status of its citizens, black or white, so
long as this characterization was not inconsistent with the federal constitution.[53] While this might have permitted blacks to
be treated as free and equal persons in some states, it also permitted others to deny blacks even the right to contract.[54]

Prior to the Civil War, then, being a member of the Negro
race clearly consigned one to an inferior constitutional status
based on that ascriptive characteristic. To put it another way,
membership in this racial group resulted in a distinct denial of
liberty in its negative sense as compared with the white majority. This special status could also be viewed in authoritarian positive freedom terms: as a social and legal position that corres-
ponded to the true nature and capacities of blacks. The actual
treatment accorded some black slaves, however, was probably
sufficiently inhumane to make even this claim implausible. With

the North's victory in the Civil War, this inferior constitutional
status was formally eliminated. The Thirteenth Amendment
to the Constitution plainly states that slavery and involuntary
servitude are not to exist within the United States. Section 1 of
the Fourteenth Amendment provides for black citizenship,
federal and state. It protects the individual against oppressive
or arbitrary state action by guaranteeing all United States
citizens certain privileges and immunities and granting to all
persons due process of law and the equal protection of the laws.
Section 2 of that amendment effectively removes Article I,
section 2's limitation on the counting of blacks for purposes of
representation. The Fifteenth Amendment guarantees blacks
the right to vote.

   This formal equality with respect to certain basic freedoms
did not radically change the actual condition of the former
slaves, however. The removal of restrictions often did not co-
exist with the personal capacity necessary for its effective utilization. The social and psychological deprivations produced by
slavery could not be quickly overcome merely by increasing
the formal negative freedom of blacks. Also, external social,
and eventually legal, restraints came to replace prior forms of
bondage. The formal equal personhood created by the post-
Civil War amendments did not prove a bar to unequal private, and
even public, treatment of the former slaves. Constitutionally,
these results were facilitated by two broad tendencies in the
Court's race-related decision making from the conclusion of the
Civil War to World War II. The first of these was the practice of
imposing a rather limited conception of racial neutrality on
governmental actors. That is, while the Court would strike
down laws that flatly disadvantaged blacks on their face, it upheld provisions that, although obviously discriminatory in purpose, administration, or impact, were arguably neutral in form.
Second, the Court usually maintained a sharp division between
the public and the private spheres by limiting both legislative
and constitutional attacks on discriminatory private behavior.

   As for the first tendency, the Court occasionally did strike
down official action clearly treating blacks in an unequal fashion. In cases like *Strauder v. West Virginia*,[55] for instance, it
invalidated racially discriminatory jury selection procedures in

criminal cases. And in *Buchanan v. Warley*,[56] it struck down a
local ordinance forbidding blacks to occupy houses in blocks
populated by a white majority. But this was about as far as the
Court was then willing to go, since legislation with even a claim
to racial neutrality usually passed constitutional muster. In its
1883 decision in *Pace v. Alabama*,[57] for example, the Court
upheld state statutes imposing stiffer penalties on interracial
adultery and fornication than on similar activities by males and
females of the same race. In the process, it asserted that no true
discrimination was present because the statutes imposed equal
penalties on members of each race. In its well-known 1896
Plessy v. Ferguson[58] decision, the Court upheld a system of
racially separate-but-equal rail passenger transportation. In that
case Justice Brown declared:

> We consider the underlying fallacy of the plaintiff's argu-
> ment to consist in the assumption that the enforced sepa-
> ration of the two races stamps the colored race with a
> badge of inferiority. If this be so, it is not by reason of
> anything found in the act, but solely because the colored
> race chooses to put that construction upon it. The argu-
> ment necessarily assumes that if, as has been more than
> once the case, and is not unlikely to be so again, the col-
> ored race should become the dominant power in the state
> legislature, and should enact a law in precisely similar
> terms, it would thereby relegate the white race to an in-
> ferior position. We imagine that the white race, at least,
> would not acquiesce in this assumption.[59]

Perhaps anticipating an objection that decisions like *Plessy*
tended to sanction social inequality, he went on to declare:
"If one race be inferior to another socially, the Constitution
of the United States cannot put them on the same plane."[60]
Much in the same general vein was a 1937 case upholding an
ostensibly neutral device like the poll tax.[61]
    The second tendency—the maintenance of a fairly sharp
public-private line—tended to limit legislative and constitutional intervention into the private sphere and thus permitted various forms of nongovernmental discrimination. As for statutory
intervention, Justice Brown's *Plessy* opinion had contended

that "[l]egislation is powerless to eradicate racial instincts or
to abolish distinctions based upon physical differences, and the
attempt to do so can only result in accentuating the difficulties
of the present situation."[62] Thirteen years earlier, in 1883, the
Court had invalidated federal legislation forbidding certain
forms of private discrimination when it struck down the Civil
Rights Act of 1875 in the *Civil Rights Cases*.[63] In one portion
of its decision there, the Court held that the act was outside
Congress's legislative powers under section 5 of the Fourteenth
Amendment (which gives Congress the power to enforce the
other provisions of the amendment), because the first section
of the amendment expressly prohibited only state (and not
private) denials of equal protection. In *Plessy*, Justice Brown
had suggested that civil rights legislation was simply inefficacious, but in the *Civil Rights Cases* Justice Bradley's opinion
for the Court seemed to regard it as unnecessary. As he
declared there:

> When a man has emerged from slavery, and by the aid of
> beneficient legislation has shaken off the inseparable con-
> comitants of that state, there must be some stage in the
> progress of his elevation when he takes the rank of a mere
> citizen, and ceases to be the special favorite of the laws,
> and when his rights as a citizen, or a man, are to be protected
> in the ordinary modes by which other men's rights are pro-
> tected.[64]

The Fourteenth Amendment's "state action" requirement also
limited the reach of constitutional attacks on private discrimination. For instance, it prevented the Court from striking down a
racially restrictive covenant in 1926.[65] And after some early de-
feats caused by too close an identification with the formal organs of government,[66] an ostensibly private white primary was
upheld in a 1935 decision.[67]

From roughly the end of the Civil War until the beginning of
World War II, then, the Court's maintenance of a distinct public-
private demarcation and its rather restricted conception of discriminatory governmental behavior tended to reinforce a racial
status quo in which black opportunities were severely limited

and black capacities were given little chance for development.
After World War II, the constitutional and legal position of
blacks changed dramatically. A variety of interrelated developments contributed to this result. Race-based or race-motivated
voting restrictions like the white primary and the poll tax were
eliminated through different judicial and amendatory efforts.[68]
The separate-but-equal doctrine of *Plessy* was definitively rejected by the Court's landmark 1954 decision in *Brown v.
Board of Education*.[69] In addition, decisions following and im-
plementing *Brown* imposed sweeping remedial duties to integrate on racially segregated school districts.[70] The private reach
of the equal protection clause in cases involving race was greatly
extended by the Court's postwar expansion of the state action
concept.[71] And the reasoning of the *Civil Rights Cases* no
longer served to block antidiscrimination legislation directed
at private behavior. In cases where public action was color
blind on its face, the Court began to direct greater attention
to the motives underlying its enactment and/or its practical
impact on blacks.[72] The equal protection guarantee, which by
its terms checks only the states, was made applicable to the
federal government as well through its incorporation within
Fifth Amendment due process.[73] Perhaps most important of
all, by the mid-1960s[74] it came to be agreed that race-based
classifications were "suspect" and had to satisfy strict scrutiny
in order to be pronounced constitutional.[75] This meant basically that such classifications were required to serve a "compelling" governmental purpose and to be "necessary" to the
promotion of that purpose if they were to survive constitutional attack.[76]

   The net result of these developments has been substantially
to equalize the constitutional status of whites and blacks.
Whether the resulting posture of formal governmental neutrality has worked to equalize tangible life chances as well is another
question. Perhaps in response to the perception that generations
of prior discrimination have severely limited black capacity,
various types of reverse discrimination—preferential private and
governmental treatment of racial minorities—became prevalent
in the 1970s. To the extent that they are constitutionally permissible, such preferences raise the possibility that race has

once more become a constitutional status, albeit one whose aim
is to *enhance* the social position of blacks and other minorities.[77]

Illegitimates

Illegitimates traditionally have been subjected to disadvantageous legislative treatment in areas such as the ability to claim
parental support, to inherit, to will to the parent, to collect
wrongful death and workman's compensation benefits, and to
reside in public housing.[78] For quite some time, such discrimination apparently was not subject to serious constitutional
challenge. Because of this indirect constitutional sanction, illegitimacy was an effective constitutional status. Since this status
involved a diminution of certain legal rights or powers, it also
amounted to a deprivation of negative liberty, one based on an
ascriptive characteristic. Unlike youth or gender, however, illegitimacy could not additionally be described as fusing status
with some idea of positive capacity. The deprivations this status
entailed hardly reflected an effort to develop the abilities of
the illegitimate, however these might be defined.

This situation began to change in 1968 when the Court invalidated portions of a state wrongful death statute that disadvantaged illegitimate children.[79] Subsequent decisions struck down
distinctions disadvantaging illegitimates in areas such as child
support, welfare, and the ability to inherit.[80] All of this took
place under equal protection auspices. Although illegitimacy is
not currently classed as a fully suspect classification requiring
maximum strict scrutiny, it is evident that something more
than the customary minimal equal protection review is employed when discrimination against illegitimates is at issue.[81]
Despite this, certain forms of discrimination against illegitimates have survived equal protection attack in the 1970s.[82]
Obviously, however, the long-term trend has been toward an
erosion of this traditional status.

Tribal Indians

While describing the status of blacks early in his *Dred Scott*
opinion, Chief Justice Taney digressed on the position of the
Indians, who, by way of comparison,

... formed no part of the colonial communities, and never amalgamated with them in social connections or in government. But although they were uncivilized, they were yet a free and independent people, associated together in nations or tribes, and governed by their own laws. . . . These Indian Governments were regarded and treated as foreign Governments, as much so as if an ocean had separated the red man from the white; and their freedom has constantly been acknowledged, from the time of the first emigration to the English colonies to the present day. . . . [T]he people who compose these Indian political communities have always been treated as foreigners not living under our Government. It is true that the course of events has brought the Indian tribes within the limits of the United States under subjection to the white race; and it has been found necessary, for their sake as well as our own, to regard them as in a state of pupilage, and to legislate to a certain extent over them and the territory they occupy. But they may, without doubt, like the subjects of any other foreign Government, be naturalized by the authority of Congress, and become citizens of a State, and of the United States; and if an individual should leave his nation or tribe, and take up his own abode among the white population, he would be entitled to all the rights and privileges which would belong to an emigrant from any other foreign people.[83]

Because of these historical considerations, the tribes have long been regarded as possessing the inherent power to regulate their internal affairs.[84] Yet along with the gradual conquest, subordination, and relocation of the tribes by an expanding America, the federal "pupilage" to which Chief Justice Taney referred has come to receive increasing emphasis. Illustrative here is the Court's statement in the much-cited 1886 case of *United States v. Kagama*:

These Indian tribes *are* wards of the nation. They are communities *dependent* on the United States. Dependent

largely for their daily food. Dependent for their political
rights. They owe no allegiance to the States, and receive
from them no protection. . . . From their very weakness
and helplessness, so largely due to the course of dealing
of the Federal Government with them and the treaties in
which it has been promised, there arises the duty of protection.[85]

These somewhat inconsistent themes of tribal self-government
and paternal federal control mark much of the law on the powers of tribal Indians to this day. It now seems to be generally
agreed that although tribal powers are inherent and not created
by Congress or the Constitution, they are subject to limitation
by treaty and by congressional authority. In fact, they are subject to total defeat by Congress at its discretion.[86] The states'
ability to regulate Indian tribes, however, is fairly limited.[87]

It follows from the special position and inherent powers of
the Indian tribes that tribal membership[88] —which is, of course,
not compulsory—creates a special status marked by diminished
constitutional protections and correspondingly greater subservience to tribal norms. Even though native-born Indians are American citizens,[89] it is routinely asserted that the federal Constitution does not apply to the tribes except where it expressly
binds them or is made applicable by treaty or by legislation.[90]
In particular, governmental checks like those imposed by the
Bill of Rights are not applicable to the tribes in governing their
members, although the states and the federal government still
must respect such norms in *their* dealings with tribal Indians.[91]
Thus, it has been held that since tribes are not federal instru-
mentalities, the Fifth Amendment's due process guarantee does
not apply to them,[92] and that, since they are not states for purposes of the Fourteenth Amendment, its guarantees are also
inapplicable.[93] In addition, the free exercise clause of the First
Amendment[94] and the Sixth Amendment's guarantee of the
right to counsel[95] have been held not to govern tribal activities.
Also, the Supreme Court has recently held that a federal prosecution occurring subsequent to a tribal court prosecution for a
lesser included offense does not violate the double jeopardy

clause of the Constitution because the tribe and the federal
government are separate sovereigns.[96] However, the requirement that the federal government compensate for takings under the eminent domain power has been found applicable to
tribal Indians.[97]

The current situation is, of course, susceptible to change
through congressional action, although historically Congress
has tended to defer to tribal norms, and its much-cited protective role has perhaps been more rhetorical than real. A conspicuous exception to this pattern of congressional deference, however, is the 1968 Indian Civil Rights Act,[98] which by its terms
makes the tribal governments subject to a variety of statutory
limitations worded much like the federal Bill of Rights.[99] Some
of the cases applying this provision, however, have stressed that
its guarantees must be read in the context of a tradition of
tribal law and custom and must be balanced against the tribe's
interest in maintaining its identity. As one federal district court
put it, for instance:

> Although Congress used language . . . from the Bill of
> Rights, this Court is of the opinion that the meaning and
> application of [the act] to Indian tribes must necessarily
> be somewhat different than the established Anglo-Ameri-
> can legal meaning and application of the Bill of Rights on
> federal and state governments. Congress has recognized as
> legitimate and has strongly supported the policy of allowing
> Indian tribes to maintain their unique governmental and
> cultural identity. The legislative record underlying the
> Indian Bill of Rights clearly shows that while Congress
> intended to establish important individual rights for per-
> sons under the jurisdiction of tribal governments, Congress
> also intended that these rights be harmonized with legiti-
> mate tribal interests. By not including certain clauses of
> the Bill of Rights and by modifying the clauses that were
> finally incorporated into [the act], Congress recognized
> as legitimate the tribal interest in maintaining traditional
> practices that conflict with constitutional concepts of
> personal freedom developed in a different social context.

The legislative history of [the act] indicates that the
scope of the individual rights contained therein is to be
determined by balancing them against the legitimate interests of the tribe in maintaining the traditional values
of their [*sic*] unique governmental and cultural identity.[100]

Thus, it has been said that the equal protection granted by the
act is not the same as the Fourteenth Amendment equal protection[101] and that the Fifteenth Amendment, as well as certain procedural provisions of the Fifth, Sixth, and Seventh
amendments, were not intended to control the tribes.[102]
The decisions dealing with the rights of tribal Indians resemble the cases establishing the other constitutional statuses discussed in this chapter. Tribal membership is clearly a status
characterized by diminished constitutional protection for the
Indian. This status also restricts negative freedom because the denial
or diminution of constitutional rights makes possible greater
external restrictions on individual behavior. This status is
basically ascriptive (one is usually born an Indian), but it does
have an achievement dimension, since the tribal Indian can
presumably always "leave the reservation" and avoid the restrictions associated with tribal life. The position of tribal Indians can also be described in terms of other status-freedom
relationships. The federal power to regulate Indian affairs, for
example, can be cast in positive freedom terms, as necessary
for developing the capacities of the tribal Indian. As one Supreme Court decision has described federal control, for instance:

In the exercise of the war and treaty powers, the United
States overcame the Indians and took possession of their
lands, sometimes by force, leaving them an uneducated,
helpless and dependent people, needing protection against
the selfishness of others and their own improvidence. Of
necessity the United States assumed the duty of furnish-
ing that protection, and with it the authority to do all
that was required to perform that obligation and to pre-
pare the Indians to take their place as independent, qualified members of the modern body politic.[103]

Practically, however, the furtherance of such purposes, if much
of a congressional concern at all, has been attempted less
through affirmative federal action than by delegation of control to the tribe. As a result, the positive freedom advanced is
less a liberal capacity for individual choice among a range of
options (that is, less devoted to making Indians "independent,
qualified members of the modern body politic") than a habi-
tuation to tribal norms. Thus the capacities developed tend to
be those of the good tribal member, and the positive freedom
promoted is arguably somewhat authoritarian. Indirectly reinforcing this perception are certain efforts at representing tribal
groups within the federal organizational structure regulating
them. In a 1974 decision upholding an employment preference
for tribal Indians in the Bureau of Indian Affairs (BIA) of the
Department of the Interior, Justice Blackmun described both
the preference and the regulatory structure in the following
terms:

> . . . this preference does not constitute "racial discrimi-
> nation." Indeed, it is not even a "racial" preference.
> Rather it is an employment criterion reasonably designed
> to further the cause of Indian self-government and to
> make the BIA more responsive to the needs of its consti-
> tuent groups. It is directed to participation by the
> governed in the governing agency. . . . Congress has sought
> only to enable the BIA to draw more heavily from among
> the constituent group in staffing its projects, all of which,
> either directly or indirectly, affect the lives of tribal In-
> dians. The preference, as applied, is granted to Indians
> not as a discrete racial group, but, rather as members of
> quasi-sovereign tribal entities whose lives and activities
> are governed by BIA in a unique fashion.[104]

Whether characterized as racial or not, this incorporation of
the tribal group and its special way of life within a larger whole
does not seem intended to dilute the integrity of tribal norms.
Rather, it appears to aim at a mosaic-like structure allowing
diversity within an overall unity, one bearing some resemblance
to the sociopolitical order sketched by Bosanquet.

Orientals

For the most part, Orientals have not occupied a distinct
status in American constitutional law. Often, however, they
have been subject to the disabilities suffered by other aliens.
Like aliens generally, Japanese and Chinese immigrants were
traditionally granted many of the same constitutional protections as American citizens. As the Court stated in 1893, for
instance:

> Chinese laborers . . . like all other aliens residing in the
> United States for a shorter or longer time, are entitled,
> so long as they are permitted by the government of the
> United States to remain in the country, to the safeguards
> of the Constitution, and to the protection of the laws,
> in regard to their rights of person and property, and to
> their civil and criminal responsibility. But they continue
> to be aliens, having taken no steps towards becoming
> citizens, and incapable of becoming such under the
> naturalization laws; and therefore remain subject to the
> power of Congress to expel them, or to order them to
> be removed and deported from the country, whenever
> in its judgment their removal is necessary or expedient
> for the public interest.[105]

The congressional powers to expel[106] and to deny citizenship[107]
were upheld in subsequent cases. Other past and present infir-
mities placed upon aliens presumably would apply to Chinese
and Japanese aliens also.

A few past Supreme Court decisions, however, deal with the
constitutional status of the Chinese and the Japanese on the
basis of their national origin. In its 1886 decision in *Yick Wo
v. Hopkins*,[108] the Court overturned on equal protection
grounds a San Francisco ordinance banning (in the absence of
official permission) the operation of laundries not housed in
buildings constructed of brick or stone, where the record revealed that most such laundries were owned by Chinese and
that prosecutions under the ordinance had been directed solely
toward Chinese. After stating that "[t]he rights of the peti-

tioners . . . are not less, because they are aliens and subjects of the Emperor of China,"[109] the Court significantly broadened the application of the equal protection clause to include individuals other than blacks when it declared:

> The Fourteenth Amendment to the Constitution is not confined to the protection of citizens. It says: "Nor shall any State deprive any person of life, liberty, or property without due process of law; nor deny to any person within its jurisdiction the equal protection of the laws." These provisions are universal in their application, to all persons within the territorial jurisdiction, without regard to any differences of race, of color, or of nationality; and the equal protection of the laws is a pledge of the protection of equal laws. . . . The questions we have to consider and decide in these cases, therefore, are to be treated as involving the rights of every citizen of the United States equally with those of the strangers and aliens who now invoke the jurisdiction of the court.[110]

On the other hand, a Chinese child's assignment to black or private schools under a Mississippi separate-but-equal education statute survived an equal protection attack in 1927.[111]

In the well-known and much-criticized[112] cases of *Hirabayashi v. United States*[113] and *Korematsu v. United States*,[114] World War II exclusion orders affecting West Coast Japanese were upheld against Fifth Amendment due process attacks. In both cases, however, the differential treatment of Orientals seems to have been based on the exigencies of the wartime situation, and both opinions were replete with rhetorical support for the ideal of racial equality. In *Hirabayashi*, the Court stated:

> Distinctions between citizens solely because of their ancestry are by their very nature odious to a free people whose institutions are founded upon the doctrine of equality . . . . We may assume that these considerations would be controlling here were it not for the fact that the danger of espionage and sabotage, in time of war and of threatened invasion, calls upon the military authorities

to scrutinize every relevant fact bearing on the loyalty of
populations in the danger areas. Because racial discrimi-
nations are in most circumstances irrelevant and therefore
prohibited, it by no means follows that, in dealing with
the perils of war, Congress and the Executive are wholly precluded from taking into account those facts and circumstances which are relevant to measures for our national
defense and for the successful prosecution of the war,
and which may in fact place citizens of one ancestry in a
different category from others. "We must never forget,
that it is *a constitution* we are expounding," "a constitution intended to endure for ages to come, and, conse-
quently, to be adapted to the various *crises* of human
affairs."[115]

Further emphasizing the uniqueness of the World War II exclusion cases is the fact that before and after the war, the Court
had struck down certain denials of economic privileges based
on lack of citizenship,[116] certain presumptions regarding citizenship in state statutes regulating the holding of real property by
aliens,[117] and certain restrictions on the ability of aliens to transfer real property,[118] all in cases involving Orientals.

    Hirabayashi and *Korematsu* are also crucial to the develop-
ment of the strict scrutiny doctrine.[119] In addition to declaring
that distinctions based on ancestry were "odious," *Hirabayashi*
stated that such distinctions were "irrelevent and therefore prohibited" in most cases.[120] And despite its result, *Korematsu*
displayed the first explicit treatment of race as a suspect cri-
terion of classification. As Justice Black stated:

> It should be noted, to begin with, that all legal restrictions
> which curtail the civil rights of a single racial group are
> immediately suspect. That is not to say that all such restric-
> tions are unconstitutional. It is to say that courts must
> subject them to the most rigid scrutiny. Pressing public
> necessity may sometimes justify the existence of such re-
> strictions; racial antagonism never can.[121]

The application of strict scrutiny to classifications disadvantaging Orientals was reaffirmed after the war.[122] Clearly, dis-

crimination based on national origin as such, like discrimination based on race, will be subjected to the fullest degree of strict scrutiny.[123]

Homosexuals

Regardless of whether homosexual behavior results from some innate predisposition with roots in physiology or early childhood experiences (as ascriptive?) or as the outcome of some autonomous personal choice (as achieved?), its discovery by the community traditionally has consigned the person so behaving to a distinct social and legal status, marked by potential criminal prosecution, employment discrimination, and social ostracism, to mention only some of the more evident possibilities. It is arguable, however, that homosexual orientation as such is not a legal or a constitutional status. At least some forms of public treatment disadvantageously affecting homosexuals, (such as sodomy statutes) typically focus on personal behavior rather than on homosexuality as a trait determining legal status in a variety of contexts. (Such statutes typically apply to male-female relations also.) Thus, it might be argued that homosexuality does not merit description as a constitutional status of the sort race and gender once were. In those cases, an immutable personal trait was definitive in establishing wide-ranging legal disabilities, while in the case of homosexuality, we confront only specific individual actions that trigger specific legal penalties. That is, homosexual behavior can be distinguished from homosexuality as a central defining characteristic of human beings, with legal disabilities being based on the former and not the latter. No one, for instance, would regard the constitutionality of rape statutes as a reason for considering rapists a constitutional status group. But it is at least as arguable that personal, social, and legal definitions of homosexuality encompass more than particular forms of behavior. As Professor Laurence Tribe has suggested, "The conduct proscribed [homosexual activity] is central to the personal identities of those singled out by the state's law."[124] It is common to see people link homosexual behavior to general personality traits of certain sorts or make it the basis of overall judgments of individual worth. In contexts like employment, the discriminatory treatment sometimes accorded homosexuals seems to spring as much from such linkages, judgments, or stereotypes as from homosexual conduct. Because these considerations cannot be readily dismissed, homosexuality will be considered as a constitutional status here, although this status seems to be on the wane.

The Supreme Court has not dealt with matters affecting homosexuals to any great degree. In the 1960s, it upheld the deportation of an alien who was a homosexual at the time of his entry into the United States.[125] In 1975, it refused to find a state statute forbidding "crimes against nature" to be unconstitutionally overbroad or vague in a case involving cunnilingus at knifepoint by a male upon a female.[126] One year later it affirmed without discussion a lower court decision upholding a Virginia statute forbidding sodomy and fellatio as applied to homosexual behavior.[127] One year after that, however, the Court stated that it had "not definitively answered the difficult question whether and to what extent the Constitution prohibits State statutes regulating [private consensual sexual behavior] among adults."[128]

Because of the Supreme Court's relative inactivity in this area, it is useful to take a brief look at a few lower federal court and state court decisions concerned with the rights of homosexuals. The highest courts of at least two states have struck down statutes proscribing certain sorts of deviant sexual behavior between adults who are not married to each other.[129] Regarding government employment, a fairly muddled picture emerges. Discharge from state or federal positions because of homosexual behavior usually can be justified only upon demonstration of some nexus or connection between that behavior and impairment of an agency's mission.[130] Factors creating such a nexus might include potential blackmail in cases involving access to classified information, emotional instability and the resulting unsuitability for certain kinds of work, and aggressive on-the-job displays of homosexual orientation.[131] In this context, the withdrawal of a security clearance from a homosexual has been overturned in at least one decision, although this is probably not the general view.[132] Decisions involving discharge from the military for homosexual activity (or even

homosexual inclinations) also seem to be mixed.[133] This is so
despite the fact that constitutional rights generally suffer some
dilution in the military context.[134] With respect to private employment, where constitutional checks typically do not apply,
hiring or promotion discrimination on the basis of homosexuality apparently is not forbidden by Title VII of the 1964 Civil
Rights Act.[135] In the educational context, several cases have
struck down state universities' denials of recognition to homosexual organizations.[136] In at least one decision, the First
Amendment right of homosexual instructors to speak out on
issues of concern to homosexuals has found support.[137]

Aliens

With a few exceptions, resident aliens historically have occupied a formal constitutional status not radically different from
that of American citizens generally. In addition, Supreme Court
decisions during the 1970s have provided aliens with an increased ability to challenge such differential legal treatment as
still applies to them. The Constitution does limit the Presidency,
as well as service in the House and the Senate, to United States
citizens,[138] and the states deny aliens the right to vote. In addition, the Congressional power to expel aliens [139] and the power
to deny them citizenship[140] seem well established. At least for
the former, however, there is a right to a formal hearing.[141]
     Despite these disabilities, it is often said that the full range
of constitutional protections is available to resident aliens.[142]
Justice Murphy once declared:

> . . . Once an alien lawfully enters and resides in this coun-
> try he becomes invested with the rights guaranteed by the
> Constitution to all people within our borders. Such rights
> include those protected by the First and the Fifth Amend-
> ments and by the due process clause of the Fourteenth
> Amendment. None of these provisions acknowledges any
> distinction between citizens and resident aliens. They ex-
> tend their inalienable privileges to all "persons" and guard
> against any encroachment on those rights by federal or
> state authority.[143]

Such broadly based individual protections did not, however, prevent the pre-World War II Court from sustaining certain forms of economic discrimination against aliens. In 1923, for instance, a state statute limiting the right of aliens to hold land was upheld in the face of due process and equal protection attacks.[144] Earlier a state's power to limit public employment to citizens had also been upheld by the Court.[145]

This attitude began to change with the Court's 1948 statement that "the power of a state to apply its laws exclusively to its alien inhabitants as a class is confined within narrow limits."[146] In the 1970s, alienage was held to be a suspect classification requiring an intermediate degree of strict scrutiny in many equal protection contexts.[147] As a result, restrictions on alien access to welfare benefits,[148] the practice of law,[149] permanent positions in the competitive classified civil service,[150] and educational benefits[151] were struck down by the Burger Court.[152] It has recently been established, however, that this more stringent standard of review will not apply to "state functions . . . so bound up with the operation of the state as a governmental entity as to permit the exclusion from those functions of all persons who have not become part of the process of self-government."[153] Coming within this classification, and upheld by the Court, were state bans on alien employment as state troopers[154] and public school teachers.[155] Thus, the Court's earlier deference toward state prohibition of alien public employment seems partially intact even today.[156]

Mental Patients

The power of the state to commit the insane under the parens patriae theory is well established.[157] Commitment obviously creates a status marked by sharply reduced constitutional protections consistent with the paternalistic purposes of the treatment and the need to protect both the patient and society. Thus, institutionalization can be regarded as a status characterized by the deprivation of negative liberty, a deprivation justified by a possible long-term increase in personal capacity. Practically, however, the social interest in institutionalization may be more significant than rehabilitative purposes. Perhaps

indicative of the traditional attitude here is Justice Holmes's
famous statement in a 1927 case presenting due process and
equal protection challenges to a state provision for the sterilization of mental defectives.

> We have seen more than once that the public welfare may
> call upon the best citizens for their lives. It would be
> strange if it could not call upon those who already sap
> the strength of the state for these lesser sacrifices . . . in
> order to prevent our being swamped with incompetence.
> It is better for all the world, if instead of waiting to exe-
> cute degenerate offspring for crime, or to let them starve
> for their imbecility, society can prevent those who are
> manifestly unfit from continuing their kind. The principle
> that sustains compulsory vaccination is broad enough to
> cover cutting the Fallopian tubes. . . . Three generations of
> imbeciles are enough.[158]

Although this holding may have been negated by subsequent
decisions,[159] the Supreme Court has not broadened the rights
of mental patients to the extent true for many of the other
statuses discussed in this chapter.

The Court has held that involuntary commitment to a mental
institution is a deprivation of liberty requiring that due process
standards be observed.[160] Due process also applies to the transfer of a prisoner to such an institution.[161] With some deference
to parental authority, it is required for the involuntary institutionalization of a minor.[162] In one case, a prisoner who refused
to cooperate in the examination necessary to determine his
status as a "defective delinquent" requiring indeterminate mental treatment and who had delayed the examination long
enough to cause his prison sentence to expire was ordered released on due process grounds.[163] Despite some recent decisions
establishing a basic right to treatment upon institutionalization,
however, the Supreme Court has refused to decide whether
mental patients possess such a positive freedom-type right.[164]
Also, a host of lower federal court decisions have been concerned with questions such as institutional maltreatment, minimum living conditions, outside communications, institutionally

compelled labor, assignment of institutional treatment levels, forced administration of drugs, the right to remain silent in a commitment proceeding, and so forth. To take just one example, plaintiffs who were tied spread-eagled to a bed for seventy-seven and a half hours and forced to scrub walls for over ten consecutive hours in short hospital gowns as apparent punishment for a homosexual act were awarded damages under a federal civil rights statute because this behavior was deemed to constitute cruel and unusual punishment and to deny due process.[165]

Prisoners

Confinement to penal institutions can be viewed as a more or less achieved status marked by obvious deprivations of liberty in its negative sense. Despite occasional claims that imprisonment can rehabilitate, this inferior status almost certainly cannot be characterized as furthering the positive capacities of most prisoners, unless an increase in criminal skills and propensities is regarded as a growth of capacity. Instead, the ends usually thought to be furthered by imprisonment are the community protection achieved by deterrence and confinement of dangerous individuals or, sometimes, the moral claims of retribution. Whatever its justifications, the inferior status created by incarceration manifests itself in a sharp diminution of many constitutional rights. Although courts now generally agree that prisoners do not forefeit such rights upon confinement, they also agree that these rights are subject to restriction because of the need to preserve institutional security, order, and discipline and that much deference will be accorded prison administrators in achieving these ends.[166]

The constitutional protections available to inmates have increased significantly since the early 1970s. Justice Rehnquist stated in 1979 in *Bell v. Wolfish:*

> There was a time not too long ago when the federal judiciary took a completely "hands-off" approach to the problem of prison administration. In recent years, however, these courts have largely discarded this "hands-off" attitude and have waded into this complex arena. The deplor-

able conditions and Draconian restrictions of some of our
Nation's prisons are too well known to require recounting
here, and the federal courts rightly have condemned these
sordid aspects of our prison systems.[167]

In so acting, the federal courts have created a sizable mass of
litigation on the constitutional rights of prisoners.[168] Generally
this body of cases represents a broad movement toward a more
equal legal status for inmates.

Racial segregation in prison facilities is now unconstitutional,[169] at least in cases not involving prison violence. Concerning
First Amendment rights, in 1974 the Supreme Court struck
down regulations giving prison officials broad powers to prevent many forms of inmate correspondence.[170] It did so by
focusing on the protected First Amendment interests of those
receiving the correspondence, thus avoiding the question of
prisoners' First Amendment rights. In two later decisions,[171]
the Court proceeded by examining the rights of the prisoner,
upholding rules forbidding media interviews with individual
inmates. The Court has also been willing to strike down regulation interfering with the practice of religions not well established in the United States.[172] It has, however, upheld prison
rules forbidding inmates to solicit other inmates to join a
prisoners' union, barring meetings of this union, and barring
bulk mailings regarding the union from outside sources.[173] Also,
the right of access to the courts has led the Court to invalidate
rules restricting jailhouse lawyers and limiting the sorts of books
available in prison libraries, and to impose an affirmative obligation to provide adequate law libraries or legal assistance.[174]
Moreover, due process standards have been found applicable to
parole revocation, probation revocation, the removal of good-
time sentence reductions for disciplinary reasons, transfer from
a prison to a mental institution, and transfer to solitary confinement,[175] but not to the transfer to another prison and the
commutation of a life sentence.[176] In a 1976 case,[177] however,
the right to counsel and the privilege of cross-examination were
held inapplicable to a prison disciplinary proceeding not involving criminal behavior, and in the same case adverse inferences
from the prisoner's refusal to answer questions were permitted

despite the constitutional privilege against self-incrimination.
During the 1970s, the lower federal courts were active in striking down certain particularly inhumane and oppressive prison
conditions as cruel and unusual punishment.[178] The Supreme
Court, though, has not actively participated in these matters.
Still, it has upheld the placement of two men in a cell designed
for one in two different cases.[179] Also, the Court has declared
that although the government has the obligation to provide
inmates with medical treatment and although deliberate indif-
ference to the serious medical needs of prisoners is unconstitutional, accidental, inadvertent, or negligent failures to provide
proper treatment do not constitute cruel and unusual punishment.[180] Finally, the federal courts often have been unwilling
to recognize positive freedom-type inmate rights to rehabilita-
tion, education, or recreation.[181]

The Court's recent tendency to extend the constitutional
rights of prisoners may be abating a bit.[182] After noting the
recent expansion of inmate rights in *Bell*, Justice Rehnquist
went on to criticize the courts' increasing willingness to "become . . . enmeshed in the minutiae of prison operations" and
thus to make frequent "judgment calls," which are not properly
part of the judicial function.[183] In that decision, the Court
upheld the following pretrial detainee center regulations or
practices: housing two inmates in a cell designed for one; prohibiting inmates from receiving hardcover books not mailed
directly from publishers, book clubs, or bookstores; prohibiting the receipt of packages of food and personal items from
outside the center; body-cavity searches following "contact"
visits; and a requirement that detainees remain outside the cell
during routine inspections. Although a return to the pre-1970s
situation is unlikely, it is equally improbable that an expansion
of prisoner rights comparable to that of the 1970s will soon occur.

The Military

As Justice Rehnquist noted in 1974, the Supreme Court
"has long recognized that the military is, by necessity, a specialized society separate from civilian society" and that "[m]ili-
tary law . . . is a jurisprudence which exists separate and apart

from the law which governs in our federal judicial establishment."[184] As a result, military service creates a distinct status
with diminished constitutional protections and reduced negative liberties for individuals so situated. This status may develop personal capacities in many cases, but for individuals killed
or wounded in the course of service it evidently reduces them
considerably. To the extent that military service is voluntary,
this status might be regarded as achieved, although it is obviously not a position from which one can separate at will. It
can also be viewed as involving an exercise of negative liberty
in which the individual freely relinquishes that liberty. For
instance, in an 1890 case where a soldier attempted to avoid
a desertion sentence by alleging that he was over age when he
enlisted, Justice Brewer viewed enlistment as a binding contract between the enlistee and the government.

> By enlistment the citizen becomes a soldier. His relations
> to the State and the public are changed. He acquires a
> new status, with correlative rights and duties; and al-
> though he may violate his contract obligations, his status
> as a soldier is unchanged. He cannot of his own volition
> throw off the garments he has once put on, nor can he
> . . . renounce his relations and destroy his status on the
> plea that, if he had disclosed truthfully the facts, the
> other party, the State, would not have entered into the
> new relations with him, or permitted him to change his
> status.[185]

This contractualistic basis for the imputation of a special sol-
dierly status diminished with the growth of the large, often
compulsory twentieth-century military establishment. With
the abolition of the draft, however, perhaps the contractualistic rationale will achieve a new relevance.

The precise contours of the special status occupied by members of the military have remained unclear to this day, often
being intertwined with procedural considerations. Federal
courts lack appellate jurisdiction over military tribunals,[186] and
service personnel wishing to obtain federal court review of military court decisions under the Uniform Code of Military Justice

(UCMJ) usually must utilize a habeas corpus petition.[187] Once,
the prevailing doctrine governing such attacks was that the
federal court's inquiry was limited to whether the military tri-
bunal had jurisdiction,[188] a rule that was often regarded as effectively putting military personnel beyond the reach of Bill
of Rights protections. As the Court wrote in 1911, "[t]o those
in the military or naval service of the United States, the military law is due process."[189] This doctrine was relaxed somewhat in a 1953 decision,[190] although the exact test to be applied
for determining the scope of the federal court review has occasioned
some disagreement since that time.[191]

Thus the prevailing contemporary view is that constitutional
protections are available to military personnel, albeit in a somewhat diluted form. Still, the exact content of such protections
is unclear and must be defined on a case-by-case basis. Apparently the only specific constitutional language on this subject
is the Fifth Amendment's exemption of cases arising in the land
or naval forces from the requirement of a grand jury indictment.
A few Supreme Court cases in the 1970s are worth mention in
this context. Perhaps the most noteworthy of these is *Parker v.
Levy*,[192] which upheld the conviction of an army physician for
refusing to provide dermatology training to members of the
Special Forces and making antiwar statements to enlisted personnel. The statements to enlisted personnel were punishable
under army regulations forbidding "conduct unbecoming an
officer and a gentleman" and "all disorders and neglect to the
prejudice of good order and discipline in the armed forces."
These regulations were subjected to First Amendment challenge
as both vague and overbroad. While rejecting Levy's vagueness
claim, Justice Rehnquist's opinion for the Court stated: "For
reasons which differentiate military society from civilian society, we think Congress is permitted to legislate both with
greater breadth and with greater flexibility when prescribing
the rules for the latter."[193] In the course of rejecting the over-
breadth claim, Rehnquist made a number of observations about
the application of constitutional norms in the military context.

> While the members of the military are not excluded from
> the protection granted by the First Amendment, the dif-
> ferent character of the military community and of the

military mission requires a different application of those
protections. The fundamental necessity for obedience,
and the consequent necessity for imposition of discipline,
may render permissible within the military that which
would be constitutionally impermissible outside it.[194]

With respect to the "character of the military community,"
Rehnquist had earlier noted "the different relationship of the
Government to members of the military," stating:

It is not only that of lawgiver to citizen, but also that of
employer to employee. Indeed, unlike the civilian situation, the Government is often employer, landlord, pro-
visioner and lawgiver rolled into one. That relationship
also reflects the different purposes of the two communities. . . . While members of the military community enjoy
many of the same rights and bear many of the same burdens as do members of the civilian community, with the
military community there is simply not the same autonomy as there is in the larger civilian community.[195]

Finally, with regard to the different "military mission," he had
also stated: "The differences between the military and civilian
communities result from the fact that it is the primary business
of armies and navies to fight or be ready to fight wars should
the occasion arise."[196]

In addition, the Court has upheld service regulations applied
so as to prohibit political activities by outsiders within the confines of an open training post.[197] It has also upheld a regulation
requiring command approval before petitions may be distributed
on base.[198] And while remarking that the applicability of the
Sixth Amendment to court-martial proceedings is unclear, it has
held that the right to counsel does not apply to summary court-
martials.[199] Finally, in 1981 the Court upheld men-only draft
registration, in part because of the way equal protection standards are altered to accommodate military requirements.[200]
There has also been a mass of lower federal court litigation on
matters such as compulsory chapel regulations and relinquishment of the right to marry in service academies, as well as hair
and wig regulations.[201]

Government Employees

Although protected by the same constitutional guarantees as are other citizens, government employees nonetheless are subject to a few specific disabilities. For instance, the Supreme Court has held the Hatch Act's limitations on political management and campaign participation by federal employees to be constitutional.[202] The Court has also upheld a similar state provision.[203] However, it has been said that the acceptance of public employment cannot be conditioned on the relinquishment of constitutional rights,[204] and the First Amendment rights of government employees have, with a few exceptions, been upheld in cases where such speech provoked dismissal. In one case, the Court struck down the dismissal of a high school teacher for writing a letter to the editor of a newspaper critical of the way his superiors handled school revenue raising and allocation.[205] In two other cases, it has overturned the dismissal of public employees because of their partisan political affiliation.[206] The Court has upheld a First Amendment challenge to payment of a service charge to a public employee union by nonunion employees concerned with the partisan and ideological uses to which the charge was being put.[207] This First Amendment-based freedom from dismissal or coercion is not absolute, however. It can be balanced against governmental interests such as effectiveness and efficiency.[208] In particular, dismissals based on partisan political affiliation may be justifiable where jobs of a policy-making or confidential nature are involved.[209] In addition, the protection against dismissal for exercising free speech rights seemingly does not apply where the expression in question is made in an intraorganizational context.[210] Turning away from First Amendment concerns, the Court has refused to apply due process standards to a dismissal from the competitive civil service[211] and to the termination of a policeman's employment.[212] Also, a local regulation limiting the length of a policeman's hair has been held constitutional.[213] Finally, as noted earlier, alienage-based restrictions on employment in certain governmental positions will receive a less stringent form of review than is typically the case when discrimination against aliens is at issue.

Notes

1. H. Maine, Ancient Law 165 (P. Smith ed. 1970).

2. When I use the terms *liberalism* or *liberal* in this book, I am usually referring to a body of related ideas generally becoming dominant in the West in the modern (roughly post-1600) period. This includes tendencies toward: materialism or positivism in the philosophic realm with a related emphasis on the distinction between facts and values; a consequent denial of Aristotelian teleology in the ethical realm; a related emphasis on values such as liberty and equality, as well as the satisfaction of least-common-denominator wants like physical security and material plenty; a view of society in which the individual is primary and society is merely an aggregate of putatively equal individuals mainly held together by external political force; and a basically manipulative and exploitive posture toward nature. Chapters 5 and 6 elaborate these ideas. This use of the term *liberalism* encompasses most of the American political tradition. Perhaps the clearest early exemplar of this syndrome of views was Thomas Hobbes.

3. R. Nisbet, The Quest for Community 4 (Oxford paperback ed. 1969). Nisbet does not regard this development as unqualifiedly good.

4. Chapter 4 discusses situations where a status position may afford increased constitutional protection or at least some practical legal advantage.

5. In this chapter, this usually involves either a situation where there is a flat statement that a particular status group will receive some kind of diminished constitutional protection or a situation where there is no such statement, but the practical application of general constitutional standards results in diminished constitutional protection for a particular status group.

6. Throughout this book, the term *group* will be used in one of two senses: as a collection of individuals united by the presence of some traits, such as blacks, or as synonymous with terms such as *organization* or *institution*. Sometimes one organization may combine both senses of the term, as for instance with the NAACP. Usually the context should make clear which sense of the term is intended.

7. Sugarman v. Dougall, 413 U.S. 634, 657 (1973) (Rehnquist, J., dissenting).

8. This paragraph is based on Bergold, *The Changing Legal Status of American Women*, 40 Current History 206 (1976). *See also* Frontiero v. Richardson, 411 U.S. 677, 684-85 (1973).

9. Minor v. Happersett, 88 U.S. (21 Wall.) 162 (1874).

10. *In re* Lockwood, 154 U.S. 116 (1894); Bradwell v. Ill., 83 U.S. (16 Wall.) 130 (1872).

11. Bradwell v. Ill., 83 U.S. (16 Wall.) 130, 141-42 (1872) (Bradley, J., concurring).
12. *See* Bergold, *supra* note 8, at 207-08.
13. In addition to the two cases discussed immediately below, *see* Riley v. Mass., 232 U.S. 671 (1914); Miller v. Wilson, 236 U.S. 373 (1915). *But see* Adkins v. Childrens Hosp., 261 U.S. 525 (1923), which was overruled in West Coast Hotel v. Parrish, 300 U.S. 379 (1937).
14. Quong Wing v. Kirkendall, 223 U.S. 59, 63 (1912).
15. Muller v. Ore., 208 U.S. 412, 421-22 (1908).
16. Goeseart v. Cleary, 335 U.S. 464 (1948).
17. Hoyt v. Fla., 368 U.S. 57 (1961). This decision was for all practical purposes overruled in Taylor v. La., 419 U.S. 522 (1975).
18. Strict scrutiny is discussed in more detail in chapter 4.
19. Craig v. Boren 429 U.S. 190, 197 (1976).
20. Frontiero v. Richardson, 411 U.S. 677, 686 (1973).
21. *See, e.g.*, Wengler v. Druggists Mutual Ins. Co., 446 U.S. 142 (1980); Frontiero v. Richardson, 411 U.S. 677 (1973); Reed v. Reed, 404 U.S. 71 (1971). On the stringency of the standard used in gender discrimination cases, *see* Perry, *Modern Equal Protection: A Conceptualization and Appraisal*, 79 Colum. L. Rev. 1023, 1045, 1055-56 (1979). The application of this standard to discrimination disadvantaging men is discussed in chapter 4.
22. Bellotti v. Baird, 443 U.S. 622, 634-39 (1979).
23. *Id.* at 638-39.
24. Prince v. Mass., 321 U.S. 158, 168 (1944).
25. U.S. CONST. art. I, § § 2, 3; art. II, § 1.
26. *E.g.*, Sturges & Burn Mfg. Co. v. Beauchamp, 231 U.S. 320, 325-26 (1913).
27. 262 U.S. 390 (1923).
28. 268 U.S. 510 (1925).
29. 321 U.S. 158 (1944).
30. *Id.* at 165.
31. For a description of the recent children's rights movement, *see e.g.*, Hafen, *Children's Liberation and the New Egalitarianism: Some Reservations About Abandoning Youth to their "Rights"*, 1976 B.Y.U.L. Rev. 605, 631-32 and the sources cited there. *See generally* the symposia in 39 Law & Contemp. Prob., No. 3 (Summer 1975) and 1976 B.Y.U.L. Rev. 605-733.
32. *See, e.g.*, Bellotti v. Baird, 443 U.S. 622, 633-39 (1979); Carey v. Population Servs. Int'l, 431 U.S.678, 693, n.15 (1977); Planned Parenthood v. Danforth, 428 U.S. 52, 74-75 (1976).
33. 390 U.S. 629 (1968).
34. 406 U.S. 205 (1972).

35. Parham v. J.R., 442 U.S. 584 (1979).
36. *See, e.g.*, *In re* Winship, 397 U.S. 358 (1970); *In re* Gault, 387 U.S. 1 (1967).
37. *See, e.g.*, Wright, *The Constitution on the Campus*, 22 Vand. L. Rev. 1027 (1969); Note, *Developments in the Law—Academic Freedom*, 81 Harv. L. Rev. 1045, 1128-57 (1968); Note, *Student Constitutional Rights on Public Campuses*, 58 Va. L. Rev. 552 (1972). Some of the leading Supreme Court cases in this area are: Tinker v. Des Moines Independent Community School Dist., 393 U.S. 503 (1969) (freedom of expression); Healy v. James, 408 U.S. 169 (1972) (freedom of association); Papish v. Bd. of Curators, 410 U.S. 667 (1973) (student press); Goss v. Lopez, 419 U.S. 565 (1975) (due process hearing before suspension).
38. The Court has also held that a fetus is not a Fourteenth Amendment "person." Roe v. Wade, 410 U.S. 113, 156-159 (1973).
39. 428 U.S. 52 (1976).
40. Carey v. Population Servs. Int'l, 431 U.S. 678 (1977).
41. Bellotti v. Baird, 443 U.S. 622 (1979).
42. H. L. v. Matheson, 450 U.S. 398 (1981).
43. *See, e.g.*, 177 New Republic (October 22, 1977), at 42, discussing the paedophile movement, whose aim is the elimination of the age of consent governing the sexual relations of adults and children.
44. The point made here is that such inclinations impose an internal check on one's autonomy. For more on this as an extension of negative liberty, *see* chapter 5.
45. Meyer v. Nebr., 262 U.S. 390, 401-2 (1923).
46. Wis. v. Yoder, 406 U.S. 205, 245-46 (1972) (Douglas, J., dissenting).
47. An exception to this generalization is Bellotti v. Baird, 443 U.S. 622, 634-39 (1979), quoted *supra* in the text accompanying note 23.
48. Actually, these provisions are still part of the formal text of the Constitution, but their practical effect was negated by the passage of the post-Civil War amendments. *E.g.*, Van Alstyne, *Rites of Passage: Race, the Supreme Court and the Constitution*, 46 U. Chi. L. Rev. 775, (1979).
49. For this interpretation of the constitutional provisions that follow, *see, e.g.*, Regents of the Univ. of Cal. v. Bakke, 438 U.S. 265, 389 (1978) (Marshall, J.).
50. Dred Scott v. Sandford, 60 U.S. (19 How.) 393, 400-27 (1857).
51. *Id.* at 449-52.
52. *E.g.*, Prigg v. Pennsylvania, 41 U.S. (16 Pet.) 539 (1842); Jones v. Van Zandt, 46 U.S. (5 How.) 215 (1847); Moore v. Ill., 55 U.S. (14 How.) 13 (1852).
53. *See, e.g.*, Strader v. Graham, 51 U.S. (10 How.) 82, 93-94

(1850); Dred Scott v. Sandford, 60 U.S. (19 How.) 393, 422 (1857).

   54. *See e.g.*, Hall v. United States, 92 U.S. 27 (1875), involving a black claimant's attempt to recover for a contractual debt occurring before the end of the Civil War.

   55. 100 U.S. 303 (1880).

   56. 245 U.S. 60 (1917).

   57. 106 U.S. 583 (1883).

   58. 163 U.S. 537 (1896). *See also* Cumming v. Richmond County Bd. of Educ., 175 U.S. 528 (1899); McCabe v. Atchison, Topeka & Santa Fe R.R., 235 U.S. 151 (1914); Gong Lum v. Rice, 275 U.S. 78 (1927).

   59. Plessy v. Ferguson, 163 U.S. 537, 551 (1896).

   60. *Id.* at 552.

   61. Breedlove v. Suttles, 302 U.S. 277 (1937).

   62. Plessy v. Ferguson, 163 U.S. 537, 551 (1896).

   63. 109 U.S. 3 (1883).

   64. *Id.* at 25.

   65. Corrigan v. Buckley, 271 U.S. 323 (1926).

   66. *See* Nixon v. Herndon, 273 U.S. 536 (1927); Nixon v. Condon, 286 U.S. 73 (1932).

   67. Grovey v. Townsend, 295 U.S. 45 (1935).

   68. U.S. Const. amend. XXIV (poll tax outlawed); Smith v. Allwright, 321 U.S. 649 (1944) (white primary outlawed under Fifteenth Amendment).

   69. 347 U.S. 483 (1954).

   70. *See, e.g.*, Brown v. Bd. of Educ. ("Brown II"), 349 U.S. 294 (1955); Green v. County School Bd., 391 U.S. 430 (1968); Swann v. Charlotte-Mecklenburg Bd. of Educ., 402 U.S. 1 (1971).

   71. *See, e.g.*, Shelley v. Kraemer, 334 U.S. 1 (1948) (racially restrictive covenant enforced by state); Burton v. Wilmington Parking Auth., 365 U.S. 715 (1961) (private restaurant in parking building owned by state agency). The expansion of state action will be discussed in more detail in chapter 3.

   72. *See, e.g.*, L. Tribe, American Constitutional Law § § 16-16, 16-18 (1978) and cases discussed there.

   73. The leading case is Bolling v. Sharpe, 347 U.S. 497 (1954). The Fifth Amendment by its terms applies to the federal government.

   74. Actually, come cases during the postwar period did not pay much attention to the standard of review to be employed for racial classifications attacked under the equal protection clause and seemed to regard such classifications as unconstitutional per se. *See* Phillips, *Neutrality and Purposiveness in the Application of Strict Scrutiny to Racial Classifications* (to be published in the Temple Law Quarterly). This is basically what the

post-Civil War Court seemed to do on the rare occasions when it struck down racial discrimination on equal protection grounds. Thus, the strict scrutiny test described below may, strangely enough, be regarded as a step backward for racial minorities. But in practice this test has usually been very stringent indeed. *E.g.,*Perry, *supra* note 21, at 1035. And as chapter 4 makes clear, the use of strict scrutiny rather than a test of per se invalidity often works to the advantage of blacks in reverse discrimination cases.

75. *See, e.g.,* Hunter v. Erickson, 393 U.S. 385, 392 (1969); Loving v. Va., 388 U.S. 1, 8-12 (1967); McLaughlin v. Fla., 370 U.S. 184, 192 (1964).

76. *E. g.,* Perry, *supra* note 21, at 1035. The second, or means, part of this test usually requires that no less discriminatory alternative method of promoting the compelling purpose be available.

77. Chapter 4 will discuss this matter in some detail.

78. *See, e.g., The Court Acknowledges the Illegitimate;* Levy v. La. *and* Glona v. Am. Guar. & Liab. Ins. Co., 118 U. Pa. L. Rev. 1, 19-34 (1969).

79. Levy v. La., 391 U.S. 68 (1968); Glona v. Am. Guar. & Liab. Ins. Co., 391 U.S. 73 (1968).

80. *See, e.g.,* Gomez v. Perez, 409 U.S. 535 (1973) (child support); N.J. Welfare Rights Org. v. Cahill, 411 U.S. 619 (1973) (welfare); Trimble v. Gordon, 430 U.S. 762 (1977) (inheritance). *See also* Weber v. Aetna Cas. & Sur. Co., 406 U.S. 164 (1972) (wrongful death benefits under workman's compensation).

81. *See, e.g.,* Lalli v. Lalli, 439 U.S. 259, 264 (1978); Trimble v. Gordon, 430 U.S. 762, 767 (1977); Matthews v. Lucas, 427 U.S. 495, 504-06 (1976).

82. *See* Lalli v. Lalli, 439 U.S. 259 (1978) (inheritance); Matthews v. Lucas, 427 U.S. 495 (1976) (social security); Labine v. Vincent, 401 U.S. 532 (1971) (inheritance).

83. Dred Scott v. Sandford, 60 U.S. (19 How.) 383, 403-04 (1857).

84. *E.g.,* United States v. Wheeler, 435 U.S. 313, 322-23 (1978).

85. 118 U.S. 375, 383-84 (1886).

86. *See, e.g.,* United States v. Wheeler, 435 U.S. 313, 323-34 (1978).

87. *See, e.g.,* the discussion in White Mountain Apache Tribe v. Bracker, 448 U.S. 136, 141-45 (1980).

88. There is no tribal power to govern non-Indians absent a congressional grant. *See* Oliphant v. Suquamish Indian Tribe, 435 U.S. 191, 195-212 (1978).

89. 8 U.S.C. §1401 (b) (Supp. II 1978).

90. *E.g.,* Groundhog v. Keeler, 442 F.2d 674, 678 (10th Cir. 1971);

Janis v. Wilson, 385 F. Supp. 1143, 1149-50 (D.S.D. 1974).
    91. *E.g.*, Santa Clara Pueblo v. Martinez, 436 U.S. 49, 56 n.7 (1978). However, differential congressional treatment of Indians does not create a suspect classification for equal protection purposes. Washington v. Yakima Indian Nation, 439 U.S. 463, 500-501 (1979).
    92. *E.g.*, Talton v. Mayes, 163 U.S. 376 (1896).
    93. *E.g.*, Barta v. Ogala Sioux Tribe, 259 F.2d 553, 556 (8th Cir. 1958); Glover v. United States, 219 F. Supp. 19, 21 (D. Mont. 1963).
    94. Native Am. Church v. Navajo Tribal Council, 272 F.2d 131 (10th Cir. 1959).
    95. Tom v. Sutton, 533 F.2d 1101, 1102-03 (9th Cir. 1976).
    96. United States v. Wheeler, 435 U.S. 313 (1978).
    97. United States v. Klamath Indians, 304 U.S. 119, 123-24 (1938).
    98. 25 U.S.C. §§1302-3 (1976).
    99. Claims under this provision are treated distinctly from claims proceeding directly under the Constitution. *See, e.g.*, Groundhog v. Keeler, 442 F.2d 674 (10th Cir. 1971).
    100. Janis v. Wilson, 385 F. Supp. 1143, 1150 (D.S.D. 1974).
    101. Wounded Head v. Tribal Council, 507 F.2d 1079, 1082-83 (8th Cir. 1975); Yellow Bird v. Ogala Sioux Tribe, 380 F. Supp. 438, 440 (D.S.D. 1974). The *Wounded Head* decision also held the Twenty-sixth Amendment and the Voting Rights Act of 1970 inapplicable to tribal elections.
    102. McCurdy v. Steele, 506 F.2d 653, 655-56 (10th Cir. 1974); Groundhog v. Keeler, 442 F.2d 674, 681-82 (10th Cir. 1971).
    103. Bd. of County Comm'rs v. Seber, 318 U.S. 705, 715 (1943).
    104. Morton v. Mancari, 417 U.S. 535, 553-54 (1974).
    105. Fong Yue Ting v. United States, 149 U.S. 698, 724 (1893).
    106. *E.g.*, Chae Chan Ping. v. United States (the Chinese Exclusion Case), U.S. 581 (1889).
    107. *E. g.*, Morrison v. Cal., 291 U.S. 82, 85-86 (1934).
    108. 118 U.S. 356 (1886).
    109. *Id.* at 368.
    110. *Id.* at 369.
    111. Gong Lum v. Rice, 275 U.S. 78 (1927).
    112. *E.g.*, A.S. Miller, Democratic Dictatorship: The Emergent Constitution of Control 82-84 (1981).
    113. 320 U.S. 81 (1943).
    114. 323 U.S. 214 (1944). *But see Ex Parte* Endo, 323 U.S. 283 (1944).
    115. Hirabayashi v. United States, 81, 100-101 (1943).
    116. Takahashi v. Fish & Game Comm'n, 334 U.S. 410 (1948).
    117. Morrison v. Cal., 291 U.S. 82 (1934).
    118. Oyama v. Cal., 332 U.S. 633 (1948).

119. Generally regarded as initiating the doctrine was Justice Stone's famous footnote in United States v. Carolene Prods. Co., 304 U.S. 144, 152-53 n.4 (1938).

120. Hirabayashi v. United States, 320 U.S. 81, 100 (1943).

121. Korematsu v. United States, 323 U.S. 214, 216 (1944).

122. Oyama v. Cal., 332 U.S. 633, 640 (1948).

123. *E.g.*, Trimble v. Gordon, 430 U.S. 762, 777 (1977) (Rehnquist, J., dissenting) (modern equal protection doctrine attacked, but clear desire to apply guarantee equally to discrimination involving race and its "first cousin," national origin). Where the discrimination in question operates against alienage as such rather than status as an Oriental, though, a lesser degree of scrutiny will apply.

124. L. Tribe, *supra* note 72, at 943.

125. Boutilier v. Immigration & Naturalization Serv., 387 U.S. 118 (1967). *See also* Rosenburg v. Fleuti, 374 U.S. 449 (1963). *But see* Nemetz v. Immigration & Naturalization Serv., 647 F.2d 432 (4th Cir. 1981).

126. Rose v. Locke, 423 U.S. 48 (1975).

127. Doe v. Commonwealth's Attorney, 403 F. Supp. 1199 (E.D. Va 1975), *aff'd mem.*, 425 U.S. 901 (1976).

128. Carey v. Pop. Servs. Int'l, 431 U.S. 678, 694 n.17 (1977) (dictum). State and lower federal court cases dealing with the question whether sexual expression is a fundamental right are a mixed lot. *See, e.g.,* Beller v. Middendorf, 632 F.2d 788, 809-12 (9th Cir. 1980), *cert. denied*, 49 U.S.L.W. 3893 (1981) (equivocal on question but discharge from Navy upheld because of deference to military); ben Shalom v. Secretary, 489 F. Supp. 964, 972-77 (E.D. Wis. 1980) (discharge from army reserves for avowed homosexual inclinations denial of various constitutional rights, including privacy); People v. Onofre, 51 N.Y.2d 476, 415 N.E.2d 936, 434 N.Y.S.2d 947 (1980) (state statute forbidding "deviant" practices between consenting adults not married to each other unconstitutional, partially on privacy grounds). *See also* L. Tribe, *supra* note 72, at 941-42 n.3 for some more cases.

129. People v. Onofre, 51 N.Y.2d 476, 415 N.E.2d 936, 434 N.Y.S.2d 947 (1980) (on privacy and equal protection grounds); Commonwealth v. Bonadio, 490 Pa. 91, 415 A.2d 47 (1980) (on equal protection grounds).

130. *E.g.*, Norton v. Macy, 417 F.2d 1161, 1164-66 (D.C. Cir. 1969).

131. *E.g., id.* at 1166. *See also* Singer v. U.S. Civil Serv. Comm'n, 530 F.2d 247 (9th Cir. 1978) (discharge of much-publicized gay activist EEOC clerk-typist who publicly stated his job affiliation upheld and *Macy* distinguished).

132. Wentworth v. Laird, 348 F. Supp. 1153 (D.D.C. 1972). *But see* Adams v. Laird, 420 F.2d 230 (D.C. Cir. 1969) (denial of security clear-

ance upheld). *See also* Gayer v. Schlesinger, 490 F.2d 740 (D.C. Cir. 1973), *order amended*, 494 F.2d 1135 (D.C. Cir. 1974).
133. *See, e.g.*, Beller v. Middendorf, 632 F.2d 788 (9th Cir. 1980), *cert. denied*, 49 U.S.L.W. 3893 (1981) (discharge upheld, largely because of deference to military); Matlovitch v. Secretary, 591 F.2d 852 (D.C. Cir. 1978) (vacated and remanded to determine basis on which denial of discretionary retention made); ben Shalom v. Secretary, 489 F. Supp. 964 . (E.D. Wis. 1980) (discharge of reservist for homosexual tendencies, not conduct, unconstitutional on various grounds); Martinez v. Brown, 449 F. Supp. 207 (N.D. Cal. 1978) (discharge regulation read as mandatory is denial of due process because no showing of nexus between homosexuality and fitness for service).
134. This is developed below in the section of this chapter discussing the rights of military personnel.
135. *E.g.*, DeSantis v. Pac. Tel. & Tel. Co., 608 F.2d 327 (9th Cir. 1979); Smith v. Liberty Mut. Ins. Co., 395 F. Supp. 1098 (N.D.Ga. 1975), *aff'd*, 569 F.2d 325 (5th Cir. 1978). Title VII generally prohibits employment discrimination based on race, sex, religion, color, or national origin.
136. Gay Lib v. Univ. of Mo., 558 F.2d 848 (8th Cir. 1977), *cert. denied*, 434 U.S. 1080 (1978); Gay Alliance v. Matthews, 544 F.2d 162 (4th Cir. 1976); Gay Students Organization v. Bonner, 509 F.2d 652 (1st Cir. 1974). *But see* Miss. Gay Alliance v. Goudelock, 536 F.2d 652 (5th Cir. 1976), *cert. denied*, 430 U.S. 982 (1977) (attempt to compel student newspaper to run advertisement for homosexual group's activities held denial of First Amendment freedom of paper, where school administration not involved in its management).
137. *See* Aumiller v. Univ. of Del., 434 F. Supp. 1273 (D. Del. 1977).
138. U.S. Const. art I, § § 2, 3; art. II, §1.
139. *E.g.*, Chae Chan Ping v. United States (the Chinese Exclusion Case), 130 U.S. 581 (1889).
140. *E.g.*, Morrison v. Cal. 291 U.S. 82, 85-86 (1934). Of course, Congress has the power not to admit aliens in the first place. *E.g.*, Bridges v. Wixon, 326 U.S. 135, 161 (1945) (dictum) (Murphy, J., concurring).
141. *See e.g.*, Kwong Hai Chew v. Calding, 344 U.S. 590 (1953); Ng Fung Hc v. White, 259 U.S. 276, 284-85 (1922).
142. This is not true, however, of nonresident enemy aliens in wartime, *see* Johnson v. Eisentrager, 339 U.S. 763 (1950), although resident enemy aliens at least have access to the courts, *see Ex parte* Kawato, 317 U.S. 69 (1942).
143; Bridges v. Wixon, 326 U.S. 135, 161 (1945) (Murphy, J., concurring). *See also id.* at 148 (freedom of speech granted to aliens); Yick Wo v. Hopkins, 118 U.S. 356, 369 (1886) (Fourteenth Amendment applies).
144. Terrace v. Thompson, 263 U.S. 197, 216-22 (1923). *See also* Ohio

ex rel. Clarke v. Deckebach, 274 U.S. 392 (1927); Webb v. O'Brien, 263 U.S. 313 (1923). *But see* Truax v. Raich, 239 U.S. 33 (1915).
145. Heim v. McCall, 239 U.S. 175 (1915). *See also* Crane v. N.Y., 239 U.S. 195 (1915).
146. Takahashi v. Fish & Game Comm'n, 334 U.S. 410, 420 (1948).
147. *E.g.*, Karst, *Foreword: Equal Citizenship under the Fourteenth Amendment*, 91 Harv. L. Rev. 1, 42 (1977).
148. Graham v. Richardson, 403 U.S. 365 (1971).
149. *In re* Griffiths, 413 U.S. 717 (1973).
150. Sugarman v. Dougall, 413 U.S. 634 (1973).
151. Nyquist v. Mauclet, 432 U.S. 1 (1977).
152. Also of interest is Hampton v. Mow Sun Wong, 426 U.S. 88 (1976), decided largely on procedural due process grounds, striking down a federal Civil Service Commission regulation barring resident aliens from employment in the competitive civil service.
153. Ambach v. Norwick, 441 U.S. 68, 73-74 (1979).
154. Folie v. Connelie, 435 U.S. 291 (1979).
155. Ambach v. Norwick, 441 U.S. 68 (1979).
156. Also, it appears that the federal government's power to classify to the disadvantage of aliens exceeds that of the states, because of the "paramount federal power over immigration and naturalization." Hampton v. Mow Sun Wong, 426 U.S. 88, 100-01 (1976). *See also id.* at 126-27 (Rehnquist, J., dissenting).
157. *Cf.* O'Connor v. Donaldson, 422 U.S. 563, 573-74 (1975); Minn. v. Probate Court, 309 U.S. 270 (1940).
158. Buck v. Bell, 274 U.S. 200, 207 (1927).
159. This is because of the apparent stress on the importance of the right to bear children in cases such as Skinner v. Okla., 316 U.S. 535 (1942); Eisenstadt v. Baird, 405 U.S. 438 (1972); and Cleveland Bd. of Educ. v. LaFleur, 414 U.S. 632 (1974). *See also* Wyatt v. Aderholt, 368 F. Supp. 1382, 1383 (M.D. Ala. 1973) (holding a sterilization law unconstitutional because of inadequate procedural protections).
160. *E.g.*, Addington v. Tex., 441 U.S. 418 (1979) ("clear and convincing" standard of proof required).
161. Vitek v. Jones, 445 U.S. 480 (1980).
162. Parham v. J.R., 442 U.S. 584 (1979) (commitment upheld); Secretary of Public Welfare v. Institutionalized Juveniles, 442 U.S. 640 (1979) (commitment upheld).
163. McNeil v. Director, 407 U.S. 245 (1972). *See also* Jackson v. Ind., 406 U.S. 715 (1972); Humphrey v. Cady, 405 U.S. 504 (1972).
164. O'Connor v. Donaldson, 422 U.S. 563, 573 (1975). This decision vacated and remanded a Fifth Circuit opinion finding such a right. Donaldson v. O'Connor, 493 F.2d 507 (5th Cir. 1974).

165. Wheeler v. Glass, 473 F.2d 983 (7th Cir. 1973).
166. *See* Bell v. Wolfish, 441 U.S. 520, 545-48 (1979).
167. *Id.* at 562.
168. *See generally* 1 Emerson, Haber & Dorsen's Political and Civil Rights in the United States 1089-1151 (4th ed. 1976) [hereinafter cited as Emerson].
169. Lee v. Washington, 390 U.S. 333 (1968).
170. *See* Procunier v. Martinez, 416 U.S. 396 (1974).
171. Pell v. Procunier, 417 U.S. 817 (1974); Saxbe v. Wash. Post Co., 417 U.S. 843 (1974).
172. Cruz v. Beto, 405 U.S. 319 (1972) (petitioner a Buddhist).
173. Jones v. N.C. Prisoners' Union, 433 U.S. 119 (1977).
174. *See* Bounds v. Smith, 430 U.S. 817 (1977) (obligation to provide law library or legal assistance); Johnson v. Avery, 393 U.S. 483 (1969) (jailhouse lawyers); Gilmore v. Lynch, 319 F. Supp. 105 (N.D. Cal. 1970), *aff'd sub nom.* Younger v. Gilmore, 404 U.S. 15 (1971) (restriction on books in library).
175. Vitek v. Jones, 445 U.S. 480 (1980) (transfer to mental institution); Enomoto v. Wright, 434 U.S. 1052 (1978), *aff'g*, 462 F. Supp. 397 (N.D. Cal. 1976) (transfer to solitary); Wolff v. McDonnell, 418 U.S. 539 (1974) (revocation of "good time" sentence reduction); Gagnon v. Scarpelli, 411 U.S. 778 (1973) (probation revocation); Morrissey v. Brewer, 408 U.S. 571 (1972) (parole revocation).
176. Conn. Bd. of Pardons v. Dumschat, 452 U.S. 458 (1981) (denial of commutation); Meachum v. Fano, 427 U.S. 215 (1976) (prison transfer). *But see* Greenholtz v. Nebr. Prison Inmates, 442 U.S. 1 (1979) (state presumption of pardon or parole; distinguished in *Dumschat*).
177. Baxter v. Palmigiano, 425 U.S. 308 (1976).
178. *See* the cases cited in Rhodes v. Chapman, 452 U.S. 337, 353-54 n.1 (1981) (Brennan, J., concurring).
179. Rhodes v. Chapman, 452 U.S. 337 (1981); Bell v. Wolfish, 441 U.S. 520, 530-43 (1979).
180. Estelle v. Gamble, 429 U.S. 97, 104-5 (1976).
181. *E.g.*, Smith v. Schneckloth, 414 F.2d 680 (9th Cir. 1969); Carey v. Settle, 351 F.2d 483 (8th Cir. 1965). *But see e.g.*, James v. Wallace, 382 F. Supp. 1177 (M.D. Ala. 1974).
182. In addition to the case discussed below, *see* Conn. Bd. of Pardons v. Dumschat, 452 U.S. 458 (1981) and Rhodes v. Chapman, 452 U.S. 337 (1981), in *supra* notes 176, 179 and accompanying text.
183. Bell v. Wolfish, 441 U.S. 520, 562 (1979).
184. Parker v. Levy, 417 U.S. 733, 743-44 (1974).
185. *In re* Grimley, 137 U.S. 147, 152 (1890).
186. *In re* Vidal, 179 U.S. 126 (1900).

187. *See* Note, *Servicemen in Civilian Courts*, 76 Yale L.J. 380 n.4 (1966). For other possible procedural devices, *see* Emerson, *supra* note 168, at 1186.

188. *E.g.*, Hiatt v. Brown, 339 U.S. 103 (1950); *In re* Grimley, 137 U.S. 147 (1890).

189. Reaves v. Ainsworth, 219 U.S. 296, 304 (1911).

190. Burns v. Wilson, 346 U.S. 137 (1953).

191. *See generally* 76 Yale L.J., *supra* note 187.

192. 417 U.S. 733 (1974).

193. *Id.* at 756.

194. *Id.* at 758.

195. *Id.* at 751.

196. *Id.* at 743.

197. Greer v. Spock, 424 U.S. 828 (1976).

198. Brown v. Glines, 444 U.S. 348 (1980).

199. Middendorf v. Henry, 425 U.S. 25 (1976). A summary court-martial is an informal proceeding conducted by a single commissioned officer who serves as judge, factfinder, prosecutor, and defense counsel. It is used for minor offenses and the penalties that it can impose are relatively limited.

200. *See* Rostker v. Goldberg, 453 U.S. 57 (1981).

201. *See* Emerson, *supra* note 168, at 1187-98.

202. U.S. Civil Serv. Comm'n v. Nat. Ass'n of Letters Carriers, 413 U.S. 548 (1973). *See also* United Public Workers v. Mitchell, 330 U.S. 75 (1947).

203. Broadrick v. Okla., 413 U.S. 601 (1973).

204. Keyishian v. Bd. of Regents, 385 U.S. 589, 605 (1967).

205. Pickering v. Bd. of Educ., 391 U.S. 563 (1968).

206. Elrod v. Burns, 427 U.S. 347 (1976) (sheriff's office employees); Branti v. Finkel, 445 U.S. 507 (1980) (public defenders).

207. Abood v. Detroit Bd. of Educ., 431 U.S. 209 (1977). However, the portions of the service charge devoted to traditional union activities such as organizing were held constitutional.

208. *E.g.*, Pickering v. Bd. of Educ., 391 U.S. 563, 569 (1968).

209. *E.g.*, Branti v. Finkel, 445 U.S. 507, 517-18 (1980).

210. Givhan v. Western Line Consolidated School Dist., 439 U.S. 410 (1979) (claim of racial discrimination in employment at junior high school communicated by teacher to principal).

211. *See* Arnett v. Kennedy, 416 U.S. 134 (1974). There, however, adequate postdismissal procedures did exist.

212. Bishop v. Wood, 426 U.S. 341 (1976).

213. Kelly v. Johnson, 425 U.S. 238 (1976).

CHAPTER 3

Informal Statuses within the Modern Occupational Structure

The overall demise of the traditional constitutional statuses and the way this supports Maine's "status to contract" generalization seem amply to bolster his reputation as a seer of emergent trends. Yet as various observers have noted,[1] Maine's statement was in significant respects overtaken by events soon after its utterance in 1861. When viewed within the individual-versus-government orientation that typifies so much American political and legal discourse, the gradual elimination of these statuses should have signaled a generalized increase in negative liberty and formal equality. What might have emerged was a condition of free and equal personhood under a regime of neutral laws in which the individual was increasingly significant as an individual. Yet when attention is directed toward other areas of social life,[2] it is evident that no such libertarian "utopia" has emerged. Despite the undoubted advance of liberal-individualist values, American life has come to be substantially dominated by large bureaucratized institutions of all sorts and, partly in response to the problems this has created, by a pervasive governmental presence. Internally, this developed institutional structure is marked by innumerable achieved status variations.[3] These tend to shape the way the negative freedoms formally granted by the legal system are actually employed. Practically speaking, the theoretically free citizen often can meaningfully exercise negative liberty only by choosing to associate with some large institutionalized group. As a result, he must adjust to its requirements, among them the restraints imposed by the organizational status position he occupies. In doing so, however, he may gain capacities that he would have lacked without this institutional involvement. Perhaps in deference to the liberal-individualist ethos, these capacities tend to be of a fairly indeterminate nature. To the extent that this is so, modern bureaucratic institutions can be said to reflect a fusion of status and liberal positive freedom. In fact, this characterization of organizational life is probably more significant than the much-discussed opposition between status and negative freedom which also typifies it.

Group Power, Positive Government, Public-Private Blurring, and the Corporate State Hypothesis: A Brief Overview

That sizable private entities like large corporations, labor unions, and universities are extremely significant actors on the American scene is no more than a truism by now.[4] Indeed, it is often said that the bureaucracy is the characteristic institution of modern societies.[5] Such institutions possess considerable social, economic, and political power. The larger corporations significantly shape the course of national production, consumption, investment, and technological advance. In oligopolistic industries, at least, they often administer prices to a significant degree. By their choice of plant and office location, they can substantially affect the economic prospects of a city, a state, or a region. More importantly for our purposes, corporations and other large groups exert substantial control over those who work within the confines of these organizations or who are otherwise significantly affected by them.[6] They determine the conditions of work and help shape the traits and values of their employees.[7] They often determine access to employment opportunities—most notably, perhaps, in the case of union closed shops.[8] They can restrict rights of a broadly constitutional nature— for instance, by discriminating in hiring or promotion, denying procedural fairness in promotion or firing, restricting expression, and invading individual privacy.[9]

Although not everyone would agree on the importance of the group, few would dissent from the proposition that the formal organs of government, both federal and state, have assumed vastly increased powers throughout the twentieth century. Left and Right may dispute the desirability, purposes, application, and consequences of different forms of regulation but not the fact of that regulation's pervasiveness. The modern positive state, says Arthur Selwyn Miller, "is a label for express acceptance by the federal government . . . of affirmative responsibility to further the economic well-being of all the people. It is a societal undertaking of a duty to attempt to create and maintain minimal conditions within the economy— of economic growth, of employment opportunities, of the basic necessities of life."[10] Here, it is not necessary to discuss the vast range of roles assumed by the modern state,[11] only to note what no one denies: that its activity is extensive.[12]

These two developments—the growth of group power and the rise of the positive state—have led to a so-called blurring of the public and the private.[13] Perhaps most significant in shaping this perception is the power exercised by the large organization. As Arthur Bentley wrote in 1908: "A corporation is government through and through. . . . Certain technical methods which political government uses, as, for instance, hanging, are not used by corporations, generally speaking, but that is a detail."[14] Much in the same spirit, Andrew Hacker has asserted: "It may well be that the time has come to alter outdated assumptions about the presumed 'private' character of our major corporations. By any reasonable measure AT&T is as important an institution in American society as the state of Alabama."[15] Still, it might be argued that there are certain functions and powers which are the sole prerogative of the state. One of these is what Wolfgang Friedmann has called its "reserve function," through which "it expresses and articulates, especially in times of crises, national policies and sentiments which do not normally express themselves in organized pressure groups."[16] This aside, though, it is not obvious how many functions traditionally associated with sovereignty reside exclusively within the province of formal governmental institutions.

Try to identify a governmental activity for which there is not an important counterpart in some private institution.

The judiciary? Mediation and arbitration play a widespread
and increasing role. Police? Pinkertons are famous in our
history; today every large company and school has its own
security force, and private eyes continue to be hired for
peephole duty; many highly innovating industries have
their own secret service working in the world of industrial
espionage. Welfare? Any listing of private, highly bureaucratized and authoritative welfare systems would be as
long as it is unnecessary. Armies? It is difficult to overestimate the significance of private armies in the past, or such
present private armies as those possessed by the Mafia and
other syndicates, not to mention the neighborhood gangs
and Minutemen.[17]

The governmental powers of organizations aside, there are
other factors conducive to public-private blurring. Due to omni-
present state activity, few areas of life can be regarded as unambiguously private. Instead, almost all such activities are colored
by the presence of the state. Roberto Mangabeira Unger tells
us that "the social law of institutions is a law compounded of
state-authored rules and of privately sponsored regulations or
practices; its two elements are less and less capable of being
separated."[18] This suggests that the distinction between those
sovereign commands aimed at intraorganizational matters, on
the one hand, and the organization's own response to these, on
the other, is often not too significant. Consider, for example,
the case where a private firm adopts its own internal affirmative action plan in response to federal employment discrimination legislation. Finally, looking at public-private blurring from
another angle, it sometimes seems that the formal organs of
government are quite privatized. It is no secret that governmental activities are substantially affected by the pressures coming
from large private groups. The reserve function perhaps excluded, some have regarded form d sovereign policy as nothing
more than the resultant of com eting group pressures.[19] In
fact, it might be said that the p litical state itself is a group distinguishable from other groups only in certain respects.[20] The
self-aggrandizing habits of administrative bodies and their resistance to legislative or executive control tend to support this
perception.

Pushing the blurring insight even further is the corporate state hypothesis. To observers of this persuasion, American society is best characterized as an organized totality marked by a substantial fusion and interpenetration of public and private bodies. To Miller, "The trend is toward the fusion of economic power (the supercorporations) and political power (the Positive State), both aided by the 'knowledge industry'; the consequence is the creation of the 'technocorporate' state."[21] In such an order, public-private blurring assumes exteme forms. "The spearhead of corporatism is the effacement both in organization and in consciousness of the boundary between state and society, and therefore between the public and the private realm."[22] Sometimes this sort of theorizing produces descriptions of the state that are remarkably similar to Hegelian and neo-Hegelian conceptions.[23] Within such an order the individual is fairly insignificant as an individual, since he or she obtains sustenance, status, power, and (perhaps) meaning only through group affiliations.[24]

For present purposes, it is not necessary to adopt the corporate state hypothesis in toto. Like any other descriptive generalization or ideal type, it can be only a more or less useful approximation of the phenomena it attempts to assimilate and make comprehensible. It may overstate the degree of coherence existing within the sociopolitical whole it postulates. Although for this reason it might be less valid than standard pluralist accounts stressing group competition,[25] it is certainly far superior to the laissez-faire model which still reigns in some circles. Lending it additional plausibility is the degree of tangible interconnection actually existing between the formal political state and ostensibly private groupings. Aside from the examples already mentioned, the well-known "triangular" industry-agency-congressional committee relationship[26] is of special importance in this respect.

Formal Constitutional Doctrine, the Rise of the
Corporation, and the Emergence of the Positive State

The law, Justice Oliver Wendell Holmes is supposed to have said, is a "magic mirror" in which we see reflected our own lives and the lives of our ancestors.[27] Certainly this is true of those constitutional provisions and doctrines whose development assisted in, or mirrored, the growth of the corporation and the positive state.[28] Since, to quote Holmes again, "[t]he substance of the law at any time pretty nearly corresponds . . . with what is then understood to be convenient,"[29] the evolution of these provisions and doctrines provides another vantage point from which to view some of the social and political developments just discussed.[30]

The Contract Clause

Article I, section 10 of the Constitution declares: "No state shall . . . pass any . . . Law impairing the Obligation of Contracts."[31] It seems to be agreed that the reason for including this language in the Constitution was to afford contract creditors protection against the debtor relief statutes passed by many states after the Revolution.

> The widespread distress following the revolutionary period and the plight of debtors had called forth in the States an ignoble array of legislative schemes for the defeat of creditors and the invasion of contractual obligations. Legislative interferences had been so numerous and extreme that the confidence essential to prosperous trade had been undermined and the utter destruction of credit was threatened. . . . It was necessary to interpose the restraining power of a central authority in order to secure the foundations even of "private faith."[32]

Soon enough, though, the clause came to be a general check on legislative infringements of so-called vested rights. Vested rights are those "which have . . . completely and definitely accrued to or settled in a person,"[33] and their constitutional protection was once felt to be a matter of extreme importance. As Edward S. Corwin has described this: "The effect of legislation on existing property rights was a primary test of its validity; for if these were essentially impaired then some clear constitutional justification must be found for the legislation or it must succumb to judicial condemnation."[34]

A significant manifestation of this drive to protect vested rights was the extension of the contract clause to block a state's

impairment of its own contracts, grants, and charters. The
debtor relief statutes of concern to the clause's drafters involved
private contracts. But, to quote Corwin again, "[i]t was necessary if the doctrine of vested rights was to do its full work that
it should enter the States themselves, and its protection through
the federal judiciary be extended to *legislative* grants, whether
of lands or charters, which, even in the States whose courts generally enforced the doctrine of vested rights, were sometimes
left to the mercy of legislative majorities."[35] The cases effecting
this extension were the well-known duo of *Fletcher v. Peck*[36]
and *Dartmouth College v. Woodward.*[37] In *Fletcher v. Peck*, an
1810 decision occasioned by the Yazoo land frauds,[38] the
Court employed the contract clause to strike down Georgia's
1796 revocation of a 1795 state grant. (The original grant was
for 35 million acres of land and occurred after speculators had
bribed the Georgia legislature.) Something of the flavor of the
times is conveyed by Justice William Johnson's concurring
opinion, with its declaration that Georgia's revocation was in-
valid "on the reason and nature of things" due to "a principle
which will impose laws even on the deity."[39] *Dartmouth College*, decided in 1819, struck down New Hampshire's attempt
to alter the 1769 charter establishing the college. That decision
was broad enough to cover corporate charters; as a result, it
gave corporations constitutional protection against subsequent
legislation impairing the privileges originally granted by the
state. The aid this provided the infant corporate movement was
not insignificant. "Before [*Fletcher v. Peck* and *Dartmouth College*], there were but a handful of manufacturing corporations
in the entire country. Under the confidence created by [these]
decisions, such corporations were to proliferate to such an
extent that they soon transformed the very face of the nation."[40]

   In part because of these decisions, the contract clause became
the most significant federal constitutional check on state regulation of the economy throughout most of the nineteenth century. Over the period 1809-1861, one source informs us, the
clause was employed 18 times to strike down state acts,[41] while
according to another, 49 state laws were struck down as unconstitutional contract impairments from 1865 to 1888.[42] In 1885,

Maine declared that the contract clause "secured full play to the
economical forces by which the achievement of cultivating the
soil of the American continent has been performed" and "is the
bulwark of American individualism against democratic impa-
tience and socialistic fantasy."[43] For all of this, though, it is
easy to overestimate the significance of the clause as a promoter
of laissez-faire and an agent of corporate growth. In Gerald
Gunther's opinion, "[h]istorians have probably exaggerated
the impact of the early contract clause decisions on American
economic and legal developments. The cases did indeed restrict;
but they did not compel legislative paralysis, they were not
the keystone of American corporate development, they did not
establish an inflexible safeguard for all vested rights."[44] First,
although it is hazardous to generalize about a number of different states over a time span of a hundred or so years, government regulation of the economy was not notable for its frequency or intensity throughout much of the nineteenth century. In
particular, the constitutional protection against charter altera-
tions provided by *Fletcher v. Peck* and *Dartmouth College* was
rendered less and less important because legislatures were de-
creasingly inclined to use charter amendments as a means of
regulating corporations.[45] This is not to say, however, that the
states were indifferent to business concerns.

> . . . [T]he state, through the tariff, could accord the entre-
> preneur protection from foreign competition; it also had
> railroad, power or other public utility franchises to grant;
> it possessed land, mineral rights, forests and other natural
> resources for private exploitation; it could offer exemption
> or mitigation of taxes; and it could provide moral or armed
> support in managing refractory workers. As a further and
> important point, these and other benefits could all be
> given or withheld in response to relatively simple decis-
> ion.[46]

This suggests what should be obvious: that there is always some
interplay between the political and economic realms and that
pure laissez-faire and economic development do not necessarily

go hand-in-hand. Nor, for that matter, did protection of vested rights always encourage commerce and growth. In the famous *Charles River Bridge*[47] decision of 1837, for instance, the Court narrowly construed a 1785 charter to build and operate a bridge over the Charles River and thus upheld a subsequent charter for a second bridge over the river. There, Chief Justice Taney clearly recognized that to treat the second charter as a contract impairment would stifle competition and innovation. If the Court decided otherwise, he asserted, "[w]e shall be thrown back to the improvements of the last century, and obliged to stand still," until the old turnpike corporations "shall consent to permit these states to avail themselves of the lights of modern science, and to partake of the benefit of those improvements which are now adding to the wealth and prosperity, and the convenience and comfort, of every other part of the civilized world."[48]

Another reason for the contract clause's limited, though quite real, impact on the growth of private economic activity was the set of doctrinal restrictions increasingly put on its reach throughout the nineteenth century. Although the clause was frequently used to strike down state legislation during that century, the range of situations to which it could be applied was progressively restricted. Probably the most significant doctrinal change was the limitation of the clause's application to regulation with a retrospective effect. This took place in the 1827 case of *Ogden v. Saunders*,[49] a contract clause decision as important as *Fletcher v. Peck* and *Dartmouth College*. What this meant was that, rather than being a check on contract impairments as such, the clause could be used only to attack laws impairing the obligations of contracts preexisting the legislation. Bernard Schwartz has contended that under a contrary approach "the Contract Clause . . . would have become an absolute bar to all governmental infringements upon contractual obligations."[50] When one considers economic regulation's usual effect on contractual freedom in the abstract, the significance of *Ogden v. Saunders* should be apparent. Another[51] significant limitation on the reach of the contract clause was the doctrine that the states' exercise of the police power[52] could not be restricted by

a prior contract, grant or charter. As the Court put the matter
in an 1880 case, "[n]o legislature can bargain away the public
health or the public morals."[53]

After the turn of the century, the contract clause fell into
increasing desuetude. It was replaced in its role as principal
check on government regulation by the doctrine of economic
substantive due process.[54] More significant in the long run was
its increasing subservience to the states' police powers.[55] Most
often cited as typifying the modern Court's hands-off attitude
in the contract clause area is *Home Building & Loan Association
v. Blaisdell*, a 1934 case where it upheld a depression-era mortgage moratorium measure. In the course of his opinion there,
Chief Justice Charles Evans Hughes virtually announced the
death of laissez-faire to justify increased state intervention in
economic life.

> The settlement and consequent contraction of the public
> domain, the pressure of a constantly increasing density of
> population, the interrelation of the activities of our people
> and the complexity of our economic interests, have inevi-
> tably led to an increased use of the organization of society
> in order to protect the very bases of individual opportun-
> ity. Where, in earlier days, it was thought that only the
> concerns of individuals or of classes were involved, and
> that those of the state itself were touched only remotely,
> it has later been found that the fundamental interests of
> the state are directly affected; and that the question is no
> longer merely that of one party to a contract as against
> another, but of the use of reasonable means to safeguard
> the economic structure upon which the good of all
> depends.[56]

Especially relevant for present purposes is Hughes's suggestion
that freedom is no longer an individual phenomenon and that
social organization is the basis of individual opportunity. By
the 1950s and 1960s, it came to be widely accepted that the
contract clause was no longer a significant part of American
constitutional law. In two late-1970s decisions,[57] however, the

Burger Court definitely gave it new life, altough its future evolution is as yet quite uncertain.[58]

Economic Substantive Due Process

   The Fifth and Fourteenth amendments to the Constitution
prevent the federal government and the states from taking liberty or property from persons unless due process of law is used.
In its usual interpretation, due process is procedural; it is basically concerned with legal administration. Guarantees such as
the right to notice of the charges brought, the right to an adequate hearing, and so forth are of this nature. This conception
of due process, however, does not exhaust the subject. At various times in the Court's history, it has given due process a substantive connotation. Substantive rules involve relations between
individuals and/or groups. Substantive due process, then, involves constitutional checks on such rules and not merely on
the procedural machinery through which they are enforced. In
its various forms, substantive due process typically involves two
operations: pumping some preferred freedom or freedoms into
the liberty protected by the Fifth and Fourteenth amendments
and subjecting deprivations of this liberty to some judicially
determined test of reasonableness. This is what the Supreme
Court did in the late nineteenth and early twentieth centuries
when it created the "economic" form of substantive due process.[59] Freedom of contract was treated as a constitutionally
protected due process liberty,[60] and infringments of that freedom were required to have some real and substantial relation
to the furtherance of a valid state purpose.[61]

   Economic substantive due process seems to express the purest
form of economic individualism. In fact, though, it often served
to protect corporate-based group interests against the various
sorts of social legislation that became increasingly common after
the turn of the century. It did so by posing a constitutional obstacle to legislation interfering with freedom of contract. The
formally equal negative liberty present where freedom of contract is maximized is an illusory freedom in fact when one party
possesses superior bargaining power. This was often the case
when large corporations confronted isolated individuals, and

protective legislation was increasingly enacted in recognition of
this fact. Such regulation, however, obviously restricted the formal contractual liberty of corporation and individual alike.
Since the corporation had been held to be a person for due process purposes in 1886,[62] it was able to challenge such legislation
on substantive due process grounds. (The contract clause was
inadequate for this purpose because of its limitation to retrospective legislation and its lack of application to the federal
government.) Freedom of contract was obviously violated in
such cases,[63] and all that remained to invalidate the legislation
was a business-oriented Court's determination that it lacked a
sufficiently close relation to a valid governmental purpose. For
this reason, courts utilizing the doctrine played a significant
economic policy-making role.[64]

Economic substantive due process did not automatically, or
even usually, work to invalidate protective social legislation,[65]
but it was effective often enough to make a difference. Two
well-known examples illustrate the point. In *Lochner* v. *New
York*,[66] the Court struck down a New York law limiting the
working hours of bakery employees. Substantive due process
was also sometimes useful in blocking the interests of organized
labor. At issue in *Coppage* v. *Kansas*[67] was a state measure
prohibiting "yellow dog" contracts: employment contracts that
required employees to agree not to join or remain a member of a
labor union. Obviously such legislation denied freedom of contract, and Justice Pitney's *Coppage* opinion declaring it unconstitutional made a ringing declaration of laissez-faire fundamentals while stressing this fact.

> Included in the right of personal liberty . . . is the right to
> make contracts for the acquisition of property. Chief
> among such contracts is that of personal employment, by
> which labor and other services are exchanged for money
> or other forms of property. If this might be struck down
> or arbitrarily interferred with, there is a substantial impair-
> ment of liberty in the long-established constitutional sense.
> The right is as essential to the laborer as to the capitalist,
> to the poor as to the rich; for the vast majority of persons

have no way to begin to acquire property, save by working for money.[68]

All things considered, though, economic substantive due process was a rearguard action by business interests and exponents of limited government. It received its death blow in the 1937 case of *West Coast Hotel* v. *Parrish*,[69] where the Court upheld a minimum wage measure for women. In that case, Chief Justice Hughes digressed on the nature of due process liberty:

> The constitutional provision invoked is the due process clause of the Fourteenth Amendment. . . . In each case the violation alleged by those attacking minimum wage regulation for women is deprivation of freedom of contract. What is this freedom? The Constitution does not speak of freedom of contract. It speaks of liberty and prohibits the deprivation of liberty without due process of law. In prohibiting that deprivation the Constitution does not recognize an absolute and uncontrollable liberty. Liberty in each of its phases has its history and connotation. But the liberty safeguarded is liberty in a social organization which requires the protection of law against the evils which menace the health, safety, morals and welfare of the people. Liberty under the Constitution is thus necessarily subject to the restraints of due process, and regulation which is reasonable in relation to its subject and is adopted in the interests of the community is due process.[70]

Considering this declaration along with Hughes's strikingly similar statement in *Blaisdell*, a variety of propositions seem to emerge. First, to Hughes, American society was by the 1930s a complex, interconnected whole and not a collection of discrete individuals. By implication, at least, this was a whole in which groups were the principal actors. Thus freedom of contract—and freedom generally—could not be a purely personal matter and certainly could not be defined simply as an absence of governmental restrictions. It was obviously conditioned in

numerous ways by the behavior of groups. To Corwin, Hughes
treated " 'Liberty' . . . as something that may be infringed by
other forces as well as government."[71] And as Miller puts it,
"these forces could only be the corporations, which by 1937
had become giant in size and which had effective control over
the terms and conditions under which most people worked."[72]
Thus freedom required positive government action to protect
against "the evils which menace the health, safety, morals, and
welfare of the people." In fact, Hughes claimed, due process
itself requires such legislation. "From being a limitation on
legislative power, the 'due process' clause becomes an actual
instigation to legislative action of a levelling character."[73] But
freedom in its modern phase was not simply protection against
abuses of group power and the ills of industrial society. It was
also "liberty in a social organization"—practically speaking, in
a group. To Hughes, obviously enough, negative freedom was
by 1937 in a state of declining significance, and liberty was
increasingly taking on a positive cast. Liberty required positive
government intervention to prevent diminutions of capacity
and it was also a group phenomenon.

After *Parrish*, substantive due process fell out of favor and
became a dirty word in American constitutional law.[74] This did
not, however, prevent its reemergence as a technique for protecting rights of a personal nature.[75] Also beginning in the 1950s,
the judicially imposed constitutional duty to which Hughes
alluded has become increasingly significant in areas such as
school desegregation, reapportionment, and the administration
of the criminal law, although not under the aegis of due process.[76] All such developments are part of the Court's post-
1930s shift from economic decision maker to protector of the
individual.

Federal Power to Regulate: The Commerce Clause

So far, we have been concerned with external checks on
government regulation of the economy, constitutional provis-
sions different from those on which the power to regulate is
based. But government regulation can be restricted internally
as well, by limiting the scope of constitutional provisions which

are the sources of regulatory authority. The federal government,
it is often said, is one of constitutionally enumerated powers
alone. Thus, federal power to regulate is not limited merely by
independent checks like due process and the contract clause,
but by the inherent reach of these enumerated powers as well.
In the twentieth century, the commerce power[77] has been by
far the most important source of federal regulatory authority.
As a result of its evolution throughout this century, it has become the major constitutional underpinning of the positive
state.

Article I, section 8 of the Constitution gives Congress the
power "to regulate Commerce . . . among the several States."
As a source of federal regulatory authority,[78] the commerce
clause occasioned little significant litigation throughout most
of the nineteenth century. With increased efforts at federal
regulation toward the end of the century, though, the clause
began to attract more attention. Sometimes it was interpreted
so as to restrict federal regulatory power and, indirectly, to
assist corporate interests. In an 1895 case,[79] for instance, the
Court found the Sherman Act inapplicable to an acquisition of
four sugar refiners by another refiner because its constitutional
basis, the commerce clause, did not apply to "manufacture."
After the turn of the century, however, two expansive commerce clause doctrines with extremely important long-term
consequences became apparent in the Court's decisions. The
first of these was the extension of Congress's powers to intrastate matters, which are not within the literal coverage of the
clause, having a significant impact on interstate commerce,
which is.[80] The other was the clause's increasing employment
for police purposes of a noncommercial nature. Here, the technique for regulating such matters as lotteries and prostitution
was to ban interstate shipments of, respectively, lottery tickets
and immoral women.[81] For a time, this technique had its limits.
In the well-known 1918 case of *Hammer* v. *Dagenhart*,[82] for
instance, the Court struck down a federal child labor statute
prohibiting the interstate shipment of goods manufactured by
offending firms.

Despite the far-reaching implications of these two doctrines,

congressional regulatory power under the commerce clause
continued to be restricted for quite some time. Early in the
New Deal, the Court found the compulsory retirement and
pension plan established by the Railroad Retirement Act, the
National Industrial Recovery Act, and the minimum wage and
maximum hours provisions of the Bituminous Coal Conservation Act to be unconstitutional assertions of the commerce
power.[83] As with economic substantive due process, the real
break with the past did not come until 1937,[84] when the Court
upheld the intrastate operation of the National Labor Relations
Act.[85] In the early 1940s, it sustained the wages and hours provisions of the Fair Labor Standards Act[86] and acreage allot-
ments set under the Agricultural Adjustment Act,[87] both as
applied to in-state operations. Today the commerce clause is a
sort of all-purpose federal police power capable of being utilized
for a wide range of noncommercial purposes and possessing an
extensive intrastate reach when so used. In the 1960s, for instance, it served as the constitutional basis for the public accom-
modations section of the 1964 Civil Rights Act.[88]

State Action

The formal constitutional doctrines just discussed assisted the
rise of the corporation and the positive state in a fairly direct
fashion. This is not true of the final constitutional area treated here,
the so-called state action requirement. Rather than facilitating the
dominance of the large group and the activist state, post-World
War II state action doctrine can instead be viewed as a response
to these social and political developments. As such, it tacitly
supports these and other contentions made in the first section
of this chapter, most notably public-private blurring.

The various individual rights provisions of the U.S. Constitution check formal governmental activity alone.[89] They do not
protect the individual against wholly private denials of personal
rights, although such private behavior may be regulated by statute. Because most of the relevant cases have arisen under the
Fourteenth Amendment, which restricts the states alone, this
limitation on the reach of constitutional protection is usually
referred to as the state action requirement. Prior to World War

II, there was a tendency to restrict state action to the activities
of formal government organs like legislatures, agencies, municipalities, and state universities. Since that time, the reach of the
doctrine has expanded considerably. As a result, state action
has become a major source of judicial and scholarly discomfiture, one observer terming it a "conceptual disaster area."[90]
    With its 1948 decision in *Shelley* v. *Kraemer*,[91] the Supreme
Court gave the state action concept a potentially broad sweep
by holding that Missouri's enforcement of a racially restrictive
private covenant made this agreement subject to constitutional
attack. Had it desired to pursue the full implications of *Shelley*,
the Court could have rendered all private behavior backed by
governmental enforcement the activity of the state. "If Shelley
were read at its broadest, a simple citation of the case would
have disposed of most subsequent state action cases. . . . Some
seemingly 'neutral' state nexus with a private actor can almost
always be found; at least by way of state backdrop for exercises
of private choice; usually, more concrete state involvement than
that."[92] In the years following *Shelley*, however, the Court
declined to follow this path. Now the dominant form of state
action inquiry focuses on the points of interaction between
formal government and the private sector, with much concern
about the role of goverment in promoting, authorizing, facilitating, aiding, or perhaps even allowing the behavior challenged
as unconstitutional. Thus, considerable judicial attention has
been devoted to factors such as the scope and intensity of government regulation, state and federal financial aid, and the
existence of a symbiotic public-private relationship approxi-
mating a joint venture. Employing such rationales for state
action, various federal courts have held subject to constitutional
checks the activities of, for instance, private hospitals, the American Stock Exchange, private universities, low-income housing
projects, a mortgage lender, a nonprofit corporation operating a
Head Start program, a corporation running a local airport, the
Long Island Railroad, a charitable foundation, and a defense
contractor.[93] Simultaneously, though, the federal courts have
also denied the existence of state action in a variety of similar
contexts. For instance, state or federal chartering is by itself

no basis for state action.[94] The existence of a regulated monopoly ordinarily seems not to suffice either.[95] Often, too, the activities of private educational institutions[96] and hospitals[97] are not regarded as state action. ConRail[98] and a community action agency[99] have been held not to qualify. In fact, there seems to have been some tendency to restrict the scope of the state action concept throughout the 1970s.[100]

Another branch of state action law, the public function doctrine, clearly emerged[101] in 1946, when the Court held First Amendment protections applicable to the activities of a company town in *Marsh* v. *Alabama*.[102] Here, the state action finding was based not on the private actor's ties to formal political organs but on its functional resemblance to a public body. The *Marsh* reasoning lay dormant until the 1960s. In 1966, it was used as an alternate basis of decision in a case striking down the exclusion of nonwhites from a public park.[103] Two years later, it was employed to overturn a local court order forbidding labor picketing within a privately owned shopping center.[104] This particular extension of the public function rationale, however, did not survive the mid-1970s.[105] In other cases, the Burger Court has seemed intent on interring the doctrine as a whole.[106] As a result, its current reach is extremely limited.

State action doctrine requires courts to draw a constitutional line between the public and the private sectors. One traditional justification for doing so is the enhancement of negative liberty: the preservation of a free zone within which individuals and groups can act without being subjected to constitutional checks.[107] The price paid is the possibility that, absent statutory restrictions, such individuals and groups will be able to limit the negative freedom of others. Preventing such private restrictions of freedom, however, might involve a thoroughgoing politicization of society. It is also arguable that because of their relatively restricted power, private actors pose less of a threat to the individual than do public bodies.

The group dominance and pervasive state presence sketched at the beginning of this chapter, however, tend to undermine these traditional assumptions. To the extent that the quasi-political powers exercised by private groups cause them to resemble formal governmental bodies, the case for subjecting them to constitutional norms is strengthened. Social factors of this sort seem best recognized by the public function doctrine, which focuses on the nature of the private actor. Of most concern here are intraorganizational exercises of power, those affecting employees and others subject to organizational control. With just such problems in mind, some observers have called for a constitutionalization of the large corporation.[108] In addition to the rise of group power, the ascendancy of activist government has undermined the traditional public-private line by rendering few activities unambiguously private. This corresponds to the main line of state action inquiry, which stresses the private actor's relations with the political state. Both of these developments contribute to public-private blurring. It would be difficult to find a clearer indication of its reality than the post-World War II evolution of the state action requirement.

Given these developments, one might expect state action to have attained a very wide reach by now. In fact, though, the area is rather muddled, and, for a variety of reasons, the scope of state action may actually be narrowing. First, many of the aims that a constitutionalization of the organization would advance have already been achieved by statute,[109] a development tending to reinforce the idea of public-private blurring. Second, real or perceived pressures from the affected private groups may deter courts from taking state action to its farthest limits. Most forms of corporativism envision ties of reciprocal influence between the formal government and major groups. Since the groups themselves have little desire to be subjected to constitutional checks, governmental organs like courts might be motivated to restrict the reach of constitutional norms. This may explain the Burger Court's tentative retreat on the state action front.[110] A third factor perhaps inhibiting the continued expansion of state action is the fear that it will eventually extend to almost all sectors of social life. Consider, to take an admittedly extreme example, the requirement that parents provide a due process hearing before confining a child to the home. To some degree, though, this difficulty can be avoided by diluting the relevant constitutional guarantee to accommodate the demands of the particular social institution in question.[111] Due process, for instance, is routinely relativized in this fashion.[112]

The Law of Large Institutions

Although it did demonstrate the interplay of formal constitutional doctrine with group power and positive government, the preceding discussion did not display constitutional status-freedom relationships. Nor did it directly bear on intra organizational statuses. In fact, there seem to be insuperable obstacles to regarding these statuses as legal, let alone constitutional, phenomena. Under the analytical positivist[113] conceptions of law which dominate American law schools and legal practice generally, norms, to be "legal," must be traceable to the command of a legitimate political sovereign. Also, such norms usually must be susceptible to more or less precise statement.[114] Obviously intraorganizational controls do not partake of the legal under such criteria. Thus, we are left to consider why a book purportedly dealing with constitutional matters should consider organizational ordering at all.

This problem can be attacked from a variety of interrelated angles. Uniting all of them are the phenomena of group dominance, positive government, public-private blurring, and nascent corporativism. These developments have tended to undermine the reigning positivist paradigm by creating systems of order rivaling the political state and dissolving the line separating group controls from formal state law. As Wolfgang Friedmann once remarked: "It is this basic differentiation between a main body of the law, which develops from the social life of the 'people,' living as nations, church congregations, business communities or families, and a limited sphere of 'state norms,' created for purposes of organization and protection, that has lost its validity and meaning in the increasingly industrialized and articulate society of our time."[115] Making the point in even more general terms is Roberto Mangabeira Unger:

> The deepest and least understood impact of corporatism is the one it has on the very distinction between the law of the state and the spontaneously produced normative

order of nonstate institutions. As private organizations
become bureaucratized in response to the same search
for impersonal power that attracts government to the
rule of law principle, they begin to acquire the features,
and to suffer the problems, of the state. At the same time,
the increasing recognition of the power these organizations
exercise, in a quasi-public manner, over the lives of their
members makes it even harder to maintain the distinction
between state action and private conduct.[116]

What all of this suggests is that private forms of control are
increasingly taking on a public cast. Also, formal state law itself has undergone changes in response to twentieth-century
social developments, coming to resemble private ordering in
certain respects. There certainly is no dearth of observers be-
moaning the decline of rule of law values in the twentieth century and their replacement by imprecise and discretionary
standards.[117] The reason for this change, some contend, is the
dilemma confronted by activist government as it tries to do
justice in a complex social environment marked by a huge
variety of group-group and individual-group relations. Ideally,
the positive state might proceed in good positivist rule of law
fashion and set out a series of precise and detailed commands
for the ordering of social life.[118] But the variety and complexity
of situations confronting it make this very difficult and in fact
seem to require open-ended, discretionary standards. To quote
Unger again:

> The first type of effect [created by the welfare state] is
> the rapid expansion of the use of open-ended standards
> and general clauses in legislation, administration, and
> adjudication. For example, the courts may be charged
> to police unconscionable contracts, to void unjust enrich-
> ment, to control economic concentration so as to main-
> tain competitive markets, or to determine whether a gov-
> ernment agency has acted in the public interest.
> . . . .
> As government assumes managerial responsibilities, it
> must work in areas in which the complexity and varia-
> bility of the relevant factors of decision seem too great

to allow for general rules, whence the recourse to vague
standards. These standards need to be made concrete
and individualized by persons charged with their administrative or judicial execution.[119]

As Unger suggests, antitrust law and the twentieth-century law
of contract[120] provide examples of this phenonenon. Consider,
for example, the range of factors relevant to decisions to permit
or not to permit corporate mergers and the difficulty of framing
these in precise terms susceptible to across-the-board application.
As Theodore Lowi has pointed out, the tendency toward discretionary fuzziness is also evident in much federal administrative
activity.[121]

Thus, although positivist conceptions of law were perhaps
appropriate to the simpler nineteenth-century social reality,[122]
they are less well suited for explaining the nature of law in
modern society. They tend to ignore the significant ordering
role played by institutionalized private groups. Because of their
emphasis on precision and certainty, they tend not to reflect
the way that "state law" has come to resemble these relatively
informal types of ordering. Perhaps as a result, other jurispru-
dential approaches with a broader conception of law and the
legal have emerged in the twentieth century. For our purposes,
the most important of these is Eugen Ehrlich's "living law,"
which went far beyond positivistic state law to embrace many
other forms of social ordering. To Ehrlich, the living law is "the
law which dominates life itself even though it has not been
posited in legal propositions," the "source[s] of its knowledge"
being "the modern legal document" and also "direct observation of life," "of commerce, of customs and usages, and of all
associations."[123] To elaborate:

> The similarity of Ehrlich's to Savigny's approach lies in
> his emphasis on the "living law of people," based on so-
> cial behavior rather than the compulsive norm of the state.
> Norms observed by the people, whether in matters of re-
> ligious habits, family life, or commercial relations, are
> law, even if they are never recognized or formulated by

the norm of the state. For Ehrlich, the main sphere of
the compulsive state norm is in the fields specifically connected with the purposes of the state, i.e. military organization, taxation and police administration. While he admits
that the sphere of essential state activities, and, therefore, of the norms created for their protection, has expanded in our time, it still remains for him an ancillary
part of the law, and one he separates from the "living law"
of the community.[124]

The living law also includes the internal norms of private associations. To Julius Stone, Ehrlich's "social law" consists of
"rules emerging from the inner ordering of social groups, including the numerous and varied associations ranging from
the simple family to vast religious or economic organizations."[125]
  Similar ideas have been expressed by the collection of French
and Italian legal thinkers whose theories have been put under
the general heading of institutionalism. These theories clearly
push the idea of law beyond simple sovereign command. In particular, they seem to regard the internal ordering of organizations as legal in nature.

> The French institutionalists thought that the very exis-
> tence of an institution imports the existence of consti-
> tutional principles of a "juridical" nature concerning its
> organization and operation, principles which emerge
> from its activities. These, as well as the constitution of
> the state [they urged], should properly be embraced
> within "constitutional law," whether or not the state has
> embodied this "law" into the positive law of the state.
> Here too, then, we must understand that the sense in
> which personality and constitutional law necessarily
> spring from institutions is not that of positive law, but
> rather the sense that these results are warranted by the
> "nature of social life."[126]

Much in the same vein is Arthur Selwyn Miller, who treats the
"living law of American constitutionalism" as including the

actions of important private groupings, such as political parties, trade unions, and corporations.[127]

Finally, even if one eschews these broader definitions of law and holds to prevailing positivist conceptions, the status features of large organizations are still relevant to the present inquiry because of their implications for human freedom. To focus on formal constitutional doctrine alone is to divert attention from the reality of group dominance and its implications for individual liberty by tacitly casting social relations in an individual-versus-government mold which by its nature cannot encompass such realities. Whatever the practical virtues of the positivist approach, it is necessarily incomplete if it fails to note how formal doctrine takes on a different aspect when viewed in a wider context.

The Organization and the Individual

If organizational power can be regarded as legal in some sense, or at least cannot be dismissed as irrelevant to a legal inquiry, it is necessary to consider the bearing of internal organizational controls on the themes of status and freedom. The description of organizational status systems and the various forms of organizational ordering set out below is brief and general. What follows is not a detailed survey of organizational behavior or the sociology of large institutions, but rather an attempt to characterize institutional life in terms of the abstract status-freedom relationships it presents.

Organizational Positions as Statuses

An obvious characteristic of large institutions like corporations, governmental agencies, labor unions, and the military is their organized, bureaucratic nature. As bureaucracies, such institutions are internally differentiated along functional lines, almost always in a hierarchical fashion.[128] The various positions occupied by individuals within the organizational hierarchy can easily be termed statuses[129] since they are distinct social places marked by different powers, duties, rights, perquisites, and so forth. In fact, they seem routinely to be so regarded.[130] This is apparent when we consider the differences between blue-collar workers and corporate executives, enlisted personnel and officers, the various grades of federal employees, or graduate students and tenured professors. The following description of an industrial firm makes the point.

> Obviously, then, the factory is arranged in a hierarchy of power; it is a pyramid with the chairman of the board at the apex and the workers at the base. Junior and senior management, clerical staff, and supervisors, occupy intermediate positions. The visitor to the factory would discover in a comparatively short time that all the employees, from the highest to the lowest, show considerable concern about the relative position they occupy in this hierarchy. They respond with great anxiety or resentment to any situation which seems to indicate that their status is in danger. Promotion in the hierarchy is not necessarily desired, but any employee who has become integrated into the structure is sensitive about his position in relation to the other employees. This attitude is seen very clearly in the canteen arangements, if we note where the workers sit and how they arrange themselves. . . . The importance attached to status is seen even more clearly if the firm is one of those in which there are separate dining rooms for the various levels within the organization: directors, management, clerical staff, and workers, may take their meals separately. Under these circumstances, there may be furious arguments and much resentment over such questions as whether a director's secretary has been unduly favoured in being permitted to dine in the managment mess rather than with the other secretaries in the office canteen.[131]

This observation can be generalized to include even such less formalized status rankings as those based on skill, seniority, and work with a more prestigious division of the organization.[132]

For the most part, organizational statuses are achieved and not ascribed.[133] In theory, at least, no one is labeled at birth as a manual laborer or a college professor. Still, different organizational status positions often do seem to be occupied by markedly different personal types. One example is the military, where the personal traits of noncommissioned officers or war-

rant officers tend to differ markedly from those of commissioned officers.[134] However, movements from one status position to another within an organization, as well as interorganizational movements, are certainly common,[135] although some types
of intraorganizational shifts appear to be largely foreclosed. It
is obviously difficult, for instance, to move from a blue-collar
job to a management position without a college degree. Finally,
although occupational statuses are not the only sorts of status relationships occupied by most individuals, occupational status does
seem to be regarded as the most significant form of status in
modern Western societies.[136] One observer has noted: "Industry
is the main source of status . . . in Western cultures, and, when
we are trying to 'place' a stranger, our first question is 'What
does he *do* ?'[137]

Organizational Control over the Individual

   Organizational statuses are just one manifestation of a more
general system of institutional control. Organizations, it has
been said, are "the most important socializing agencies in America" and "our major agencies of social control."[138] However,
American life is not (or is not yet) completely dominated by
bureaucratized groups, and it is evident that no one is directly
compelled to join up. Yet is is equally plain that significant
forces push most people in that direction. "In a society dominated by a fusion of big government and big business," Arthur
Selwyn Miller contends, "freedom means the attenuated liberty
to decide which group to join—and not much more. . . . Join up
or drop out are the *only* choices, and the former will prevail."[139]
There are several fairly obvious reasons why this tends to be so.
Entrepreneurial success of the traditional sort is probably less
attainable than in the past, at least in established industries.
Now large corporations[140] are increasingly perceived as offering
the most favorable environment for those strongly oriented
toward material success. For people generally, institutional affiliation is often—with justice—regarded as offering the best opportunity for earnings, prestige, security, and all of life's other
tangible goods. Sometimes such affiliations represent the course
of least resistance for those who are uncertain of what direction
to pursue.[141] The American educational system, with its strong
emphasis on specialization and vocationalism, tends to reflect

organizational needs and to shape individuals to fit organizational requirements.[142]

Once within the confines of the organization, the individual
is subjected to a range of external restrictions. Merely to occupy an organizational status position is to be required to perform the duties associated with the position. Obviously, too,
organizational life may involve restrictions on attire, intragroup speech,[143] demeanor, and so forth. Sometimes the organization's demands may spill over into the private sphere;
corporate executives, for instance, may be expected to maintain a certain life-style. Some of these restrictions are less likely to be present at the lower rungs of the organization, where
remuneration and other benefits are generally lower. But here
unions frequently will impose their own particular restraints.
In fact, membership in a trade union can be regarded as a status
in which workers exchange their largely formal freedom to
contract with the employer for the tangible benefits accruing
from group solidarity and are subjected to the restrictions that
inevitably accompany this.[144] Finally, private organizations
may even infringe rights that, were it not for the state action
requirement, would be of a constitutional nature. Privacy, procedural fairness, and extramural speech are examples.[145]

These external restrictions usually apply only so long as the
individual remains affiliated with the group imposing them.
The sanctions making them effective typically are dismissal
from the organization or the failure to advance within it, plus
the accompanying material losses. Such sanctions are not the
only sources of group control over the individual. At least since
the publication of William H. Whyte's *The Organization Man*
in 1956, it has been a commonplace that there are powerful
social and psychological forces tending toward the adjustment
of individual inclination to group demands. John Kenneth Galbraith, for instance, speaks of "identification," a process by
which individuals come to find group goals superior to their
own and thus take on these goals, as one of the major forces
creating loyalty to the organization in his new industrial
state.[146] In a recent book on the individual and the organization, William Scott and David Hart assert that in order to advance the overriding goal of institutional "health,"[147] modern

organizations become "managerial systems using universal
behavioral techniques ["methods drawn from the behavioral sciences and instructed by humanistic psychology"] to integrate
individuals and groups into mutually reinforcing relationships
with advancing technology in order to achieve system goals
efficiently."[148] The purpose of this is "achievement of a general
harmony between the individual and the organization through
a mutually shared set of values."[149] One requirement for attain-
ment of this harmony is that "individuals must be schooled in
behaviors appropriate to their organizational roles."[150] This, in
turn, requires that successful professionals[151] make organizational values "an intrinsic part of their lives" by creating "an
efficient and harmonious relationship" between these values
and "their entire personality."[152] For some theorists of management, in fact, the desideratum is "reduction of self to a
series of organizational functions."[153] This seems to be most
important (and pronounced) at the highest levels of the organization.[154] It may be particularly true within the corporation
where, it is said, those who aspire to high-echelon positions must
continually affirm, and genuinely believe, that business and business values are central to American life, that their firms' products are essential to national well-being, and that their com-
panies are making forceful efforts to tackle a wide range of
social problems.[155] The drive to accomodate individual inclination to group need, Scott and Hart insist, is common to organizations in general, and not to corporations alone.[156]

   To say that the individual's identification with group goals is
desired is not to say that attempts at personal socialization are
always effective. A number of background factors conduce
toward this, however. To the extent that organizations satisfy
rationally calculated desires for money, prestige, a good life-
style, security, and so forth, they usually attract a certain
degree of loyalty. Since it is hardly unusual for people to adopt
attitudes that benefit them in tangible ways, further attachment
to organizational values is a likely consequence of individual
efforts to advance within the organization. Another set of background factors assisting personal identification with group demands involves the depersonalization and anomie often said to
characterize modern life.

In a transformed society, managers and workers alike are uprooted, but it is the former—the middle class—who seek adjustment and new roots because of the profound changes they have undergone in environment, expectations and status. Eastman Kodak's medical plans, IBM's country clubs, Richfield Oil's model homes, du Pont's psychiatrists, Reynolds Tobacco's chaplains, and even RCA's neckties with the corporate insignia— all are symptomatic of the effort to establish a feeling of community within the corporation. The middle class employee no longer has an alternative community in which he can find a sense of belonging. . . . Thus there has emerged the equivalent of a new kind of citizenship: corporate citizenship.[157]

This citizenship, in turn, gives the displaced individual a status otherwise unavailable in an individualistic climate.

The white-collar employee of the corporation possesses status as well as contract, for the corporation has begun to assume rather broad obligations toward him, regardless of his value to—or even his performance in—the company. The member of a contract system is regarded simply as an employee whose contract with his employer lasts as long as he does his job. The member of a status system is regarded as a person: the benefits he receives stem less from his performance as an employee than from his stature as an individual.[158]

Finally, these background factors aside, the organization itself obviously takes many steps to ensure the required fit between personal inclination and the requirements of a group-based status. Psychological testing sometimes eliminates those who fail to display the needed malleability or slots people according to their perceived characteristics.[159] Another step is the collection of techniques that has been given the label "therapeutic paternalism."[160] In its broadest sense, this can involve the whole package of material and psychic benefits provided to the individual by the organization.

The bureaucratization of benevolence is a function of the depersonalization of work. Pats on the back by the entrepreneur-owner and an extra day off around the time of the accouchement of the worker's wife were the equivalents of the fringe benefits that are now written with scrupulous and mechanical generosity into union contracts. Bureaucratized benevolence for the lower classes of corporate society is paralleled by the development of corporate welfarism for the middle classes of that society. Millions are bound in a system of tribal dependence through paternalistic personnel policies, conformitarian training programs, tax-deductible expense accounts, an ever-ringing celebration of corporate interest through advertising propaganda, and the growth of the new company towns in suburbia and exurbia. The new middle class of suburban split-level Babbits, riding the 8:05 into the city and the 5:05 out of it, wearing the status badges that mark their level in the corporate world, more anxious than yearning, looks for solace and safety in the "togetherness" of the corporate collective. For the upper classes of corporate society, bonuses play an important part in the reward system, as do the numerous opportunities for beating the tax laws; and the risk of loss of status is a powerful incentive to conform when the juniors are being looked at closely to see whether they will "fit." For all classes the threat of deprivation of these social sweets is a strong sanction that makes the cruder forms of discipline less necessary.[161]

Therapeutic paternalism can also involve more specific practices, such as sensitivity training or T groups, and the use of participatory management as a tool of control.[162] Finally, although present efforts in this direction seem not to have advanced too far, it may come to involve more direct means of psychological manipulation, including the use of drugs, electrical stimulation of the brain, and Skinnerian methods generally.[163]

Status and Freedom in Large Organizations

Status and Freedom as Opposed or Complementary?

If organizational life is seen in terms of the external restrictions it places on individuals, the opposition between status

and negative freedom is the point of reference. But if attention
is directed toward the numerous forces tending to produce a
coalescence of individual motivation and organizational requirements, something like the Hegelian fusion of status, positive
freedom, and duty, with its "adjustment of inclination and individual capacity to the performance of socially significant
work,"[164] is being envisioned. Here, organizational status is
largely constitutive of personal identity and thus of individual
capacity. Which abstract relationship affords a superior descriptive picture, model, ideal type, or paradigm? Obviously, there
is abundant evidence to support either interpretation, just as
devotees of the laissez-faire and corporate state models of the
economy can adduce much evidence to make their respective
cases. When dealing with matters like freedom, our focus should
be primarily at the level of personal perceptions and behavior.
If, for instance, the status-versus-negative-freedom model is to
be counted as a superior description of organizational life, institutional restrictions should be perceived as such by the individual, should create some personal discomfiture, and should
provoke as much opposition as is possible under the circumstances. If such perceptions and reactions tend not to occur,
we should conclude that although the opposition between status
position and negative liberty is no doubt present in some sense,
its ability to explain organizational life as actually lived is highly
suspect. A corresponding line of argument can be advanced to
test the fusion-of-status-and-positive-freedom model of the organizational milieu.

Perhaps these points can be concretized a bit by introducing
a more or less familiar American type. The negative freedom
picture would seem to presuppose an individual who undertakes
an organizational affiliation with a fairly clear recognition that
he is trading off a certain loss in the ability to act as he wishes
in exchange for the tangible benefits the affiliation offers. This
person would clearly perceive organizational restrictions as restrictions and would be ready to urge practicable means for
their reduction when possible. Such a picture of individual motivation arguably underlies some of the current concern for
rights within the organization initiated by lawyers and others
sensitive to the realities of group power.[165] The recurrent desire
to constitutionalize the corporation through an expansion of

the state action concept[166] is just one example. The positive
freedom model of organizational life, in contrast, might presuppose one of two personal types, or some combination of
the two. Here individuals might, on the one hand, possess innate
drives that find satisfaction in the organizational context,[167] or
they might be essentially indeterminate and malleable and thus
ready subjects for organizational conditioning.[168] In either case,
organizational controls generally would not be perceived as
checks on one's will but rather as forces with which that will is
and should be identified.

With the numerous qualifications such a view inevitably en-
tails, the positive freedom account of organizational life appears
superior to the negative alternative. The general perception
underlying this position is that the personal capacities making
opposition between the individual and the organization meaningful seem in fairly short supply in the America of the 1970s
and 1980s. A variety of observations indirectly support this perception; taken as a whole, they are difficult to square with the
idea that organizational life displays an acute conflict between
personal drives and organizational demands. Large organizations
do not create a closed circle totally limiting one's ability to act
as one wishes. Although opting out of the system may be an
unattractive alternative for many, there is no direct external
compulsion to join up. The principal sanctions against the failure to conform to group requirements are the inability to advance within the organization, or ultimately, to be discharged
from it. Thus, organizational dictates can readily be avoided by
those possessing the personal capacity to do so. In this sense,
America is still a (negatively) free country, if one is willing to pay
the price for exercising that freedom. The relative infrequency
with which this choice is made suggests both that such capacities
tend to be lacking and that the conditions obtaining in modern
organizations are not generally perceived as imposing onerous
restraints. This initial line of argument, however, ignores the
numerous material inducements leading ostensibly freedom-
loving Americans to affiliate with bureaucratic groups. But this
raises yet another question: why, if the opposition between negative liberty and organizational demands is a living reality for
most people, do large organizations dominate the American
scene to the extent that they do? Whatever social forces may

have led to the rise of modern bureaucracy,[169] its eventual triumph would almost certainly have been accomplished less easily had its implications for negative liberty been widely perceived and opposed. Such opposition as existed obviously was inefficacious in the long run. This again suggests that the supposed antimony between individual and group has, for a great many people, not been a fact to be deplored.

Another set of factors more directly tending to support the positive freedom conception of organizational life concerns the nature of that life as tangibly lived. The identification of the individual with the group, although not verbalized in Hegelian terms, has been a commonplace of twentieth-century sociology and organizational theorizing generally. More concretely, anyone who has observed large organizations cannot help but be aware of their tendency to shape individual desires and behavior to fit group demands. For most people most of the time, this does not seem to be perceived as a crushing burden or a denial of personal identity. Instead, most individuals pursuing organizational careers appear to assume the existence of a rough harmony between personal inclination and group demands or not to consider the question at all.

One example may help to bolster the general point that intragroup life today tends toward a fusion of individual inclination and the dictates of the institution. All are familiar with the contemporary tendency to see organizational misdeeds as springing from the machinations of bureaucratic elites operating from positions of unfettered power. Such views tend to ignore the fact that although such actions often require decisions by elites, elite behavior itself is conditioned by organizational requirements.[170] The pronounced tendency for those high up in the bureaucracy to internalize the goals of the organization has already been noted. And the idea that high-level managers are unfettered agents would surely come as a surprise to those occupying such positions. What this suggests is a view of the organization as an entity with goals and purposes transcending those brought to it by its constituent human parts—a sort of "group-person," to use Miller's term.[171] The recurrent tendency to refer to organizations as if they are organisms[172] is symptomatic here.

The argument for the fusion-of-status-and-positive-freedom

model has been stated in a fairly unqualified fashion, mainly to emphasize what is probably an unfamiliar view of organizational life. While descriptively superior to its competitor, this model does not even begin to cover every relevant personal case. In innumerable situations, the clash between the demands of an organizational status and a person's negative freedom—a clash that technically is always "there"—assumes importance to the individual. The current concern for employee rights would seem to increase the need for such a concession; in fact, this concern might be adduced to invalidate the whole argument just made. If people generally identify with the groups in which they work, it might be contended, why do we see so many attacks on organizational controls? Some of this discomfiture no doubt reflects the inescapable fact that the conflict between organizational status and negative liberty is quite real in many instances. The drive for increased freedom within the organization, however, while superficially an expression of traditional American rugged individualism, actually seems to be something less than, or at least different from, this. Demands for greater freedom within the large group do not involve a widespread rejection of organizational life as such. Some observers, in fact, feel that the power and legitimacy of the organization have actually increased since the Silent 1950s, the disturbances of the 1960s to the contrary notwithstanding.[173] And the drive for employee rights has occurred during a period in which the use of indirect therapeutic controls seems to have increased. Impressionistically, at least, it appears that these controls have been subjected to less criticism than have overt forms of external coercion or mistreatment. (To the archetypal rugged individualist, in contrast, the former sort of control might appear most insidious, while the latter, though disliked, might at least be regarded as honest and out in the open.) Perhaps, then, the current concern over the conditions of organizational life mainly reflects a desire that the conditions of work be more pleasant, humane, and satisfying and that controls take therapeutic rather than overtly authoritarian forms. Although the achievement of such an agenda would no doubt increase negative liberty to some degree, this would be of dubious significance if indirect controls produce the needed conformity. In fact, some employee rights are com-

patible with the positive freedom model of organizational identification. For example, concern about the need for greater
worker participation is common, but participatory management
is often a socializing device in practical effect. Finally, external restrictions like denials of privacy and free speech have little
to do with the nurturing and capacity-supplying role the positive freedom model assumes organizations will fulfill.[174]

The Capacities Fostered by Organizational Life

The positive liberty with which organizational status has been
identified involves the enhancement of capacity; it remains to be
seen what abilities modern institutional statuses tend to promote. Organizational statuses impart certain skills, and the acquisition of these is undoubtedly a growth in capacity, but a
more abstract characterization is needed. Generally, the capacities that organizations now promote are largely of an open, liberal nature, although the older identification of status position
and duty is inescapably present.

Our first candidate for consideration is the strongly authoritarian idea of capacity, which is often linked with ascriptive
forms of status. Underlying this are traditional conceptions of
virtue,[175] as well as the view that the virtues whose exercise
constitutes a realization of a person's true nature sometimes
vary from ascriptive class to ascriptive class. But success in modern
modern organizations does not require one to identify with the
Guardian class in Plato's *Republic*, to spend nights reflecting
on Aristotle's *Ethics*, or to be influenced by those who do. In
fact, organizational success may not even require adherence to
nineteenth-century American conceptions of ethical worth. As
Irving Kristol, surely no foe of the corporation, has noted about
the qualities needed for executive advancement:

> It is still believed, and it is still reasonable to believe, that
> worldly success among the working class, lower middle
> class, and even middle class has a definite connection with
> personal virtues such as diligence, rectitude, sobriety, hon-
> est ambition, etc., etc. And, so far as I can see, the connec-
> tion is not only credible but demonstrable. It does seem
> that the traditional bourgeois virtues are efficacious among

these classes; at least, it is rare to find successful men
emerging from these classes who do not to a significant
degree exemplify them. But no one seriously claims that
these traditional virtues will open the corridors of corporate power to anyone, or that those who now occupy the
executive suites are—or even aspire to be—models of bourgeois virtue.[176]

And although racial and sexual discrimination in hiring, assignment and promotion no doubt remains, the long-run trend
be toward its disappearance.[177]

The next possibility is the fusion of status, positive freedom,
and duty characteristic of Hegel and the British neo-Hegelians.
Here, the effects of post-seventeenth-century individualism are
apparent: group statuses tend to be achieved, not ascribed, and
there is little overt reference to ascriptive classifications. To some
degree, this status-freedom relationship finds reflection in organizations today. No institution could function for long if it did
not assign individuals more or less definite places and tie these
to duties of a fairly specific nature. Also, modern organizational
statuses, like those of the Hegelian model, generally depend on
personal achievement. Yet the congruence between this status-
freedom relationship and life in contemporary bureaucracies is
far from complete. While Hegel and the British idealists often
proceeded at a level of generality sufficient to cover twentieth-
century developments, traditional moral ideals are quite promi-
nent in their writings, and generalizations about ascriptive
groups are occasionally present also.[178] In addition, their writings tended to legitimize a social order in which both sorts of
ideas were alive in a way that is not true today. Nowhere in
Hegel's *Philosophy of Right*, Green's *Lecture on the Principles
of Political Obligation*, Bosanquet's *Philosophical Theory of the
State*, or the societies they tended to celebrate is one likely to
find a picture of intragroup life quite like that presented by,
say, Joseph Heller's *Something Happened*.

Thus, we are left with the open-ended liberal idea of capacity,
whose goal is the individual ability to entertain and pursue a
wide range of potential options. It is doubtful whether this
conception of capacity is viable or meaningful if pushed to its
logical extreme,[179] and certainly no organization could function,

or exist, if within its confines all things were possible to all people at all times. Still, something like this idea of capacity does seem to be promoted within modern bureaucracies. First, when compared with the conditions out of which they arose, today's institutional statuses represent an increase in human possibilities. As Wolfgang Friedmann once remarked about modern forms of status in general:

> . . . the new status, while limiting this often theoretical freedom of decision of the individual—a freedom that led to the degradations, the slums, the miseries of the many, compared with the wealth and power of a very few—has at the same time released new energies and given new opportunities. The worker who is dependent on whatever his employer and union may work out for him between them has, at the same time, far greater opportunities of education and intellectual development. The law ensures for him minimum standards of work, housing, and compensation, which free him from the incessant toil of the feudal peasant and the early industrial worker. In modern democracies the law has gradually . . . diminished or removed the status barriers that kept people relentlessly within their class, race or religion. In particular—and here we see the main principle still working itself out in a kind of delayed action effect—the woman now enjoys a legal freedom of movement . . . which she has never before enjoyed in the history of Western civilization.[180]

Second, the proper functioning of twentieth-century organizations seems to demand a certain degree of openness and flexibility on the part of those who inhabit them. The industrial psychologist Elton Mayo, for instance, frequently stressed that an "adaptive society" where technological change has rendered all fixed reference points and stable social structures indefinite requires correspondingly flexible social skills.[181] Similarly, David Riesman's well-known other-directed man was to some extent a consequence of—or at least well adapted to—the conditions of modern bureaucratic life. Perhaps the most striking aspect of this emergent character type is its sensitivity to external signals and thus its indeterminacy. Riesman wrote:

What is common to all the other-directed people is that
their contemporaries are the source of direction for the
individual—either those known to him or those with
whom he is indirectly acquainted, through friends and
through the mass media. This source is of course "internalized" in the sense that dependence on it for guidance
in life is implanted early. The goals toward which the
other-directed person strives shift with that guidance: it
is only the process of striving itself and the process of
paying close attention to the signals from others that
remain unaltered throughout life.[182]

"[O]ther direction," he asserted, "is becoming the typical
character of the 'new' middle class—the bureaucrat, the salaried
employee in business, etc."[183] Due to the network of complex
relationships modern managers confront both within and without the organization and the growing importance of communications technology, "[p]eople . . . become the central problem
of industry," and there is a need "for the work of men whose
tool is symbolism and whose aim is some observable response
from people."[184] And while Riesman's relatively rigid inner-
directed man may possess these skills, "for manipulation of
others, there is a somewhat greater compatibility between characterological other direction and sensitivity to others' subtler
wants."[185]
   Fairly similar observations emerge from Michael Maccoby's
recent examination of several high-technology industries.[186]
The character type most often assuming leadership roles there,
he found, was the "Gamesman,"[187] a type coming to replace
Whyte's organization man and Riesman's other-directed man in
social significance.[188] Although the Gamesman perhaps is more
innovative and aggressive, he seems every bit as flexible and
open as his predecessors.

   The modern gamesman is best defined as a person who
   loves change and wants to influence its course. He likes
   to take calculated risks and is fascinated by technique and
   new methods. He sees a developing project, human relations, and his own career in terms of options and possibili-

ties, as if they were a game. His character is a collection of
near paradoxes understood in terms of its adaptation to
the organization [sic] requirements. He is cooperative but
competitive; detached and playful but compulsively driven
to succeed; a team player but a would-be superstar; a team
leader but often a rebel against bureaucratic hierarchy;
fair and unprejudiced but contemptuous of weakness;
tough and dominating but not destructive. . . . His main
goal is to be known as a winner, and his deepest fear is to
be labelled a loser.[189]

The Gamesman is "unbigoted, nonideological and liberal. . . .
He is open to new ideas, but he lacks convictions."[190]
Also suggestive in this context is Scott and Hart's description
of the organizational imperative, which plays so pronounced a
role in ordering bureaucratic life. Based on the general propositions that individual well-being derives from the organization
and that all behavior must enhance organizational health, it em-
braces three rules: (1) technological rationality (the most efficient use of available means to produce chosen ends); (2) stew-
ardship (loyalty to the organizational imperative and to all in
whose interest the organization is managed); and (3) pragma-
tism (a focus on existing short-term problems at the expense
of longer-range concerns).[191] Assuming that such values, and
not many others, are widely internalized within the organizational milieu, that milieu assumes a rather indeterminate character.
    Third, organizational life inevitably must reflect extant ten-
dencies in the larger society within which large groups operate.
While catch-phrases like the "Me Generation" and the "New
Narcissism" can be overused, their prevalence suggests that
American life increasingly is typified by a preoccupation with
the self. If the survey data amassed and interpreted by Daniel
Yankelovich are representative, the desires to be relieved from
tangible commitments, to maximize personal options, and to
grow in generalized ways are coming to typify significant seg-
ments of the population.[192] Since organizations recruit from a
society in which such sentiments are prevalent, it is difficult
to imagine that their internal life has gone unaffected by these

traits. Some recent tendencies such as participatory management, employee rights, and the desire for a more humane and
pleasant work environment seem congruent with such an atmosphere. Developments of this sort can be viewed in fairly
optimistic terms. Consider the following comment by David
Ewing:

> Employee rights is part of a new wave of individualism
> that has spread across society. The new individualism
> is more qualitative than quantitative. It is fed by length-
> ening leisure hours, modern education with its stress on
> individual attitudes and interpretation, moral relativism,
> burgeoning communication, technological profusion, and
> social affluence.
>   . . . .
> Individualism today must not be measured against the
> individualism of the past, for it is different in quality.
> The affluent individualism of today doesn't entertain
> Horatio Alger-like dreams of becoming a president or a
> railroad tycoon. It dreams of expressing oneself, of being
> a free, unfettered, unbeholden, hobby-loving, vacation-
> taking member of a good company and liver of the good
> life; and it values belonging—not so much belonging to
> God, Mammon, or *Who's Who*, as in the age of Alger, as
> belonging to the community and the regional web of life.
> Yesterday's "rugged individual" sought security through
> accomplishment and estate building; today's affluent in-
> dividual seeks security through affiliation with co-workers,
> neighbors, social clubs, sports fans, and the environment.
> His motto is not "Onward and upward" but "O Brother
> Man."[193]

It is also possible to see the contemporary social scene and
the organizational environment it influences as an abyss of
alienation, emptiness, superficiality, and neurotic self-seeking.
This is more or less the tack taken by Christopher Lasch,
whose "narcissist" personality type, whatever else might be
said about him, does not possess many settled, determinate
moral attributes.[194] The narcissist, Lasch insists, often thrives
in modern bureaucracies.

The narcissist comes to the attention of psychiatrists for some of the same reasons that he rises to positions of prominence not only in awareness movements and other cults but in business corporations, political organizations, and government bureaucracies. For all his inner suffering, the narcissist has many traits that make for success in bureaucratic institutions, which put a premium on the manipulation of interpersonal relations, discourage the formation of deep personal attachments, and at the same time provide the narcissist with the approval he needs in order to validate his self-esteem. Although he may resort to therapies that promise to give meaning to life and to overcome his sense of emptiness, in his professional career the narcissist often enjoys considerable success. The management of personal impressions comes naturally to him, and his mastery of its intricacies serves him well in political and business organizations where performance now counts for less than "visibility," "momentum," and a winning record.[195]

What unites the otherwise-divergent accounts offered by Ewing and Lasch is the fairly indeterminate nature of the characters they highlight and their common residence within the organization. (One is almost tempted to guess that the authors are describing the same people, but Ewing seems to focus on younger, lower-level individuals while Lasch appears to be depicting achievers.) Whatever the exact nature of modern individualism, it seems compatible with organizational demands and capable of influencing the internal life of the organization to a significant degree.[196]

Notes

1. *See, e.g.*, W. Friedmann, Law in a Changing Society 498-99 (Penguin ed. 1972); J. Stone, Social Dimensions of Law and Justice 120 (1966).

2. A later section of this chapter attempts to justify the inclusion of these formally nonlegal and nonconstitutional phenomena. Also, formal constitutional doctrines relating to these phenomena will be discussed at various points.

3. More or less achieved statuses like those obtaining for the military, government employees, prisoners, and mental patients—which are organizationally based and thus resemble the institutional statuses discussed within—were generally more resistant to the liberal-individualist impulse than the ascriptive statuses discussed in chapter 2; however, ascriptive criteria will reemerge in chapter 4.

4. The account of group power sketched here is derived from sources like the following: W. Friedmann, *supra* note 1; J. K. Galbraith, The New Industrial State (2d ed. 1971); A. Hacker, The End of the American Era (1970); T. Lowi, The End of Liberalism (1st paperback ed. 1969). This account must be qualified, however, because of the fact that large corporations do not totally dominate the American economy. *See, e.g.*, Galbraith's distinction between the "planning system" and the "market system" in his Economics and the Public Purpose (1973).

5. *E.g.*, M. Weber, *Bureaucracy*, in H. Gerth & C. Mills (eds.), From Max Weber 196 (Oxford paperback ed. 1958).

6. For example, students or hospital patients.

7. *E.g.*, A. Hacker, *supra* note 4, at 59-63, 66, 70-72.

8. *E.g.*, Miller, *Toward "Constitutionalizing" the Corporation: A Speculative Essay*, 80 W. Va. L. Rev. 187, 195 (1978).

9. *See* D. Ewing, Freedom Inside the Organization (1977).

10. A. S. Miller, The Modern Corporate State 86-87 (1976).

11. For a listing of these, *see, e.g.*, W. Friedmann, *supra* note 1, at 495-96.

12. This is not to say that this activity is always effective. *See, e.g.*, A. S. Miller, Democratic Dictatorship: The Emergent Constitution of Control ch. 9 (1981).

13. R. M. Unger, Law in Modern Society 193 (paperback ed. 1976).

14. A. Bentley, The Process of Government 268 (1908).

15. A. Hacker, *supra* note 4, at 64.

16. W. Friedmann, *supra* note 1, at 325.

17. T. Lowi, *supra* note 4, at 44.

18. R. M. Unger, *supra* note 13, at 202.

19. *See, e.g.*, W. Friedmann, *supra* note 1, at 323-25 and T. Lowi, *supra* note 4, at 71 (both noting the tendency to do this and both critical of it).

20. *See* A. Bentley, *supra* note 14, at 261.

21. A. S. Miller, *supra* note 10, at 113 (italics omitted).

22. R. M. Unger, *supra* note 13, at 200-201.

23. *Compare* A. S. Miller, *supra* note 12, at 54-69 *with* the discussion of Hegel and Bosanquet in chapter 1.

24. *E.g.*, A. S. Miller, *supra* note 10, at 188-89.

25. For example, the interest group liberalism described and criticized in T. Lowi, *supra* note 4.

26. This is described, not without criticism, in Weaver, *Regulation, Social Policy and Class Conflict*, Pub. Interest, No. 50 (Winter 1978) 45, 46-50.

27. B. Schwartz, The Law in America 15 (American Heritage ed. 1974). Unfortunately, this edition does not quote Holmes directly or provide a citation for this remark.

28. The doctrines discussed here do not exhaust the interrelations among formal constitutional development, the corporation, and activist government.

29. O. W. Holmes, The Common Law 5 (paperback ed., M. Howe ed. 1963).

30. Public-private blurring and the corporate state hypothesis do not figure in the formal constitutional discussion that follows. Their significance should become apparent in the next section of this chapter. Also, the corporate state hypothesis will reemerge in chapter 6.

31. On the contract clause generally, *see, e.g.*, B. Schwartz, A Commentary on the Constitution of the United States, Part II. The Rights of Property (1965); Hale, *The Supreme Court and the Contract Clause* (pts. 1-3), 57 Harv. L. Rev. 512, 621, 852 (1944); Phillips, *The Life and Times of the Contract Clause*, 20 Am. Bus. L. J. 139 (1982). As its language indicates, the clause applies only to the states. A few decisions, however, apply something like contract clause standards to the federal government under Fifth Amendment due process.

32. Home Building & Loan Ass'n v. Blaisdell, 290 U.S. 398, 427 (1934).

33. Black's Law Dictionary 1735 (4th ed. 1951).

34. E. Corwin, Liberty against Government 72 (1948) (italics omitted). Citations are to the 1978 Greenwood Press reprint.

35. *Id.* at 83 (emphasis added).

36. 10 U.S. (6 Cranch) 87 (1810).

37. 17 U.S. (4 Wheat.) 518 (1819).

38. For discussions of this, *see* A. S. Miller, *supra* note 10, at 42; B. Schwartz, *supra* note 31, at 274-75; Hale, *supra* note 31, at 630-33.

39. Fletcher v. Peck, 10 U.S. (6 Cranch) 87, 143 (Johnson, J.).

40. B. Schwartz, *supra* note 31, at 278.

41. A. S. Miller, *supra* note 10, at 42.

42. B. Schwartz, *supra* note 31, at 268.

43. H. Maine, Popular Government 247-48 (1885), quoted in G. Gunther, Cases and Materials on Constitutional Law 555 n.4 (10th ed. 1980).

44. G. Gunther, *supra* note 43, at 555.

45. For instance, while it was generally agreed that the states could evade *Dartmouth College* by including within the charter a reserved right to amend it, many states often failed to do so. G. Gunther, *supra* note 43, at 555. Also, even where such a reservation was made, the states often showed little inclination to employ it later. A. S. Miller, The Supreme Court and American Capitalism 38 (1968).

46. J. Galbraith, *supra* note 4, at 291. Citation is to the Mentor paperback edition.

47. Charles River Bridge v. Warren Bridge, 36 U.S. (11 Pet.) 420 (1837).

48. *Id.* at 552-53.

49. 25 U.S. (12 Wheat.) 213 (1827).

50. B. Schwartz, *supra* note 31, at 272. Whether the bar would have been absolute, though, is questionable.

51. Three other limitations deserve brief mention. First, there was a tendency to distinguish between contract obligations (which could not be impaired) and contract remedies (which could). Second, as stated in note 45 *supra*, the states could reserve a power to amend in the charter. Third, there was a tendency to construe the original grant narrowly and thus avoid later impairments, a tendency quite evident in the *Charles River Bridge* case.

52. The police power is a general state power to regulate for the health, safety, morals, and well-being of the people. Also, the contract clause typically did not bar a state's exercise of the eminent domain power.

53. Stone v. Miss., 101 U.S. 814, 819 (1880).

54. On this, *see* Phillips, *supra* note 31, at 155-58, economic substantive due process is discussed below.

55. *See id.* at 158-62.

56. Home Building & Loan Ass'n v. Blaisdell, 290 U.S. 398, 442 (1934).

57. United States Trust Co. v. N.J., 431 U.S. 1 (1977); Allied Structural Steel Co. v. Spannaus, 438 U.S. 234 (1978).

58. For more on this, *see* chapter 6. For more on these cases, *see* Phillips, *supra* note 31, at 163-70; Schwartz, *Old Wine in Old Bottles? The Renaissance of the Contract Clause*, 1979 Sup. Ct. Rev. 95.

59. For early language anticipating the doctrine, *see, e.g.*, Mugler v. Kan., 123 U.S. 623, 660-61 (1887); Butchers' Union Co. v. Crescent City Co., 111 U.S. 746, 754-60, 760-66 (1883) (Field, J., and Bradley, J., concurring); Munn v. Ill., 94 U.S. 113, 136-54 (1976) (Field, J. dissenting); The Slaughterhouse Cases, 83 U.S. (16 Wall.) 36, 83-111 (1972) (Field, J., dissenting).

60. *E.g.*, Allgeyer v. La., 165 U.S. 578, 589 (1897).

61. *E.g.*, Mugler v. Kan., 123 U.S. 623, 661 (1887).

62. Santa Clara County v. Southern Pac. R.R., 118 U.S. 394 (1886).

63. Actually, the real and substantial relation test was applied to deprivations of property also.

64. However, even when the economic variant of substantive due process was dominant, it did have its application to noneconomic areas of life. *E.g.*, Meyer v. Neb., 262 U.S. 390 (1923); Pierce v. Soc'y of Sisters, 268 U.S. 510 (1925), both discussed in chapter 2.

65. *E.g.*, G. Gunther, *supra* note 43, at 517. *See* Bunting v. Ore., 243 U.S. 426 (1917); Holden v. Hardy, 169 U.S. 366 (1898). Often, as suggested in chapter 2, the doctrine did not block legislation aiming to protect working women. *E.g.*, Muller v. Ore., 208 U.S. 412 (1908).

66. 198 U.S. 45 (1905).

67. 236 U.S. 1 (1915).

68. *Id.* at 14.

69. 300 U.S. 379 (1937).

70. *Id.* at 391.

71. E. Corwin, *supra* note 34, at 161,

72. A. S. Miller, *supra* note 10, at 95.

73. E. Corwin, *supra* note 34, at 161 (italics omitted).

74. *See, e.g.*, Ferguson v. Skrupa, 372 U.S. 726 (1963).

75. Perhaps the best example is Roe v. Wade, 410 U.S. 113 (1973).

76. *See* Miller, *Toward a Concept of Constitutional Duty*, 1968 Sup. Ct. Rev. 199.

77. The taxing and spending powers, among others, have also been fairly important sources of federal regulatory authority.

78. The original purpose of the commerce clause was to nationalize commerce by restricting certain forms of state protectionism. In line with this purpose, state regulation may be unconstitutional if it unduly hinders or burdens interstate commerce. Commerce clause cases of this sort have been fairly common in both the nineteenth and twentieth centuries.

79. United States v. E. C. Knight Co. 156 U.S. 1 (1895).

80. *See, e.g.*, Houston E. & W. Texas Ry. v. United States, 234 U.S. 342 (1914).

81. Champion v. Ames, 188 U.S. 321 (1903) (lotteries); Hoke v. United States 227 U.S. 308 (1913) (the Mann Act).

82. 247 U.S. 251 (1918).

83. R.R. Retirement Bd. v. Alton R.R. Co., 295 U.S. 330 (1935) (Railroad Retirement Act); Schechter Poultry Corp. v. United States, 295 U.S. 495 (1935) (NIRA); Carter v. Carter Coal Co., 298 U.S. 238 (1936) (Coal Conservation Act).

84. In that year, the court also upheld the Social Security Act under the spending power. Steward Machine Co. v. Davis, 301 U.S. 548 (1937);

Helvering v. Davis, 301 U.S. 619 (1937).
  85. National Labor Relations Bd. v. Jones & Laughlin Steel Corp.,
301 U.S. 1 (1937).
  86. United States v. Darby, 312 U.S. 100 (1941).
  87. Wickard v. Filburn, 317 U.S. 111 (1942).
  88. *E.g.*, Heart of Atlanta Motel v. United States, 379 U.S. 241 (1964).
  89. L. Tribe, American Constitutional Law 1147 n.1 (1978).
  90. Black, *The Supreme Court, 1966 Term—Foreward: "State Action."*
Equal Protection, and California's Proposition 14, 81 Harv. L. Rev. 69,
95 (1967).
  91. 334 U.S. 1 (1948).
  92. G. Gunther, *supra* note 43, at 1002.
  93. *E.g.*, Ginn v. Matthews, 533 F.2d 477 (9th Cir. 1976) (Head Start);
Holodnak v. AVCO Corp., 514 F.2d 285 (2d Cir. 1975) (defense contrac-.
tor); Jackson v. Statler Foundation, 496 F.2d 623 (2d Cir. 1974) (foundation); O'Neill v. Grayson County War Memorial Hosp., 472 F.2d 1140
(6th Cir. 1973) (hospital); Intercontinental Indus., Inc. v. Am. Stock
Exch., 452 F.2d 935 (5th Cir. 1971) (stock exchange); Capers v. Long
Island R.R., 429 F. Supp. 1359, 1367 n.11, *aff'd sub nom.* Harris v. Long
Island R.R., 573 F.2d 1291 (2d Cir. 1977) (dictum) (railroad); Niswonger
v. Am. Aviation, Inc., 424 F. Supp. 1080 (E.D. Tenn. 1976) (airport);
Short v. Fulton Redevelopment Co., 390 F. Supp. 517 (S.D.N.Y. 1975)
(housing project); Rackin v. Univ. of Pa., 386 F. Supp. 992, 995-1005
(E.D. Pa. 1974) (private university); Brown v. Lynn, 385 F. Supp. 986
(N.D. Ill. 1974) (mortgage lender).
  94. *E.g.*, Cohen v. Ill. Inst. of Technology, 524 F.2d 818, 824 (7th
Cir. 1975).
  95. *E.g.*, Jackson v. Metropolitan Edison Co., 419 U.S. 345, 351-52
(1974).
  96. *E.g.*, Cohen v. Ill. Inst. of Technology 524 F.2d 818 (7th Cir. 1975).
  97. *E.g.*, Schlein v. Milford Hosp., 561 F.2d 427 (2d Cir. 1977).
  98. Wenzer v. Consolidated Rail Corp., 464 F. Supp. 643 (E.D. Pa),
aff'd, 612 F.2d 576 (3d Cir. 1979).
  99. Hines v. Cenla Community Action Comm., Inc., 474 F.2d 1052
(5th Cir. 1973).
  100. The best example is Jackson v. Metropolitan Edison Co., 419 U.S.
345 (1974).
  101. The doctrine was perhaps foreshadowed by the so-called white-
primary cases. On these, *see, e.g.*, G. Gunther, *supra* note 43, at 997-99.
  102. 326 U.S. 501 (1946).
  103. Evans v. Newton, 383 U.S. 296 (1966).
  104. Food Employees v. Logan Valley Plaza, 391 U.S. 308 (1968).

105. *See* Lloyd Corp. v. Tanner, 407 U.S. 551 (1972); Hudgens v. NLRB, 424 U.S. 507 (1976).

106. *See* Jackson v. Metropolitan Edison Co., 419 U.S. 345 (1974); Flagg Bros., Inc. v. Brooks, 436 U.S. 149 (1978).

107. L. Tribe, *supra* note 89, at 1149.

108. *E.g.*, Miller, *A Modest Proposal for Helping to Tame the Corporate Beast*, 8 Hofstra L. Rev. 79 (1979).

109. An obvious example is antiemployment discrimination legislation such as Title VII of the 1964 Civil Rights Act.

110. This will be briefly discussed in chapter 6. The point made there is that the limitation of state action tends to assist group control of the individual.

111. This was suggested in Holodnak v. AVCO Corp. 514 F.2d 285 (2d Cir. 1975).

112. *See, e.g.*, Bd. of Curators v. Horwitz, 435 U.S. 78 (1978).

113. Here, analytical positivism will be regarded as defining law as the command of a formal, legitimate political authority; expressed in clear written rules; backed by sanctions; and valid irrespective of moral goodness or badness. Employing (where needed) the concept of delegation, this conception of law would include at least express constitutional norms, statutes, common law and constitutional court rulings, administrative regulations and decisions, executive orders, and local governmental rules such as ordinances. The internal status differentiations contained within most large organizations would not qualify as law under such a definition because they do not issue from a formal, legitimate political authority but rather from an ostensibly private entity. The internal norms of a governmental bureaucracy, however, probably would fit within this particular positivistic conception of law.

114. On analytical positivism's preoccupation with conceptual order, *see* W. Friedmann, Legal Theory ch. 23 (5th ed. 1967).

115. W. Friedmann, *supra* note 1, at 20-21.

116. R. M. Unger, *supra* note 13, at 210-2.

117. *See, e.g.*, F. Hayek, The Road to Serfdom ch. 6 (1944); Lowi, *supra* note 4, ch. 5.

118. Something like this may actually have occurred in the case of the "new regulation" of the 1970s. *See e.g.*, Lilly v. Miller, *The New "Social Regulation,"* Pub. Interest (Spring 1977), at 49; Weaver, *Regulation, Social Policy and Class Conflict*, Pub. Interest (Winter 1978), at 45.

119. R. M. Unger, *supra* note 13, at 193-94, 196.

120. *See* Metzger & Phillips, *Promissory Estoppel and the Evolution of Contract Law*, 18 Am. Bus. L.J. 139, 153-58 (1980).

121. T. Lowi, *supra* note 4, ch. 5. Lowi, to be sure, is critical of this

and recommends something he calls juridical democracy in its stead.

122. *See* W. Friedmann, *supra* note 114, at 290; Trubeck, *Toward a Social Theory of Law: An Essay on the Study of Law and Development*, 82 Yale L.J. 1 (1972).

123. E. Erhlich, Fundamental Principles of the Sociology of Law 493 (W. Moll tr. 1936).

124. W. Friedmann, *supra* note 1, at 20.

125. J. Stone, Social Dimensions of Law and Justice 732 (1966).

126. *Id.* at 525.

127. A. S. Miller, *supra* note 10, at 17-18.

128. *See, e.g.*, M. Weber, *supra* note 5; R. Michels, Political Parties (1911).

129. Although the point is not especially important here, a role is distinguishable from a status. "The concepts of 'status,' 'role' and 'prestige' are often confused. Generally speaking, status implies a position within a group, role the appropriate behavior which goes with that position, and prestige is something more personal which the individual brings to his status and role." J. Brown, The Social Psychology of Industry 141 (Penguin ed. 1954).

130. *E.g.*, Gardner & Moore, *Status and Status Hierarchies*, in 1 J. Litterer (ed.), Organizations: Structure and Behavior 189-96 (2d ed. 1969). *Cf.* R. Bierstedt, The Social Order 268-72 (4th ed. 1974).

131. J. Brown, *supra* note 129, at 100.

132. *E.g.*, *id.* at 138-43.

133. *E.g.*, T. Parsons, Essays in Sociological Theory 78-79 (rev. ed. 1954). For instance, it has been said that the top executives of major American corporations are not predominantly of upper-class origins. A. Hacker, *supra* note 4, at 60-61. However, the statement in the text needs to be qualified in light of continuing, if diminishing, organizational discrimination against women and various minorities. It also needs to be qualified by the observation that even a perfectly meritocratic system of organizational hiring, assignment, and promotion inevitably will reflect the effects of prior discrimination on the basis of ascriptive traits.

134. *See* J. Brown, *supra* note 129, at 105.

135. For a suggestion that interorganizational movements are not too significant for the individual because of the way large organizations resemble each other, *see* W. Scott & D. Hart, Organizational America 101 (paperback ed. 1979). For a further suggestion that they are not as common as frequently believed, *see id.* at 149-150, 173-74.

136. *E.g.*, R. Bierstedt, *supra* note 130, at 255, 260-61.

137. J. Brown, *supra* note 129, at 189 (italics in original).

138. W. Scott & D. Hart, *supra* note 135, at 2, 36.

139. A. S. Miller, *supra* note 10, at 188-89 (italics in original).

140. The following discussion focuses on the corporation, but it is generally applicable, with variation from context to context, to large institutionalized groups generally.

141. Consider for instance second- or third-year law students who went to law school to postpone the making of choices and drift toward practice in a large law firm because jobs of this sort are most prestigious and remunerative and because the law school's placement office tends to emphasize large firms.

142. W. Scott & D. Hart, *supra* note 135, at 140, 152-58. This is especially true of business schools.

143. *E.g.*, Forbes, *Freedom and Organization Reconsidered*, 31 Am. J. Econ. & Soc. 189, 192 (1972).

144. *Cf.* W. Friedmann, *supra* note 1, at 347-66.

145. *See generally* D. Ewing, *supra* note 9.

146. *See* J. Galbraith, *supra* note 4, chs. 11,13.

147. W. Scott & D. Hart, *supra* note 135, at 47.

148. *Id.* at 4 (italics omitted).

149. *Id.* at 101.

150. *Id.* at 85.

151. This is generally less true at lower levels of the organization. Consider the stereotypical alienated assembly line worker. At this level, however, the union may sometimes be an intense object of identification for the worker, though it is likely that this attachment has diminished over the years.

152. W. Scott & D. Hart, *supra* note 135, at 150.

153. *Id.* at 147 (discussing the work of Harland Cleveland).

154. *Id.* at 86, 162, 172-73.

155. A. Hacker, *supra* note 4, at 63.

156. W. Scott & D. Hart, *supra* note 135, at 148-49.

157. A. Hacker, *supra* note 4, at 72. This argument will be very important in chapter 5; however, it is open to question whether large contemporary organizations are adequate substitutes for lost forms of community.

158. *Id.* at 71-72.

159. *See, e.g.*, W. Whyte, The Organization Man 171-201 (1951).

160. W. Scott & D. Hart, *supra* note 135, at 76.

161. Latham, *The Body Politic of the Corporation*, in E. S. Mason (ed.), The Corporation in Modern Society 232 (1959).

162. W. Scott & D. Hart, *supra* note 135, at 76-77, 114-15, 141-42.

163. *See, e.g., id.* ch. 8. These will be discussed in chapter 6.

164. G. Sabine, A History of Political Theory 655 (3d ed. 1961).

165. However, as will become apparent later, I do not think that this is the best way to characterize the employee rights phenomenon.

166. *See, e.g.*, Miller, *supra* note 8, at 187; A. Berle, *Constitutional Limitations on Corporate Activity—Protection of Personal Rights from Invasion through Economic Power*, 100 U. Pa. L. Rev. 933 (1952).

167. This is equivalent to the authoritarian positive freedom model presented in chapter 1. Here, the duties associated with a group status would both express the individual's real nature and develop abilities that are themselves part of that nature.

168. Human malleability seems to be assumed in management thinking. *See* W. Scott & D. Hart, *supra* note 135, at 55-61. Various attempts at reconciling these two views of the individual will be found in chapters 5 and 6.

169. Some of these will be discussed in chapter 5.

170. *Cf.* W. Scott & D. Hart, *supra* note 135, at 6-8.

171. A. S. Miller, *supra* note 10, at 157-58 (referring to the state).

172. As noted disapprovingly in W. Scott & D. Hart, *supra* note 135, at 37.

173. *Id.* at 7-8, 51-52.

174. Chapter 5 will attempt an overall explanation of the matters discussed above. By way of anticipation, the argument advanced there will be roughly as follows. Liberal individualism creates substantial forces for identification with the organization. It has destroyed traditional forms of community, but the individual's need for this still exists, and the organization offers a possible substitute community. Also, the advance of liberal individualism tends to dilute those capacities that would provoke opposition to the organization and thus leaves people relatively unequipped to resist organizational conditioning. It is likely, however, that modern organizations are inadequate replacements for lost forms of community, and the advance of liberal individualism, while leaving people dependent on the organization, makes them resentful of overt coercion yet still amenable to therapeutic controls. Thus, the individual seems to be simultaneously dependent on organizations and resentful of organizational controls when these assume authoritarian forms.

175. *Cf.* A. MacIntyre, After Virtue chs. 10-13 (1981).

176. I. Kristol, Two Cheers for Capitalism 263 (1978).

177. Conspicuous exceptions to this statement are the reverse statuses discussed in chapter 4. These, however, hardly resemble traditional ascriptive characterizations.

178. For example: "Women are capable of education, but they are not made for activities that demand a universal faculty such as the more advanced sciences, philosophy, and certain forms of artistic production. Women may have happy ideas, taste, and elegance, but they cannot

attain to the ideal. The difference between men and women is like that between animals and plants. Men correspond to animals, while women correspond to plants because their development is more placid and the principle that underlies it is the rather vague unity of feeling. When women hold the helm of government, the state is at once in jeopardy, because women regulate their actions not by the demands of universality but by arbitrary inclinations and opinions. Women are educated—who knows how?—as it were by breathing in ideas, by living rather than acquiring knowledge. The status of manhood, on the other hand, is attained only by the stress of thought and much technical exertion." Hegel's Philosophy of Right (T. M. Knox tr.) § 166 (Addition). "Additions" were derived from student notes to Hegel's lectures.

179. This will be argued in chapter 5.
180. W. Friedmann, *supra* note 114, at 499.
181. *See* E. Mayo, The Social Problems of an Industrial Civilization 11-13, 31, 70, 75, 112, 117 (1945).
182. D. Riesman, The Lonely Crowd 21 (abridged paperback ed. 1961).
183. *Id.* at 20.
184. *Id.* at 127-28.
185. *Id.* at 128.
186. M. Maccoby, The Gamesman (1976). All citations are to the Bantam paperback. Maccoby apparently has recently argued that his Gamesman is not too well adapted to organizations of the near future, but this would not seem to disturb his earlier findings.
187. To Maccoby, however, there are three other significant corporate personality types; the craftsman (motivated by standards peculiar to his skill or practice; the jungle fighter (the traditional American entrepreneurial type); and the company man (more or less like Whyte's organization man).
188. *See* M. Maccoby, *supra* note 187, at 24-26.
189. *Id.* at 100. *See also id.* chs. 5-6.
190. *Id.* at 107.
191. W. Scott & D. Hart, *supra* note 135, at 43-46.
192. *See generally*, D. Yankelovich, New Rules (1981).
193. D. Ewing, *supra* note 9, at 68-69 (paperback ed.).
194. Lasch's development of the narcissist personality type relies heavily on Freudian psychology. *See* C. Lasch, The Culture of Narcissism 33-41 (1978).
195. *Id.* at 43-44. *See also id.* at 46-47.
196. Of course, it can be argued that corporations contribute to the present climate in no small degree through advertising and the promotion of consumerism generally.

CHAPTER 4

The Reverse Statuses

Although the liberal individualist advance has hardly eliminated status differentiation as such, it would seem to have
left ascribed statuses in a state of conspicuous desuetude.
Whatever else might be said about organizational statuses,
they are not formally[1] ascriptive in nature. Of the traditional
statuses, those most clearly classifiable as ascribed—for example, race, gender, and illegitimacy—were least resistant to the
liberal movement. Thus, unequal legal impediments based on
immutable traits now seem a thing of the past.

Ascriptive classifications, nevertheless, have not been banished
from the American legal system. Since the late 1960s, such
attributes increasingly have been made the basis for new
statuses conferring positive benefits on certain groups, mainly
minority racial groups.[2] Unlike the inferior statuses, such reverse
discrimination often increases the negative freedom of those
it benefits by eliminating external impediments to their advance. In fact, it can readily be viewed as a means of facilitating minority access to large modern organizations. In
addition, these positive or reverse statuses tend to fuse the
concepts of status and positive freedom, albeit in a fashion
quite different from the inferior statuses. First, they are often
correctives for the denials of capacity likely to occur where
past deprivations have inhibited the ability to compete and
thus tend to perpetuate themselves despite the existence of
neutral laws. Second, they often promote minority access to

an institutional structure with its own tendency to fuse status and positive liberty. In both cases, the capacities promoted seem mainly of a liberal nature.

Currently, reverse or positive statuses arguably exist in five areas: (1) the portion of modern equal protection doctrine involving so-called suspect classifications; (2) professional education; (3) public and private employment; (4) elementary and secondary schooling;[3] and (5) voting. These statuses usually benefit racial groups, and with the exception of the employment area, they are mainly of formal constitutional dimensions.

The Status Implications of Equal Protection
Suspect Classifications

The Fourteenth Amendment's equal protection clause states: "No State shall . . . deny to any person within its jurisdiction the equal protection of the laws." Despite the generality of this language, early interpretations of the clause viewed it as primarily intended to attack discrimination against blacks.[4] (Even here, its impact was fairly limited for quite some time.) But soon the equal protection guarantee was applied to governmental[5] classifications concerning aliens, orientals, and other groups.[6] Before the end of the nineteenth century, it came to apply to all instances of unequal treatment by public organs, irrespective of the group affected. As the Court stated in 1886, the clause's guarantees "are universal in their application, to all persons within the territorial jurisdiction, without regard to any difference of race, of color, or of nationality; and the equal protection of the laws is a pledge of the protection of equal laws."[7] In spite of its wide-ranging potential application, though, the equal protection clause was applied in a relatively unaggressive fashion prior to World War II. Its existence did not pose much of a threat to the various inferior statuses. Justice Holmes, in fact, contemptuously dismissed the clause as "the usual last resort of constitutional arguments" in a 1927 case involving the sterilization of mental defectives.[8] Race cases perhaps excepted, the usual equal protection standard employed during this period was the rational basis test, which merely required that classifications bear some reasonable relation to the furtherance of a valid governmental purpose.[9]

Although the rational basis test is still the standard of choice in other areas, after World War II it came to be supplemented by the strict scrutiny now applied to certain specific kinds of classifications. In its purest form, the strict scrutiny test requires that such governmental distinctions be "necessary" to the effectuation of a "compelling" governmental purpose.[10] Now subjected to this stringent form of equal protection review are two broad sets of classifications: (1) those discriminating with respect to certain fundamental rights such as procreation, voting, and interstate travel, and (2) those involving the suspect categories of race or national origin, gender, alienage, and illegitimacy. The suspect classification aspect of this new doctrine was intimated by Chief Justice Stone's 1938 *Carolene Products* footnote, with its suggestion that discrimination against certain "discrete and insular minorities" might require "more searching judicial inquiry."[11] The actual degree of scrutiny applied in cases involving each particular suspect classification has been the subject of some disagreement. At this time, there seems to be a rough consensus on a sliding scale, in which racial discrimination is subject to very stringent tests, with classifications based on the other suspect traits receiving a somewhat less searching examination.[12] The standard in cases involving sex-based discrimination, for instance, is whether the classification "serve[s] *important* governmental objectives and [is] *substantially* related to achievement of those objectives."[13] The existence of a weaker test has also been expressly noted in the area of illegitimacy.[14]

There is little doubt that the suspect classification doctrine was originally intended to help eliminate official discrimination against groups such as blacks, Orientals, women, aliens, and illegitimates. The language of the *Carolene Products* footnote suggests as much, and virtually all pre-1975 applications of the doctrine involved classifications of this sort. Thus, the emergence of strict scrutiny in suspect classification cases can readily be viewed as part of the liberal individualist advance. Discrimination on the basis of traits like race, national origin, gender, alienage, and illegitimacy, along with the constitutional sanction it received, was precisely what constituted the inferior statuses discussed in Chapter 2, and it is just such discrimination that the suspect classification doctrine attacks. As the doctrine is typically formulated, however, it contains no explicit limitation to classifications disadvantaging the "deprived" group encompassed by the suspect category. This raises the possibility that it might be employed by the "dominant" group also contained within this category. To say, for instance, that racial classifications trigger strict scrutiny without specifying which groups are to receive enhanced protection suggests that whites as well as racial minorities may be able to utilize this stringent form of review to challenge official action disadvantaging them. To all appearances, this possibility went unrecognized for quite some time. The rise of governmental reverse discrimination and the increasing tendency for men to challenge sex-based regulations disadvantaging them relative to women made confrontation of the question inevitable by the mid-1970s.

If strict scrutiny is applied only where discrimination against a previously deprived group is at issue—is applied in a one-sided, asymmetrical, or unequal fashion—it clearly creates a constitutional status benefiting the deprived group. An enhanced ability to invalidate offical action working to one's disadvantage is, formally at least, a legal right or power, and its absence a relative legal disability. For instance, to grant women (but not men) the power to subject sexually differentiating governmental behavior to some form of strict scrutiny is to confer upon women a practical power to avoid legal disabilities that is not granted to men. It might plausibly be argued, however, that this formal status does not confer much of a practical advantage where existing public discrimination largely works against the deprived group. Here, unequal access to strict scrutiny may work more to equalize the practical legal positions of the two sexes than to create an overall legal benefit for the deprived group. That is, inequality at the constitutional level may be necessary for eliminating various disabilities created by legislatures, administrative bodies, municipalities, and all the other formal organs of government. But with the virtual elimination of overt official discrimination against such groups, it is doubtful whether this situation still obtains.

Where strict scrutiny is applied in an equal, neutral, or symmetrical fashion, on the other hand, no formal constitutional

status exists. Here, both groups falling within the particular
suspect category (for example, men and women) would have
the power to subject governmental discrimination to some
degree of enhanced scrutiny. This would not restore previously
existing legal statuses; rather, all public action classifying on the
basis of the suspect trait would be imperiled.

The Supreme Court's treatment of this symmetry question
has been tortured and confused. The problem has not arisen in
the contexts of alienage and illegitimacy. Barring the enactment
of preferential measures favoring these groups, it is not likely to
occur in either case. As for sex discrimination, whose rise to
suspect status began in the early 1970s, many of the early cases
establishing the change involved laws disadvantaging women.[15]
For some time after this shift, the Court seemed inclined to
treat classifications disadvantaging men under rational basis
standards. In a 1974 case,[16] for instance, it upheld a property
tax exemption for widows but not widowers by using something like a rational basis test. One year later, it also rejected
a male challenger's claim that navy "up or out" policies imposing less stringent retention standards on female officers than
on their male counterparts denied equal protection, again on
what seemed to be a rational basis footing.[17] In that same year,
the Court did strike down a legislative classification burdening
men, but the way it did so cast doubt on its willingness to treat
gender-based discrimination in a truly symmetrical fashion. At
issue in *Weinberger* v. *Wiesenfeld*[18] was a widower's challenge
to Social Security Act provisions stating that survivors' benefits be paid to the wife and child of a deceased husband and
father but only to the children of a deceased wife and mother.
In that case, the Court examined the legislation from the viewpoint of the female wage earner (not the uncompensated widower who was the actual litigant in the case) and thus was able
to invalidate it by employing strict scrutiny.

These preliminary skirmishes set the stage for the Court's
1976 shift in *Craig* v. *Boren*,[19] the well-known Oklahoma 3.2
beer case. *Craig*, which announced the "substantial relation to
important governmental objectives" test for sex discrimination
cases, used this intermediate test to sustain a male-based challenge to an Oklahoma statute prohibiting the sale of 3.2 beer to

men below the age of twenty one and to women below the age of
eighteen. While the *Craig* majority did not expressly consider the
neutrality question, Justice Rehnquist's dissent left little doubt a-
bout the significance of the step the Court was taking. Criticizing
the majority's treatment of gender discrimination as a "talisman
which—without regard to the rights involved or the persons affected—calls into effect a heavier burden of judicial review,"
he noted that "before today, no decision of this Court has applied an elevated level of scrutiny to invalidate a statutory
discrimination harmful to males."[20] After *Craig*, the Court used
the intermediate standard to strike down an Alabama alimony
statute providing that ex-husbands alone could be required to
pay alimony; a New York domestic relations enactment requiring consent of the mother, but not the father, for adoption of
an illegitimate child; and a Missouri workman's compensation
provision establishing recovery standards for spousal death that
disadvantaged widowers as against widows.[21] While doing so,
it has stated that the same degree of scrutiny is to be applied
to enactments burdening both men and women.[22] Nevertheless,
there is still some doubt whether the Court's application of
strict scrutiny in gender discrimination cases has always been
genuinely neutral. In a 1977 case,[23] it upheld Social Security
Act provisions giving retired female wage earners a pecuniary
advantage over their male counterparts because the provisions
"substantially" advanced the "important" purpose of reducing
the economic disparity between men and women. In 1981 the
Court rejected equal protection challenges to a gender-biased
California statutory rape provision[24] and to men-only draft
registration.[25] During the same period, sex discrimination
against women almost invariably has been found to be unconstitutional.[26] Thus, in the practical application of the *Craig*
test, it appears that a certain degree of intersexual differentiation still remains.

In the area of race, the two Supreme Court cases dealing with
the question of strict scrutiny's symmetry are *Regents of the
University of California* v. *Bakke*[27] and *Fullilove* v. *Klutznick*.[28]
In *Bakke*, the Court struck down a University of California-
Davis medical school admissions plan establishing quota-like
preferential entry standards for certain chosen minorities and
ordered the white male challenging this plan admitted to medi-

cal school. The case, however, left considerable room for admissions officers to consider an applicant's race as an ostensible means of promoting student body diversity. In *Fullilove*, the Court upheld a federal public works provision ordering that 10 percent of each grant under the act be expended for minority contractors and suppliers. *Bakke* and *Fullilove* defy complete, yet succinct, recapitulation, and no attempt at the former will be made here.[29] Both are graced with a collection of discordant concurring and dissenting opinions. Neither gives much indication that the Court has been able to achieve a coherent collective position on the constitutional treatment of reverse racial discrimination.[30] Out of the confusion, however, two[31] more or less identifiable positions on the question of strict scrutiny's neutrality emerge.

The first position, enunciated most forcefully by Justice Powell,[32] is that strict scrutiny should be applied in a neutral fashion in race cases. Powell's *Bakke* opinion is emphatic on the point. "The guarantee of equal protection," he asserted, "cannot mean one thing when applied to one individual and something else when applied to a person of another color." "If both are not accorded the same protection, then it [the guarantee] is not equal."[33] Later, he added, "It is far too late to argue that the guarantee of equal protection to *all* persons permits the recognition of special wards entitled to a degree of protection greater than that accorded others."[34] In justifying this position, Powell stressed the importance of formal ascriptive neutrality at the constitutional level.

> Once the artificial line of a "two-class theory" of the Fourteenth Amendment is put aside, the difficulties entailed in varying the level of judicial review according to a perceived "preferred" status of a particular racial or ethnic minority are intractable. The concepts of "majority" and "minority" necessarily reflect temporary arrangements and political judgments. As observed above, the white "majority" itself is composed of various minority groups, most of which can lay claim to a history of prior discrimination at the hands of the state and private individuals. Not all of these groups can receive preferential treatment and corresponding judicial tolerance of distinctions drawn in

terms of race and nationality, for then the only "majority" left would be a new minority of White Anglo-Saxon Protestants. There is no principled basis for deciding which groups would merit "heightened judicial solicitude" and which would not. Courts would be asked to evaluate the extent of the prejudice and consequent harm suffered by various minority groups. Those whose societal injury is thought to exceed some arbitrary level of tolerability then would be entitled to preferential classifications at the expense of individuals belonging to other groups. Those classifications would be free from exacting judicial scrutiny. As these preferences began to have their desired effect, and the consequences of past discrimination were undone, new judicial rankings would be necessary. The kind of variable sociological and political analysis necessary to produce such rankings simply does not lie within the judicial competence—even if they otherwise were politically feasible and socially desirable. . . .

By hitching the meaning of the Equal Protection Clause to these transitory considerations, we would be holding, as a constitutional principle, that judicial scrutiny of classifications touching on racial and ethnic background may vary with the ebb and flow of political forces. . . . [T]he mutability of a constitutional principle, based upon shifting political and social judgments, undermines the chances for consistent application of the Constitution from one generation to the next, a critical feature of its coherent interpretation. . . . In expounding the Constitution, the Court's role is to discern principles sufficiently absolute to give them roots throughout the community and continuity over significant periods of time, and to lift them above the level of the pragmatic political judgments of a particular time and place.[35]

The full strict scrutiny used in race cases imposes very stringent tests of constitutionality. Thus, one would think that Powell's determination to apply it in a racially neutral fashion would have doomed the *Bakke* quota and the *Fullilove* preference in his eyes. Yet his actual application of strict scrutiny belied the color-blind abstractions he used to justify its employment.

While application of strict scrutiny did invalidate the rigid Davis
quota in *Bakke*, it did not, said Powell, defeat race-conscious
admissions procedures designed to further student body diversity.[36] In *Fullilove*, Powell took the virtually unprecedented[37]
position that an outright racial classification can survive full
strict scrutiny by voting to uphold the preference at issue
there.[38] The concrete application of a constitutional test, it
seems, is every bit as important as its abstract formulation.
Reinforcing this observation is Justice Stevens's *Fullilove* dissent, where he voted to strike down the preference despite
using a test not much different from Powell's.[39]

The second position on the application of strict scrutiny to
racial classifications burdening whites—a position adopted by
Justices Brennan, Marshall, Blackmun, and perhaps White—is
an interesting improvisation. According to these justices, racial
discrimination disadvantaging minorities should be accorded
full strict scrutiny, but preferences benefiting these groups
should be treated under the intermediate standard used in sex
discrimination cases. Full strict scrutiny is inappropriate for
minority preferences, Brennan's *Bakke* opinion declared, because whites as a class lack "traditional indicia of suspectness"
like personal disabilities, continuing discrimination, and political powerlessness, and because such discrimination does not
"stigmatize" them.[40] However:

> . . .[T]he fact that this case does not fit neatly into our
> prior analytic framework for race cases does not mean
> that it should be analyzed by applying the very loose
> rational-basis standard of review that is the very least
> that is always applied in equal protection cases. . . . In-
> stead, a number of considerations—developed in gender
> discrimination cases but which carry even more force
> when applied to racial classifications—lead us to conclude
> that racial classifications designed to further remedial pur-
> poses "must serve important governmental objectives
> must be substantially related to achievement of those ob-
> jectives."[41]

These considerations included the possibility that benign discrimination might reinforce existing stereotypes about racial

minorities and the fact that all race-based classifications conflict with the meritocratic values so deeply rooted in American
life.[42] The intermediate standard did not prove much of an
obstacle to finding the *Bakke* quota and the *Fullilove* preference constitutional.[43] In fact, Justice Marshall triumphantly
announced in *Fullilove*, "the question is not even a close one."[44]

Any generalizations in this area are hazardous, but it appears
that the Court as a whole has tended to invoke and apply strict
scrutiny non-neutrally or asymmetrically in *Bakke* and *Fullilove*. First, it upheld the racial preference at issue in *Fullilove*.
The *Bakke* exception for diversity-oriented race consciousness
creates a substantial loophole for tacit admissions preferences.
The Court's performance in *United Steelworkers* v. *Weber*,[45]
which sustained a private firm's voluntary quota for access to
a craft training program despite an attack under a neutrally
worded federal employment discrimination statute, is similar
to *Bakke* and *Fullilove* in its practical result. Second, at least
three justices clearly desire that comparatively lenient tests of
constitutionality be applied to racial classifications benefiting
minorities at the expense of the white majority. Third, even
Powell's ringing declaration of ascriptive neutrality did not
prevent him from finding the *Fullilove* preference constitutional and from opening an escape route for covert quotas in
Bakke. *Bakke* and *Fullilove*, however, both leave the Court
considerable freedom for maneuver when it next confronts a
constitutional challenge to reverse racial discrimination. In the
emergent political climate of the 1980s, it may well resolve
such a case in a fashion less congenial to minority interests.
Perhaps a harbinger of future developments is the position
taken by Justices Stewart and Rehnquist in *Fullilove*. There,
they apparently abandoned strict scrutiny in race cases, instead
adopting a flat per se ban on racial classifications, no matter
what the nature of such classifications.[46]

Despite much judicial rhetoric to the contrary, it appears
that equal protection strict scrutiny has tended to favor the
deprived group encompassed by a suspect heading over its
dominant counterpart. That is, groups such as blacks and
women, plus aliens and illegitimates, tend to have easier access
to the more stringent forms of equal protection review and to

find the actual application of these standards somewhat tilted in their favor.[47] Thus, race, national origin, sex, alienage, and illegitimacy are once again constitutional statuses, although admittedly fairly qualified ones in the cases of race and gender. These new statuses differ radically from those of the past. Now, occupation of a status position provides a constitutional benefit: a heightened ability to invalidate governmental action working to one's disadvantage. What remains to be examined is the relationship between this new status and the various conceptions of freedom. Generally, this status tends to enhance negative liberty and may in certain circumstances promote positive freedom as well.

Access to strict scrutiny can increase the negative liberty of its beneficiaries. This follows from the fact that it provides them with enhanced power to invalidate disadvantageous external regulations. In many instances[48] where a claimant sucessfully uses this test to attack some discriminatory measure, his or her field of effective action is increased because an external impediment has been removed. Thus, the emergence of strict scrutiny in suspect classification cases is one aspect of the liberal individualist movement, since its effect is to eliminate restrictive legal status differentiations. As Justice Brennan once put it while arguing for the adoption of strict scrutiny in gender discrimination cases:

> There can be no doubt that our Nation has had a long and unfortunate history of sex discrimination. Traditionally, such discrimination was rationalized by an attitude of "romantic paternalism" which, in practical effect, put women, not on a pedestal, but in a cage. As a result of notions such as these, our statute books gradually became laden with gross, stereotyped distinctions between the sexes, and, indeed, throughout much of the 19th century the position of women in our society was, in many respects, comparable to that of blacks under the pre-Civil War slave codes. . . .
>   It is, of course, true that the position of women has improved markedly in recent decades. Nevertheless, it can hardly be doubted that, in part because of the high visibil-

ity of the sex characteristic, women still face pervasive,
although at times more subtle, discrimination in our educational institutions, in the job market and, perhaps most
conspicuously, in the political arena.[49]

Here, the reason for urging a more stringent form of equal protection review was precisely to eliminate external obstacles to
female self-assertion.

Thus, the constitutional status created by the asymmetry of
strict scrutiny often increases negative liberty for the suspect
groups benefited by the status. Here, status and negative freedom are linked or fused, and not opposed. If the purpose of
this status were merely to advance its beneficiaries' negative
liberty, though, there would be little reason for its existence.
This is so because the elimination of traditional restrictions
could be just as expeditiously advanced by allowing both groups
contained within the suspect heading to invoke strict scrutiny.
For instance, giving men increased power to attack gender-
biased laws burdening them would not of itself affect women
challenging stereotypic measures like those condemned by
Justice Brennan. As a result, there might seem to be little reason for refusing to make strict scrutiny symmetrical in suspect
classification cases.

For those advocating neutrality, however, this approach generates its own problems.[50] For one thing, it tends to ignore the
way that negative liberties can conflict, especially in the context
of a zero sum game. For instance, if men are able to invalidate
a state's allocation of scarce good X to women alone, both sexes'
practical access to that good may be somewhat diminished because of the price increases created by increased demand.[51] For
another thing, this approach tends to assume the existence of
those personal abilities necessary for increased negative liberty
to be meaningful.[52] Equal opportunity under a regime of neutral law is a merely formalistic equality where past deprivations
cause some competitors to enter the race with built-in handi-
caps.[53]

Both problems—scarcity and diminished capacity—are plainly
present in cases like *Bakke*. Entry to medical schools cannot
(or will not) be expanded indefinitely, and it is clear that mi-

norities tend on the average to possess a lesser store of entry-related abilities than do their white counterparts.[54] It is in response to this predicament that some universities have enacted preferential admissions policies like those challenged in *Bakke*. Such policies can be viewed as correctives for the denials of personal capacity created by generations of slavery and discrimination.[55] They can also be seen as means for promoting such capacities in future generations. As Professor John Hart Ely has written:

> The real hope lies, I think, in the fact that parents seem to make a difference. . . . If we underwrite a generation of Black professionals, even a generation that does not do quite as well in professional school as their White classmates, their children and their children's children may grow up with interests, motivations and aptitudes that are not dissimilar from those the rest of us grew up with, and, consequently, may do as well in school as Whites from similar backgrounds. The case for "reparations" or payments for two hundred years of oppression may be an uneasy one, but those two hundred years cannot but have made a difference. No matter how plausible this reasoning sounds, however, it remains a speculation, and the question must be reached whether it can sustain what is, after all, a racial classification.[56]

If strict scrutiny is made truly symmetrical and applied with full vigor to programs preferring racial minorities,[57] the programs' survival is imperiled. A measure of inequality in its invocation and application, on the other hand, should usually permit their continuance in one form or another. Thus, if it is assumed that reverse racial preferment does tend to enhance minority capacity,[58] inequality at the constitutional level can help to further this end. In such cases, the existence of a constitutional status can be linked with the positive conception of liberty. Obviously, this fusion of status and positive freedom differs considerably from its Hegelian and neo-Hegelian counterparts, which tended to define capacity in limited and determinate ways. Since many current programs of minority prefer-

ment promote access to large institutions,[59] the capacities
advanced by the newer forms of status are likely to be of a
liberal variety.

Professional School Admissions

Professional schools[60] are significant points of access to the
modern occupational structure and the rewards it offers. Programs giving certain minorities preferential admission to these
schools clearly display the status implications of aggressive efforts at equalized access to both higher education and, ultimately, to the occupational structure itself. The principal decision on the constitutionality of such programs is *Bakke*.[61]
There, the Supreme Court declared an outright admissions
quota unconstitutional while leaving much room for covert
minority preferences rationalized as a means of promoting
student body diversity. The *Bakke* compromise probably has
not restricted race-conscious state university[62] admissions preferences to any great degree. As Professor Laurence Tribe once
noted: "The headlines could cry 'Bakke Wins Admission,'
while lawyers and admissions officers would quietly read the
subtitle: 'affirmative action upheld.'"[63]

To the extent that they afford the relevant groups a practical
admissions edge over whites, minority entry preferences,
whether open or covert, make these minorities favored status
groups. To the extent that these preferences are protected from
equal protection attack, the status is of constitutional dimensions as well. This status increases negative freedom for benefited minorities since it weakens the external obstacle that
strictly meritocratic procedures impose. (But minority admissions preferences also tend to reduce the negative liberty of
whites because they impose an obstacle to applicants like Alan
Bakke.) In addition, this status can assist in developing the
capacities of its beneficiaries and thus can be regarded as fused
with positive freedom goals. Presumably, exposure to a professional school curriculum will aid in the development of abilities
not previously possessed. Moreover, successful completion of
a professional school program provides the certification (and,
one hopes, the capacity) for entry into an organizational status
position. This, in turn, should enhance the development of

those abilities encouraged by organizational affiliation. Finally, these successes may also help to advance the capacities of future generations of minorities.

In addition to these status themes, other characterizations of minority admissions preferences are possible. If these preferences involve quotas based on the minority's percentage of some relevant population, they approach a system of proportional representation within the professional school context. Thus, they can be said to create a system of group rights.[64] This point is usually made by claiming that now it is the ascriptively defined group, and not the individual, which is the entity entitled to educational opportunity and that the individual's fate is increasingly tied to his or her status as a group member. Perhaps more plausibly, it might be asserted that although individuals obviously still exist as discrete units, for some purposes social life is more coherently described by taking the group to be primary. This is often true for institutionalized groups, and the point might be extended to cover ascriptively defined collections of individuals as well. In the minority admissions context, though, all such assertions must be qualified. Current practices do not even begin to approach a system where access to educational opportunity is determined by, say, one's caste. Even the rigid *Bakke* quota, for example, relied heavily on the usual indicia of academic merit.[65] Additionally, even ascriptively neutral selection criteria will usually have decided group implications in practice. Whites, for instance, will generally fare better under such criteria than will non-whites. The presumed difference is that under neutral procedures, individual merit, and not some immutable trait unrelated to ability, will be the determinant of personal advance.

Employment

Another fairly clear set of reverse statuses can be found in the area of public and private employment. Here, the statuses are usually not of formal constitutional dimensions, but their practical significance is nonetheless considerable. Under Title VII of the 1964 Civil Rights Act and other civil rights statutes,[66] quota-like entry or promotion policies favoring racial minorities[67] routinely have been held to be an appropriate remedy[68] against private employers,[69] labor unions,[70] and governmental employers[71] found guilty of employment discrimination.[72] Statistical data comparing minority representation in the employment unit to the minority percentage in some relevant local population can assist in establishing such discrimination.[73] Apparently because of their remedial nature, the Supreme Court has often implied that these preferences do not pose constitutional problems.[74] Preferential employment plans have also been enforced against federal contractors pursuant to executive order.[75] In fact, a "voluntary" craft training program undertaken by a private employer doing government business and fearing federal reprisals survived a Title VII attack by a white worker when the Supreme Court decided *United Steelworkers v. Weber*[76] in 1979. *Bakke* and *Fullilove* apparently have had little impact on this set of employment-related preferential statuses.[77]

Quota-like minority employment preferences typically create a legal status favoring the minorities they benefit. They establish a system of differential access to a valued activity and do so on the basis of an ascribed trait.[78] Like the statuses already discussed, these preferences tend to increase the negative liberty of favored minorities. They accomplish this by breaking down an external obstacle—disadvantageous hiring and promotion practices—to minority advance.[79] They also seem to be intended to augment long-term minority capacity. As one decision upholding a racial preference put it:

> It is now well understood . . . that our society cannot be completely color-blind in the short term if we are to have a color-blind society in the long term. . . . Discrimination has a way of perpetuating itself, albeit unintentionally, because the resulting inequalities make new opportunities less accessible. Preferential treatment is one partial prescription to remedy our society's most intransigent and deeply rooted inequalities.[80]

Implicit in this language is the assumption that, due to the diminution of minority capacity created by past discrimination, meritocratic neutrality does not create equal opportunity in fact. Also tacitly asserted is the expectation (or hope) that preferential treatment eventually will enhance minority abilities to such an extent that its continuance will be unnecessary and a truly color-blind society will be possible. Once again, a reverse status seems to be linked with the furtherance of personal capacity and thus to be fused with positive freedom values. Mainly, the liberal variant of positive freedom is promoted, since the legal status facilitates access to an occupational structure where open-ended conceptions of capacity tend to predominate.

As with professional school admissions preferences, these employment-related statuses lend themselves to some additional characterizations. First, they can be said to set up a system of group rights. Their aim is to assist certain ascriptive groups, and they often make individual advance dependent upon group membership.[81] One fairly recent federal court of appeals decision is frank on this point. While denying an equal protection challenge to a plan discriminating in favor of women and racial minorities, it established the existence of a compelling governmental interest by stating:

> The federal interest in the present case is that of remedying the effect of a particular pattern of employment discrimination upon the balance of sex and racial groups [which] would otherwise have obtained—an interest distinct from that of seeing that each individual is not disadvantaged by discrimination, since it centers on the distribution of benefits among groups. . . . The governmental interest in having all groups fairly represented in employment is . . . substantial, and since that interest is substantial the adverse effect on third parties is not a constitutional violation.[82]

In short, the governmental interest in achieving the proper intrafirm group balance was sufficient to overcome an individual's putative right to equal protection of the laws.[83] As this language also suggests, quota-like employment programs often appear to aim at a system of ascriptively based proportional representation in the firms and unions where they are imposed.

This is similarly evident in cases where the quota is based on the affected group's percentage of some relevant surrounding population.[84] It also can be inferred from the use of statistics in the initial proof of discrimination, since this suggests that the optimum condition is one of proportional representation for certain minority groups.[85]

School Integration

Elementary and secondary education is a vital point of access to the American occupational structure. The first and most famous of the Court's school desegregation decisions, *Brown* v. *Board of Education*,[86] displayed an acute awareness of education's importance in promoting access to and the capacity for success within the organized social life of modern America.

> Today, education is perhaps the most important function of state and local governments. Compulsory school attendance laws and the great expenditures for education both demonstrate our recognition of the importance of education to our democratic society. It is required in the performance of our most basic public responsibilities, even service in the armed forces. It is the very foundation of good citizenship. Today it is a principal instrument in awakening the child to cultural values, in preparing him for later professional training, and in helping him to adjust normally to his environment. In these days, it is doubtful that any child may reasonably be expected to succeed in life if he is denied the opportunity of an education. Such an opportunity, where the state has undertaken to provide it, is a right which must be made available to all on equal terms.[87]

In rejecting the notion that separate-but-equal schools for blacks could adequately serve these purposes, the Court also stated: "To separate [black children] from others of similar age and qualifications solely because of their race generates a feeling of inferiority as to their status in the community that may affect their hearts and minds in a way unlikely to ever be undone."[88] This suggests that to the Court, segregated schooling necessarily impaired capacity for blacks subjected to it. Integrated schooling, on the other hand, enhanced capacity or increased positive freedom. It seems fairly clear that this capacity was viewed in an open-ended sense, as involving a generalized ability to utilize the options made available by American life today.

Effectuation of this goal has necessarily involved explicit consideration of racial differences, generally in the form of a judicially imposed duty to distribute black students on a more or less equal basis throughout a given locality's school system.[89] This means that the educational right enjoyed is one granted blacks as a group. As one federal court of appeals described the process set in motion by the "all deliberate speed" command of *Brown's* implementation decision:[90]

> The gradual transition the Supreme Court authorized was to allow the states time to solve the administrative problems inherent in the change-over. No delay would have been necessary if the right at issue in *Brown* had been only the right of individual Negro plaintiffs to admission to a white school. Moreover, the delay of one year in deciding *Brown II* and the gradual remedy *Brown II* fashioned can be justified only on the ground that the "personal and present" right of the individual plaintiffs must yield to the overriding right of Negroes *as a class* to a completely integrated education.[91]

This approach, undoubtedly motivated by the exigencies of school integration in the South, was also apparent in decisions such as *Green* v. *County School Board*.[92] There, the Court struck down a freedom-of-choice plan as inadequate for promoting the ultimate goal of a "unitary nonracial system of public education" in the particular county involved.

Thus, the Supreme Court's school desegregation cases seem to reflect positive freedom goals and do so by effectively creating a system of group rights. Although they no doubt confer advantages on blacks as a group, it is not clear that these cases provide blacks a positive status as compared with the white majority. In theory, at least, such decisions aim at an immedi-

ate equality of educational opportunity. They do not involve
favoritism of the sort presented by *Bakke* or by remedial employment discrimination quotas. Elementary and secondary
education is compulsory and thus is not nearly so much a
finite good as professional school admissions slots or employment positions.

Also, it is not clear whether school integration increases the
negative liberty of black students. It does eliminate a previous
restriction on attendance at all-white schools, but it often compels attendance at such schools. The group right granted blacks
as a class—a right to a very rough proportional representation
throughout the school district—can restrict the negative freedom
of the individual black person who prefers a predominantly
black neighborhood school.[93] Illustrating these points is the little-
known late 1960s case of *Norwalk CORE* v. *Norwalk Board of
Education*,[94] a decision that is grist for the mill of neo-Wallace-
ites and black separatists alike. The case involved a black and
Puerto Rican equal protection challenge to a local school integration plan providing, among other things, that minorities be
bused to formerly white schools but that there be little or no
busing of whites to minority schools. In rejecting this challenge,
the federal district court basically concluded that the plan did
not discriminate against the minority plaintiffs.

> ... the Board ... has not abridged the rights of the Black
> and Puerto Rican community: there is no right to a neigh-
> borhood school; there is no right not to be bused; and
> there is no right requiring equal treatment of that which
> is in fact unequal (here, neighborhoods). Although *people*
> are equal and governmental classification by race will not
> be tolerated, *neighborhoods* are not.[95]

Addressing the fact that the plan did subject minorities to
greater practical burdens than whites, the court opined that
"[s]pecial burdens may be imposed upon a defined class to
achieve a permissible purpose where the definition of class has
been reached in a manner highly relevant to the purpose being
sought."[96] Finally, as if to dispel all further argument, it
declared that to hold otherwise would "be to discourage vol-

untary action by enlightened public officials attempting to
correct one of the underlying causes of racial tension in this
Nation."[97]

Although decisions like *Norwalk CORE* are easy enough
targets, the tactic of forced integration would appear to be
necessary if *Brown*'s premises and assimilationist goals are
sound. The formal negative liberty established by freedom-of-
choice plans was a fairly illusory freedom in many southern
school districts throughout the 1950s and 1960s. In this context, compulsory school integration was an obvious corrective
to the array of social forces conditioning black students' choice.
But such reasoning would not apply where individual blacks—
for example, traditionalist southerners or cultural nationalists
of all sorts—genuinely desire all-black local schools. Here, the
liberal positive freedom thrust of the school integration decisions seems to require some restrictions on negative liberty, at
least until the debilitating effects of slavery and discrimination
are eliminated and blacks can make truly free choices. As Theodore Lowi once wrote:

> Most of the burdens of such a [busing] plan fall upon
> Negro children, but of course this is one of the advan-
> tages of such an approach, since they and their families
> have the most to gain from it. . . .[N]o plan of this sort
> will work without the use of benign quotas, or positive
> discrimination. . . .
> Many Negro parents . . . fear such a system, but they
> must balance their fears against present educational
> opportunities that doom their child far more certainly
> than commuting. . . . Ghetto schools are perpetuating
> the inferior culture that second-class citizenship created,
> and the cycle can be broken only by abandonment of
> those schools. The real problem is whether the Negro
> community is as yet mature enough to accept positive
> discrimination.[98]

If this argument is taken seriously, it follows that recalcitrant
blacks, like the inhabitants of Rousseau's polity, must be
"forced to be free."[99]

Voting

Political participation as such is not a direct means of access to the modern occupational structure, yet its importance for groups seeking representation within this structure can hardly be doubted. For instance, denying blacks the right to vote was quite useful in maintaining the inferior social status they long occupied and still occupy today to some degree. The famous one man-one vote principle announced and applied by *Baker v. Carr*[100] and its progeny, passage of the Voting Rights Act of 1965,[101] and the declaration that voting is a fundamental right relative deprivation of which triggers strict scrutiny[102] have provided the courts with powerful tools for giving minorities equal political access and the tangible benefits that presumably will flow from it.

These legal developments are yet another instance of the liberal individualist movement. Their application, however, has not always been a straightforward process. Underlying many of the difficulties this presents is the fact that one man-one vote is a principle whose validity is something less than self-evident. As Justice Frankfurter noted in his largely forgotten *Baker* v. *Carr* dissent:

> One cannot speak of "debasement" or "dilution" of the value of a vote until there is first defined a standard of reference as to what a vote should be worth. What is actually asked of the Court in this case is to choose among competing bases of representation—ultimately, really, among competing theories of political philosophy —in order to establish an appropriate frame of government for the State of Tennessee and thereby for all the States of the Union.[103]

In short, one man-one vote is just one theory of democracy and thus is not an infallible guide to the ordering of political activity. Moreover, the principle is a classic case of what Michael Oakeshott has called political rationalism: the imposition of an abstract, schematic model on a society's customary political arrangements.[104] Thus, the simple majoritarianism represented by the principle can negate what used to be called the permanent interest of the community in favor of transient popular enthusiasms. To take just one example, Chief Justice Earl Warren's famous declaration that "[l]egislators represent people, not trees or acres"[105] should provide food for thought to those environmentalists inclined to pursue its obvious implications. In addition, the principle is an inadequate descriptive guide to a pluralist social reality in which groups of all sorts are extremely significant actors.[106] Warren's assertion that "[l]egislators are elected by voters, not farms or cities or economic interests,"[107] while correct in a narrow technical sense, seems an empty ideological platitude when one considers the manifest influence that groups exert on the formal political processes.[108] Finally, the one man-one vote principle can sometimes deny effective representation to certain groups. A neutral territorially based legislative districting scheme, for example, can dilute the electoral strength of widely dispersed minorities.

In light of the difficulties that the one man-one vote principle presents, it is not surprising that the Court has sometimes deviated from its announced norm of personal political equality by creating effective statuses giving certain groups extra political weight relative to this norm. As before, the principal beneficiaries of this activity have been racial minorities, although the practical benefits received have usually not been too great. A relatively early, but significant, instance of this was the Court's 1966 decision in *Katzenbach* v. *Morgan.*[109] This case concerned a conflict between a New York statute requiring voters to be literate in English and a provision of the Voting Rights Act establishing the right to vote for anyone educated to the sixth grade in a Puerto Rican school. At issue was the extent of congressional authority under section 5 of the Fourteenth Amendment, which gives Congress the power to enforce the substantive provisions of the amendment. Here, the relevant substantive provision was the equal protection clause, and New York's literacy requirement was concededly no denial of equal protection. Concluding that Congress's enforcement powers were operative even where no direct constitutional violation existed, Justice Brennan's opinion for the Court declared: "Correctly viewed, §5 is a positive grant of legislative power authorizing Congress to exercise its discretion in determining

whether and what legislation is needed to secure the guarantees
of the Fourteenth Amendment."[110] Then Brennan went on to
justify the federal provision as a means for securing nondiscrim-
inatory governmental treatment and as a permissible congressional response to possible discriminatory motives in the enactment of the literacy requirement. Since it appears that the New
York law remained in effect so far as other classes of voters
were concerned,[111] the *Katzenbach* Court effectively sanctioned
unequal access to the polls.

Similar inequalities are apparent in some of the Court's redistricting decisions in the 1970s. In *White* v. *Regester*,[112] it overturned portions of a state legislative redistricting plan because
of a uniquely local pattern of past discrimination against blacks
and Mexican-Americans. In concluding, it suggested that not
every racial or political group had a similar right to representation in the state legislature.[113] In *Beer* v. *United States*,[114] the
Court, while refusing to strike down New Orleans' reapportionment of councilmanic districts, did interpret the relevant portion of the Voting Rights Act as requiring that there be no
retrogression in the voting rights of racial minorities. More significantly, in the 1977 case of *United Jewish Organizations* v.
Carey,[115] the Court upheld a New York reapportionment
scheme despite Fourteenth and Fifteenth amendment challenges by a geographically concentrated contingent of Hasidic
Jews whose population was split between two districts as a
result of the plan. As Justice Brennan's concurring opinion
conceded, the plan was clearly designed to produce definite
numbers of nonwhite representatives in the state's legislature.

> The one starkly clear fact of this case is that an overt
> racial number was employed to effect petitioners' assign-
> ment to voting districts. In brief, following the Attorney
> General's refusal to certify the 1972 reapportionment
> under his §5 powers, unnamed Justice Department offi-
> cials made it known that satisfaction of the Voting Rights
> Act in Brooklyn would necessitate creation by the state
> legislature of 10 state Assembly and Senate districts with
> threshold nonwhite populations of 65%. . . . The result
> of this process was a county-wide pattern of districting
> closely approximating proportional representation.[116]

In its 1980 decision in *City of Mobile* v. *Bolden*,[117] the Court upheld a system of city government with three commissioners chosen by at-large voting despite Fourteenth and Fifteenth amendment challenges asserting that the voting rights of blacks as a group were diluted by this majoritarian scheme.[118] But on the same day as the *Bolden* decision, the Court also upheld the U.S. Attorney General's denial of a clearance for a city's shift to a similar form of government in *City of Rome* v. *United States*.[119] Although under *Bolden* the city's new form of government was constitutional, this case involved federal power under the Voting Rights Act and turned on Congress's enforcement powers under section 2 of the Fifteenth Amendment, which resembles section 5 of the Fourteenth Amendment. Here, the Court concluded that these powers were sufficient to justify the attorney general's decision despite the absense of a constitutional violation.

Taken as a whole, these cases[120] suggest a judicial tendency to legitimize federal and state attempts to establish a rough system of proportional political representation for certain minority groups. Since other groups are not so blessed, minorities again occupy a preferred—if rather qualified—legal status position as compared with these groups. Whatever the merits of this result, it cannot be readily reconciled with the vision of political equality underlying the one man-one vote principle. In some cases, at least, this preferential treatment is a response to the way that minority voting power can be diluted by facially equal and neutral electoral schemes. It is difficult to regard this status as increasing the negative freedom of the minorities it benefits since it does not eliminate a direct impediment to action. To the extent that minorities use their preferred position to enhance their social standing, however, some long-term increases in capacity may result. To that extent, a fusion of status and positive freedom can be said to exist in the voting rights context. In theory, one supposes, this qualified status will disappear once minorities achieve something resembling equal capacity. But preferred positions of this sort, like those enjoyed by the major political parties, may well persist so long as political realities permit the favored groups to retain them. It is factors of this sort that are likely to determine their fate in the long run.

146 The Dilemmas of Individualism

Notes

1. Informal patterns of ascriptively based hiring, job assignment, and promotion do exist within modern organizations, although they have been increasingly subject to attack since the 1960s.

2. Technically, such positive classifications also create an inferior legal status position for the groups whom they relatively disadvantage.

3. It is questionable, however, whether any real status differentiation exists in this case.

4. *See, e.g.*, Slaughterhouse Cases, 85 U.S. (16 Wall.) 36, 71-72 (1873); Strauder v. W. Va., 100 U.S. 303, 306-7 (1880). *See also* R. Berger, Government by Judiciary 166-83 (1977); Perry, *Modern Equal Protection: A Conceptualization and Appraisal*, 79 Colum. L. Rev. 1023, 1026-28 (1979).

5. The text of the Fourteenth Amendment's equal protection guarantee mentions only state activities. In 1954, however, the Supreme Court made equal protection standards applicable to the federal government as well. Bolling v. Sharpe, 347 U.S. 497 (1954). Thus, the term *governmental* will be employed in the text, even for historical periods in which the equal protection clause applied only to the states.

6. *E.g.*, Truax v. Raich, 239 U.S. 31, 41 (1915) (aliens); Yick Wo v. Hopkins, 118 U.S. 356 (1886) (Chinese).

7. Yick Wo v. Hopkins, 118 U.S. 356, 369 (1886).

8. Buck v. Bell, 274 U.S. 200, 208 (1927).

9. An early example is F. S. Royster Guano Co. v. Va., 253 U.S. 412, 415 (1920).

10. *E.g.*, Perry, *supra* note 4, at 1035. Satisfying the requirement that the classification be necessary to the fulfillment of a compelling purpose often means that no less discriminatory alternative means of furthering that purpose be available.

11. United States v. Carolene Prods. Co., 304 U.S. 144, 152-53 n.4 (1938).

12. Karst, *Foreword: Equal Citizenship under the Fourteenth Amendment*, 91 Harv. L. Rev. 1, 42 (1977).

13. Craig v. Boren, 429 U.S. 190, 197 (1976) (emphasis added).

14. Trimble v. Gordon, 430 U.S. 762, 767 (1977); Matthews v. Lucas, 427 U.S. 495, 504-6 (1976).

15. The case that initiated the change was Reed v. Reed, 404 U.S. 71 (1971). *See also* Frontiero v. Richardson, 411 U.S. 677 (1973); Stanton v. Stanton, 421 U.S. 7 (1975). Altough not marked by majority adoption of a full-fledged strict scrutiny approach, these cases certainly established that sex discrimination was no longer to be treated under rational basis standards. The enunciation of the intermediate standard now used in gender discrimination cases first came in Craig v. Boren, 429 U.S. 190 (1976).

16. Kahn v. Shevin, 416 U.S. 351, 355 (1974).
17. Schlesinger v. Ballard, 419 U.S. 498, 508-10 (1975).
18. 420 U.S. 636 (1975) *See also* Califano v. Goldfarb, 430 U.S. 199 (1977).
19. 429 U.S. 190 (1976).
20. *Id.* at 219-220 (Rehnquist, J., dissenting).
21. Orr v. Orr, 440 U.S. 268 (1979); Caban v. Mohammed, 441 U.S. 380 (1979); Wengler v. Druggists Mutual Ins. Co., 446 U.S. 142 (1980).
22. *E.g.*, Orr v. Orr, 440 U.S. 268, 279 (1979).
23. Califano v. Webster, 430 U.S. 313 (1977). Also worth note in this general context is Parham v. Hughes, 441 U.S. 347 (1979).
24. Michael M. v. Superior Court, 450 U.S. 464 (1981).
25. Rostker v. Goldberg, 453 U.S. 57 (1981).
26. *E.g.*, Kirchberg v. Feenstra, 450 U.S. 455 (1981); Califano v. Westcott, 443 U.S. 76 (1979); Davis v. Passmann, 442 U.S. 228 (1979) (finding a private right of action for a constitutional violation).
27. 438 U.S. 265 (1978).
28. 448 U.S. 448 (1980).
29. For more detail on these cases, *see* Phillips, *Neutrality and Purposiveness in the Application of Strict Scrutiny to Racial Classifications* (to be published in the Temple Law Quarterly).
30. Two further sources of confusion deserve brief mention. First, four *Bakke* justices decided the case on statutory grounds and did not reach the constitutional question. Second, *Fullilove* involved federal legislation, and for three of the justices this definitely affected the equal protection analysis.
31. In addition to the positions discussed, *Fullilove* saw two more possibilities emerge. The first of these is the flat ban on all racial classifications, even benign classifications, apparently adopted by Justices Stewart and Rehnquist. The second is Chief Justice Burger's rather muddled attempt to emasculate traditional equal protection analysis because of a felt need to defer to Congress.
32. Justice Stevens probably agrees with Powell on this general point. *See* Phillips, *supra* note 29.
33. Regents of the Univ. of Cal. v. Bakke, 438 U.S. 265, 289-90 (1978).
34. *Id.* at 295.
35. *Id.* at 295-99.
36. *See id.* at 311-24.
37. Prior to *Fullilove*, the only decisions upholding a racial classification in the face of strict scrutiny were the World War II Japanese exclusion cases. Perry, *supra* note 4, at 1035-36.
38. *See* Fullilove v. Klutznick, 448 U.S. 448, 495-517 (1980) (Powell, J., concurring). However, this was partially due to Congress's enforcement

powers under section 5 of the Fourteenth Amendment, powers that past cases suggested could be used in a very race-conscious fashion. *See id.* at 507-14. *See also infra* text accompanying notes 109-11.

39. *See id.* at 532-54 (Stevens, J., dissenting). *See also* Phillips, *supra* note 29.

40. Regents of the Univ. of Cal. v. Bakke, 438 U.S. 265, 357-58 (1978) (Brennan, White, Marshall and Blackmun, JJ., concurring and dissenting).

41. *Id.* at 358-59.

42. *Id.* at 360-61.

43. *See id.* at 362-79; Fullilove v. Klutznick, 448 U.S. 448, 520-22 (1980) (Marshall, J., concurring). In each case, the preference was treated as substantially related to the important purpose of compensating minorities for past social discrimination.

44. Fullilove v. Klutznick, 448 U.S. 448, 519 (1980) (Marshall, J., concurring).

45. 443 U.S. 193 (1979).

46. *See* Fullilove v. Klutznick, 448 U.S. 448, 523, 525-26 (1980) (Stewart, J., dissenting). For some elaboration, *see* Phillips, *supra* note 29.

47. Although the point was not discussed to any great degree above, one reason for this is that eliminating the effects of prior discrimination—sometimes specific and identifiable, sometimes societal—is often regarded as a compelling or important governmental purpose.

48. This, however, is usually not true where government denies or confers a benefit on the basis of a status attribute. For instance, striking down a statute denying death benefits to illegitimates cannot readily be characterized as increasing the negative freedom of illegitimates because only in a very indirect sense can an external impediment to action be said to have been eliminated.

49. Frontiero v. Richardson, 411 U.S. 677, 685-86 (1973).

50. For a more detailed discussion of this whole area, *see* Phillips, *supra* note 29.

51. This example is based on Craig v. Boren, 429 U.S. 190 (1976), although in the case of 3.2 beer the effect is likely to be minimal. A related matter with some zero sum implications involves situations where government confers or denies a benefit on the basis of a status attribute. If, for example, social security provisions benefiting women are struck down, governmental actors theoretically can make the benefit available to men as well or eliminate it entirely.

52. An increase in negative liberty can sometimes enhance capacity. Consider the case of a woman or minority member who is able to obtain a previously denied job under meritocratic employment discrimination legislation and as a result develops a variety of new abilities.

53. As chapter 5 will make clear, though, the theoretical implications

of attempts to correct this are themselves unappetizing.

54. This was obviously true in *Bakke*. *See* Regents of the Univ. of Cal. v. Bakke, 438 U.S. 265, 277-78 n.7 (1978).

55. *See, e.g.*, Horwitz, *The Jurisprudence of* Brown *and the Dilemmas of Liberalism*, 7 Harv. Civ. Rts.-Civ. Lib. L. Rev. 599, 610 (1979).

56. Ely, *The Constitutionality of Reverse Racial Discrimina*ʳ⁻⁻, 41 U. Chi. L. Rev. 723, 726 n.22 (1974).

57. This is what tended not to happen in Powell's *Bakke* and *Fullilove* opinions.

58. This assumption has been challenged. *See, e.g.*, the claims discussed in Phillips, *supra* note 29.

59. Some examples will be discussed immediately following.

60. Much of the discussion applies to college and university admissions generally.

61. Regents of the Univ. of Cal. v. Bakke, 438 U.S. 265 (1978). *See also* DeFunis v. Odegaard, 82 Wash. 2d 11, 507 P.2d 1169 (1973), *dismissed as moot*, 416 U.S. 312 (1974). The latter case is notable mainly because of Justice Douglas's attempt to fashion genuinely meritocratic admissions criteria capable of taking minority status into account. His principal assertion was that sometimes minority status may be an indicator of long-term academic and professional potential. *See* DeFunis v. Odegaard, 416 U.S. 312, 331-32 (Douglas, J., dissenting).

62. Because of the state action requirement, *Bakke* has no application to wholly private universities; however, factors such as government funding may make the activities of a formally private university subject to constitutional checks.

63. Tribe, *Perspectives on* Bakke: *Equal Protection, Procedural Fairness or Structural Justice*, 92 Harv. L. Rev. 864, 864-65 (1979).

64. *See, e.g.*, Kurland, *Ruminations on the Quality of Equality*, 1979 B.Y.U. L. Rev. 1, 18-19. For more on the subject, *see* Phillips, *supra* note 29.

65. *See* Regents of the Univ. of Cal. v. Bakke, 438 U.S. 265, 275 (1978) (describing how meritocratic criteria were used within the class of minority applicants).

66. 42 U.S.C. §§ 1981, 2000e, 2000e-2, 2000e-16 (1976).

67. In this area, the vast majority of the reported cases involve racial discrimination and preferences favoring racial minorities.

68. This includes employment preferences enacted as part of a consent degree after a civil rights suit by the government under these statutes. *See, e.g.*, United States v. City of Miami, 614 F.2d 1322 (5th Cir. 1980).

69. *See, e.g.*, United States v. N. L. Industries, Inc., 479 F.2d 354 (8th Cir. 1973).

70. *See, e.g.*, United States v. Int'l Union of Elevator Constr., 538

F.2d 1012, 1017-20 (3d Cir. 1976). For more such cases *see* Phillips, *Status and Freedom in American Constitutional Law*, 29 Emory L.J.3, 86 n.338 (1980).

71. *See, e.g.*, Carter v. Gallagher, 452 F.2d 315, 327-32 (8th Cir. 1971), *cert. denied*, 406 U.S. 950 (1972). For more such cases, *see* Phillips, *supra* note 70, at 86 n.339.

72. This is not universally true, however. *See, e.g.*, Sledge v. J. P. Stevens & Co., 585 F.2d 625, 645-52 (4th Cir. 1978), *cert. denied*, 440 U.S. 981 (1979).

73. For some Supreme Court pronouncements on this point, *see* Dothard v. Rawlinson, 433 U.S. 321, 329-31 (1977); Hazelwood School Dist. v. United States, 433 U.S. 299, 307-12 (1977); Teamsters v. United States, 431 U.S. 324, 337-40 (1977).

74. *See, e.g.*, Regents of the Univ. of Cal. v. Bakke, 438 U.S. 265, 301-2 (1978); Fullilove v. Klutznick, 448 U.S. 448, 483 (1980).

75. *See, e.g.*, Associated Gen. Contractors v. Altshuler, 490 F.2d 9 (1st Cir. 1973), *cert. denied*, 416 U.S. 957 (1974). The executive orders in question are Exec. Order No. 11246 and Exec. Order No. 11375. Under the aegis of these orders and rules issued pursuant thereto, the Office of Federal Contract Compliance Programs has had the authority to monitor the affirmative action performance of federal contractors. Its sanctions include the power to terminate federal contracts with non-complying firms and, in extreme cases, to blacklist recalcitrant offenders. At this writing, there have been intimations that the Reagan administration will restrict federal power under these orders.

76. 443 U.S. 193 (1979). In *Weber*, the defendant acted under the threat of the sanctions described in *supra* note 75.

77. *See* Phillips, *supra* note 29.

78. For a few academic quibbles and qualifiers to this general proposition, *see* Phillips, *supra* note 70, at 86-87 n.343.

79. They also tend to restrict the negative freedom of excluded white workers.

80. Associated Gen. Contractors v. Altshuler, 490 F.2d 9, 16 (1st Cir. 1973), *cert. denied*, 416 U.S. 957 (1974).

81. For many of the same reasons discussed in the case of professional school admissions preferences, this assertion needs to be qualified a bit.

82. EEOC v. Am. Tel. & Tel. Co., 556 F.2d 167, 179-80 (3d Cir. 1977), *cert. denied sub nom.* Communications Workers v. EEOC, 438 U.S. 915 (1978).

83. Actually, as if to reinforce the point of group predominance, the parties raising the equal protection claim in this case were various unions.

84. *See, e.g.*, Davis v. County of Los Angeles, 566 F.2d 1334, 1336-37, 1343-44 (9th Cir. 1977), *vacated as moot*, 440 U.S. 625 (1979).

85. This might be justified as an attempt to replicate the results that presumably would have occurred had the long history of racial maltreatment never taken place and minority groups thus had come to possess equal capacity, but this does not change the practical effect of such methods of proof.

86. 347 U.S. 483 (1954).

87. *Id.* at 493.

88. *Id.* at 494.

89. *See, e.g.,* Swann v. Charlotte-Mecklenburg Bd. of Educ., 402 U.S. 1, 24-25 (1971), where the Court stated that although strict mathematical quotas were not constitutionally required, "mathematical ratios" could be used as "a starting point in the process of shaping a remedy."

90. Brown v. Bd. of Educ., 349 U.S. 294, 301 (1955) (*"Brown* II").

91. United States v. Jefferson County Bd. of Educ., 372 F.2d 836, 868 (5th Cir. 1966) (italics omitted and emphasis added in the last line).

92. 391 U.S. 430 (1968).

93. An October 1971 Gallup survey, for instance, reported a 47 to 45 margin against busing among blacks. N. Glazer, Affirmative Discrimination 84 (1975).

94. 298 F. Supp. 213 (D. Conn. 1969), *aff'd,* 423 F.2d 121 (2d Cir. 1970). *See also* Coppage v. Franklin County Bd. of Educ., 394 F.2d 410 (4th Cir. 1968).

95. Norwalk CORE v. Norwalk Bd. of Educ., 298 F. Supp. 213, 223 (D. Conn. 1969) (italics in original).

96. *Id.* at 225.

97. *Id.* at 226.

98. T. Lowi, The End of Liberalism 278-79 (1st paperback ed. 1969).

99. Of course, Rousseau's conception of freedom differs from the sort of freedom ultimately to be promoted here.

100. 369 U.S. 186 (1962).

101. 42 U.S.C. § 1971 *et seq.* (1976).

102. *E.g.,* Kramer v. Union Free School Dist., 395 U.S. 621 (1969).

103. Baker v. Carr, 369 U.S. 186, 300 (1962) (Frankfurter, J., dissenting).

104. *See* M. Oakeshott, Rationalism in Politics and Other Essays (1962). Oakeshott, however, contends that political rationalism is never what it purports to be—an independent exercise of reason dissociated from social circumstance—and instead urges that political ideologies are abridgements of an existing state of affairs. *See id.* at 119-23. Thus, one man-one vote can be seen as the product of an increasingly individualistic and formally egalitarian social and political climate.

105. Reynolds v. Sims, 377 U.S. 533, 562 (1964).

106. *Baker* v. *Carr* and decisions like it were not without their group

implications, since they tended to advance the interests of urban groups at the expense of rurally based concerns. *Cf.* W. Elliot, The Rise of Guardian Democracy ch. 4 (1974).

107. Reynolds v. Sims, 377 U.S. 533, 562 (1964).

108. For an extreme statement of the view that formal democracy is a facade masking and legitimating group control, *see* A. S. Miller, Democratic Dictatorship: The Emergent Constitution of Control ch. 7 (1981).

109. 384 U.S. 641 (1966).

110. *Id.* at 651.

111. The Court specifically held that "the New York English literacy requirement cannot be enforced to the extent that it is inconsistent with § 4(e) [of the Voting Rights Act]." *Id.* at 647. Presumably, this meant that literacy requirements still could be enforced as to groups other than the affected Puerto Ricans.

112. 412 U.S. 755 (1973).

113. *Id.* at 769.

114. 425 U.S. 130, 140-41 (1976).

115. 430 U.S. 144 (1977).

116. *Id.* at 169 (Brennan, J., concurring).

117. 446 U.S. 55 (1980).

118. There, Justice Stewart's opinion for the Court characterized Justice Marshall's dissent as advocating a constitutional right of proportional representation for minorities.

119. 446 U.S. 545 (1980).

120. Also relevant in the context of political representation is Morton v. Mancari, 417 U.S. 535 (1974), described in chapter 2 in the section on tribal Indians. There, the Court upheld a portion of the Indian Reorganization Act providing that qualified tribal Indians receive hiring and promotion preferences in the Bureau of Indian Affairs.

CHAPTER 5

Status and the Liberal Individualist Advance

The variety of status-freedom relationships presented in chapters 2 through 4 requires some overall explanation. One promise of the liberal individualist movement was the demise of status restrictions, yet in its ongoing advance, it has everywhere been accompanied by new forms of status. This might be attributed to illiberal social and personal forces aligned against the movement. On the other hand, there might be something about liberal individualism itself that causes its recurrent entanglements with status systems to which it is theoretically opposed.

The Inadequacies of Liberal Individualism

The liberal individualist movement has been the general background force framing the developments sketched in this book. This movement generally involves the progression toward a condition in which maximum effect is given to the choices of a person's ego, "I," or self. Its thrust is toward removing restrictions on individuals of assumed stability and rationality and thus providing them with an environment in which their innate potentialities will flower.[1] In its early forms, liberal individualism involved the elimination of external status restrictions. This was roughly the period comprehended by Maine's status-to-contract generalization. It includes the gradual demise of the traditional status relationships. At this time, it was not unusual for people to see history as a "progressive emancipation of the individual from the tyrannous and irrational statuses"[2] of the past. Thus, because this involved the elimination of external restraints, the liberal individualist advance originally represented an increase in negative freedom. Usually the individual's ability to utilize the field of action thus cleared was assumed. Theoretically, though, this whole effort was problematical. Negative freedom alone—the mere absence of external impediments and nothing more—cannot provide the individual with criteria of choice. As Alasdair MacIntyre once noted:

> Liberalism always appears accompanied by and allied to, not only philosophical theories, but also political and economic stances of a non-liberal kind. . . . The reason that this is always so and must always be so is that liberalism by itself is essentially negative and incomplete. It is a political doctrine about what cannot be justified and what ought not to be permitted: interference of a variety of kinds with individual liberty. This essentially negative character of liberalism derives from its eighteenth-century antecedents. Liberalism was the doctrine used to undermine the authoritarianism and the authority of the *ancien régime*. What is liberal in the writings of Jefferson and of Robespierre and their like are their demonstrations of the unjustifiable character of censorship, of alien rule, of denial of the suffrage, of arbitrariness in the courts, and of the enforcement of religious practice. It is from them that liberalism inherits its character as a series of denials.
>
> From this negative character derives both the virtue and the vice of liberalism. The virtue resides in the affirmation of the values of toleration and of freedom of expression. . . . The vice of liberalism derives from the continuous refusal of liberals to recognize the negative and incomplete character of their liberalism. The precepts of liberalism enjoin upon us certain constraints on our political activities; but they set before us no ends to pursue, no ideal or vision to confer significance upon our political action. They never tell us what to do. Hence no institution, no social practice can be inspired solely or even mainly by liberalism; and every such institution or social practice that claims to be so inspired—such as the "liberal" university or the "liberal" state—is always a fraud.[3]

The example of the catatonic sitting unimpeded in an open field reinforces the point.

At first glance, the liberal version of positive freedom would seem to correct this deficiency. This sort of positive freedom involves the capacity to entertain and pursue a wide, theoretically infinite, range of options. To Ronald Dworkin, its furtherance is (or should be) a major goal of the contemporary liberal, who, he says, "is concerned to expand imagination without imposing any particular choice upon imagination."[4] To some extent, this idea of capacity seems to have been realized in twentieth-century America. All are familiar with people who, while maintaining a certain coherence of personality, appear capable of responding to experience in creative ways and integrating their responses with the personality in a process that can only be called growth. Certainly the modern positive state and contemporary organizational life have expanded both the range of options available to many people and their capacity to pursue them. Thus, to the extent that promotion of such abilities is a concern of public policy, liberal positive freedom can be said to have a nurturing aspect—the bringing to bear of latent abilities residing within, as well as the strengthening of whatever internal traits enable creative response to new stimuli. In the case of the catatonic, this would require elimination of whatever internal psychological forces block activity and stimulation of such potentialities (including potentials for responsiveness and creative growth) as exist within him. In such cases, we can imagine the state or other capacity-producing agent effectively saying something like the following to the benefited individual: "You have within you certain potentialities, and it is the aim of public policy to promote the conditions of your growth, but we don't too much care what these potentialities are or what form your growth takes, so long as both are genuinely yours."

From a thoroughly liberationist point of view, however, this would not result in complete freedom unless the agent of choice—the ego, "I," or self—is totally unaffected by internal factors that nonetheless are external to it. If the self is influenced by such factors, its choices are necessarily constricted, and the individual cannot possess the ability to entertain and pursue all options. What would seem necessary for complete liberation to occur is a self that operates as a sort of mental command center whose choices are not affected by anything—internal or external—extraneous to it. This self would have to be a simple, pure ego or "I" because, if it possesses any determinate qualities, these will inevitably influence the choices it makes. It is difficult to imagine a self having definite traits, yet still retaining the ability to choose or act in a completely open fashion.[5] This liberationist aspect of liberal freedom can easily be viewed as involving the transfer of negative freedom goals from the external to the internal sphere. That is, since the elimination of external obstacles is obviously insufficient if internal checks still limit the ability to choose, these too must be de-deprived of influence for choice to be truly free.

It may be, however, that this sort of self-liberation is not possible, or, more precisely, is possible only through the self's complete destruction. As F. H. Bradley, tracing the path from negative freedom to libertarian positive freedom, tells us:

> . . . what is freedom? "It means not being made to do or be anything. 'Free' means 'free from.' " And are we to be quite free? "Yes, if freedom is good, we cannot have too much of it." Then, if "free"="free *from*," to be quite free is to be free from everything—free from other men, free from law, from morality, from thought, from sense, from—Is there anything we are *not* to be free from? To be quite free from everything is to be—nothing. Only nothing is quite free, and freedom is abstract nothingness. If in death we cease to be anything, then there first we are free, because there first we are—not.[6]

For Bradley, then, the drive for complete autonomy requires the negation of all determinate mental content and culminates in the perfect freedom of a rationally required suicide.[7] The key line in this quotation is Bradley's statement: "To be quite free from everything is to be—nothing." This statement may not be persuasive on its face, but its meaning becomes clearer if we assume the view, often associated with philosophical idealists,[8] that all aspects of experience are internally related to each other. This means that each such aspect derives its qualities from the other aspects to which it stands in relation and that a thing's relations thus determine its nature. Nothing simply *is* apart from its relations. (There seems to be some similarity between this position and any approach seeing phenomena in systemic terms and noting the ways that all elements of the system shape each other. Certain theories of the personality, some renderings of twentieth-century physics,[9] and some environmentalists' views of the ecological system might serve as examples.) If this is so, the idea of a totally unrelated, undetermined free self is ridiculous and ultimately vacuous. On these assumptions, moreover, the effort to achieve absolute freedom could be quite destructive. If internal and external phenomena inevitably shape the self and thus limit its choices, self-liberation requires their elimination. Perhaps Hegel had this negating, destructive tendency in mind when he called negative freedom

> . . . the freedom of the void which rises to a passion and takes shape in the world. . . . [W]hen it turns to actual practice, it takes shape in religion and in politics alike as the fanaticism of destruction. . . . Only in destroying something does this negative will possess the feeling of itself as existent. Of course it imagines that it is willing some positive state of affairs, such as universal equality or universal religious life, but in fact it does not will that this shall be positively actualized, and for this reason: such actuality leads at once to some sort of order, to a particularization of organizations and individuals alike; while it is precisely out of the annihilation of particularity and objective characterization that the self-consciousness of this negative freedom proceeds. Consequently, what negative freedom intends to will can never be anything in itself but an abstract idea, and giving effect to this idea can only be the fury of destruction.[10]

If the self were to succeed in eliminating the surrounding external and internal worlds, it would be left with nothing to which it could stand in relation. To the idealists at least, it then would itself cease to exist.

Still, it is obviously possible to reject the idea that the self is determined by its relations to other phenomena. But if its complete liberation from external and internal stimuli were possible, what would this entail? Most likely, it would lead to perfectly random behavior. To quote Bradley again:

> . . . Free-will means non-determinism. The will is not determined to act by anything *else*; and, further, it is not determined to act by anything *at all*. Self-determination means that the self . . . *may* realize itself by and in this, that, and the other particular; but it also implies that there is no reason why it should identify itself with this one, rather than with that one; . . . there is nothing in the self which brings this, and not that, act out of it. . . . Freedom means *chance*; you are free, because there is no reason which will account for your particular acts, because no one in the world, not even yourself, can possibly say what you will, or will not, do next.[11]

The key here is the indeterminancy and impoverishment of the self that absolute freedom seems to require. As Bradley says: "there is nothing in the self which brings this, and not that, act out of it." To give the self some criteria for choosing would be to provide it with some determinate characteristics, however broadly defined, and thus to limit its options somewhat. Lacking any internal standards, it can only latch onto such experiential stimuli as are presented to it and should do so in an utterly unpredictable fashion. Actually, even this would restrict the options available to the free self, since its choices would be limited by the range of particulars actually before it. This, Frithjof Bergmann has argued, can make the liberated individual very resentful of himself and everything around him: "[T]his type feels genuinely free only when he performs an utterly capricious act, when the act is prompted neither by a rational consideration, nor by anything else that is either within or without him. . . . If he feels free only in these actions, then he must live with an almost constant sense of being victimized and managed. No man can perform very many capricious actions."[12]

Thus, the absolute self-liberation required by the attempt to maximize the capacity for choice seems to lead to absurd consequences. Obviously, such extremes of behavior are very uncommon, if not impossible. They are comparable to a limiting case in mathematics. Yet, as Bergmann notes, one reason for examining such extremes "is the possibility . . . that our own culture fosters the crystallization of this type."[13] This will involve approximations of the extremes just discussed. One wishing to maximize personal autonomy might be required never to act at all, since to do so would ensnare oneself in some definite course of behavior that would foreclose other alternatives. Total inaction is not usually appealing, however, so one desiring to act while retaining as many alternatives as possible would seem advised to undertake tentative commitments only, always taking care to keep options open. This would be necessary both because tangible commitments usually involve external restraints (for example, the legal obligations accompanying marriage) and because they may impose internal checks as well (for example, the emotional entanglements created by marriage). That these tendencies are becoming more and more prevalent is by now a cliche. If any verification of this is needed, one example from Daniel Yankelovich's *New Rules* may suffice to convince the skeptic.[14]

Mark and Abby Williams, Yankelovich tells us, are two "strong formers," people who take the new self-fulfillment ethic to an extreme. Both are in their early thirties. Mark works for a public interest law firm, and Abby is a magazine editor for a multinational chemical company. They have been married for six years. Each values the freedom modern life provides, and each seeks to maximize it. Without discussing the matter openly, Mark and Abby have drifted into a sort of "open marriage" in which it is understood that each party may "work late" several nights a week" with no questions asked. Mark is sleeping with one of his clients, Robin, who came to him after being arrested for selling cocaine. Abby has also pursued several brief affairs but usually felt guilty afterwards. Although Abby likes being married, "she says her needs for sexual fulfillment and intimacy are not being fully met by her husband." Despite all this, though, Abby wants to have a baby "to fulfill my maternal needs." She is reluctant to do so, however, because of the

state of her marriage and because raising a child would interfere
with her career. Mark wants Abby to have the child but is
troubled by the loss of family income this will entail and by
the likelihood that fatherhood would require him to be home
most evenings. Mark, who is dissatisfied with his job, also is
tempted by the possibility of moving to Maine, where Robin's
brother has a house, and going into private practice there. Com-
menting on these people, Yankelovich need only note the obvious: "[T]hey value their personal freedom so intensely that
they regard each new choice and commitment demanded of
them as a threat to their freedom and a challenge to other possibilities they might also exercise. The question of what to
commit to and sacrifice for thus remains forever open, making
their lives unsettled." Yankelovich also emphasizes Abby's
constant references to her "needs," suggesting that "she [al-
most] believes the process of filling her unmet needs is like
filling a set of wine glasses at a dinner party." Here, the comparison to a detached self taking inventory of its psychic requirements is evident. Although this note is muted, Mark and
Abby also display a bit of the liberation ethic's tendency
toward negation and resentment. Their marriage, for instance,
is fairly shaky, and Mark seems somewhat willing to abandon
his job, a job whose public service aspects he often finds praise-
worthy. Mark also states that he "walk[s] around in a state of
constant anger." Abby has "mini-anxiety attacks" in which
"her optimism is drained as if by vacuum, and she feels dry-
mouthed and empty."

As Yankelovich is careful to note, Mark and Abby are not
typical of contemporary Americans—at least not yet. At this
point, it is not crucial to assess the degree to which their pursuit of liberation has become a national pastime, only to note
that it is an obvious and growing social tendency. The purpose
of the argument advanced thus far is not to develop some
general theory of personality or to examine the extent to
which liberal positive freedom is practicable. Instead its aim
is, first, to establish a negative proposition: that the idea of
liberation entailed by liberal individualism, if pushed to an
extreme in isolation from other values, leads to absurd and
destructive results. The utterly unrestrained free self is ultimately a vacuous, and perhaps dangerous, concept. From this

negative conclusion, a positive argument emerges: liberal freedom, if it is to be viable, always requires determinate restraints.
To say this is only to repeat old, if neglected, truisms, like
"Freedom implies limits" or "Liberty requires order." Depending on the intensity and completeness with which liberal freedom manifests itself at various times and places, a variety of
relations between it and its complementary "order" requirement is possible. The need for limiting controls may be met
primarily by restraints external to the individual, mainly by
internal checks, or by some combination of the two. Also,
there can be different kinds of external or internal checks. This
conclusion has definite implications for the different status-
freedom relationships presented in this book, and it is to these
that we now turn.

The Traditional Inferior Statuses: Status and Freedom
as Opposed yet Complementary

Most obvious about the traditional or inferior constitutional
statuses is the conceptual clash between status and negative
freedom that they present.[15] Now we are in a position to sup-
plement this characterization. If freedom always implies restraints, might not the traditional statuses have helped play
such a compensatory role? This was more or less the case; these
statuses were part of a network of social checks serving a critical
ordering function for a society in which direct political controls
were, comparatively speaking, few. Thus status and freedom,
while conceptually opposed, were often practically complementary during this period.

As manifested in American constitutional law, the inferior
statuses generally were at their apogee in the nineteenth century. For most of that century, affirmative government regulation of society, while never totally absent, was relatively restricted. This was generally the era of limited government and
the negative, "nightwatchman" state. Although American government has never been truly indifferent to business,[16] this
hands-off posture was usually most evident in the economic
realm. But as the presence of the traditional constitutional
statuses suggests, nineteenth-century America was hardly a
libertarian society in noneconomic areas of life. The laissez-
faire posture that prevailed for most of the century did not

prevent the legislation of traditional morality.[17] This period
was also one in which the restraining influence of the family,
the church, and the local community was of paramount importance in shaping the lives of most people.[18] In addition, Irving
Kristol tells us, the bourgeois ethic characterizing this era
stressed the values of "thrift, industry, self-reliance, self-discipline [and] a moderate degree of public-spiritedness."[19] To
David Riesman, the nineteenth century was part of the era in
which the personally rigid inner-directed man, with his "gyro-
scopic" self-direction and his "hard enduringness and enterprise," was prevalent.[20]

This conjunction of liberal and illiberal patterns seems to
have been no accident. The restraints imposed by family, locality, religion, traditional morality, and character type played
a vital ordering role in a society where direct political controls
were, by twentieth-century standards, relatively few. As Robert
Nisbet has remarked about the restraints imposed by family and
locality:

> What has so often been called the natural economic order
> of the nineteenth century turns out to be . . . a special
> set of political controls and immunities existing on the
> foundations of institutions, most notably the family and
> local community, which had nothing whatsoever to do
> with the essence of capitalism. Freedom of contract, the
> fluidity of capital, the mobility of labor, and the whole
> factory system were able to thrive and to give the appear-
> ance of internal stability only because of the continued
> existence of institutional and cultural allegiances which
> were, in every sense, precapitalist. Despite the rationalist
> faith in natural economic harmonies, the real roots of
> economic stability lay in groups and associations that
> were not essentially economic at all.[21]

Also, the "fortunate legacy" of premodern religious values like
altruism, self-abnegation, social obligation, truth telling, and
trust provided vital social cement during this period. Fred
Hirsch writes:

> Religious obligation therefore performed a secular func-
> tion that, with the development of modern society, be-

came more rather than less important. It helped to recon-
cile the conflict between private and social needs at the
individual level and did it by internalizing individual
norms of behavior. It thereby provided the necessary
social binding for an individualistic, *non*altruistic market
economy. This was the non-Marxist social function of
religion.

. . . .

. . . The market system was, at bottom, more dependent
on religious binding than the feudal system, having abandoned direct social ties maintained by the obligations of
custom and status.[22]

Supplementing these controls, and presumably operating even
when they were not present, were internal restraints of the
sort possessed by the inner-directed man. To quote Kristol
again:

. . . The liberal-individualist vision of society is not an
abstract scheme which can be imposed on any kind of
people. For it to work, it needs a certain kind of people,
with a certain kind of character, and with a certain cast
of mind. Specifically, it needs what David Riesman calls
"inner-directed" people—people of firm moral convictions, a people of self-reliance and self-discipline, a people
who do not expect the universe to be offering them something for nothing—in short, a people with a non-utopian
character even if their language is shot through with utop-
ian cliches.[23]

These different restraints were interrelated to some degree. It
is hard to imagine how the inner-directed type, for instance,
could have internalized his rigid norms so strongly without
familial, religious, and community support in his formative
years.
    Seen in this context, the traditional constitutional statuses
take on a different aspect. Now they can be seen as reflecting,
and to some degree forming, a variegated pattern of social ordering in which basically illiberal, often authoritarian, controls
played a vital role. First, the traditional statuses facilitated

direct political controls. Since they amounted to a diminution
of constitutional rights due to a status attribute, they made
possible greater sovereign control of the groups they encompassed. However, because political checks were relatively weak
in the nineteenth century, this is probably the least important
function served by the inferior statuses. Second, some of these
constitutional statuses mirrored social status relationships
which were significant ordering factors in the last century. The
social statuses occupied by women and children were vital to,
if not constitutive of, the family and the stabilizing and socializing functions it fulfilled. (Perhaps the social and legal oppro-
brium visitd upon homosexuals and illegitimates had a slight
effect in the same direction.) Although it is difficult to find
anything good to say about black slavery and the conditions
most blacks still faced after the Civil War, the inferior status
they occupied was part of a social hierarchy that, if nothing
else, was ordered. Perhaps an analogous argument could be
made with respect to tribal Indians. Many of the inferior
statuses admittedly do not fit this pattern. For instance, restrictions on the rights of mental patients and prisoners are inevitable in almost any period and continue today. Also, the positions occupied by the military and government employees
resemble modern bureaucratic statuses. Third, some social
statuses and their constitutional counterparts were related in
various ways to the general social stabilizers of family, locality,
religion, and traditional morality. The role of statuses like wo-
manhood, youth, and maybe homosexuality or illegitimacy in
reinforcing the family has already been mentioned. Obviously
such statuses, and others, received religious sanction as well.
These family-oriented statuses also tended to reinforce the
values of localism and community by putting some restraints
on social and geographical mobility. In their own, less praise-
worthy, ways, the statuses occupied by blacks and tribal Indians
occasionally may have done much the same.[24]

Another Look at the Organizational Statuses

Without embracing such egregious features of nineteenth-
century life as slavery, contemporary American conservatives
tend to defend a reconciliation of freedom and order much like

that just described. Republican politicians and conservative intellectuals alike typically advocate both free market policies
and traditional virtues and social institutions.[25] The political
rhetoric of Ronald Reagan is an obvious example. At an abstract level, this conservative reconciliation leaves much to be
desired, since it attempts to combine essentially antagonistic
liberal and premodern ideas.[26] Worse yet, the continuing advance of liberal individualist values has left the traditionalist
portion of the conservative synthesis less and less in touch with
social reality. (Some might assert that the resurgence of traditional attitudes represented by the Moral Majority undermines
this observation, but it is difficult to imagine that such groups
would be nearly so vociferous and defensive were they not in
fact a minority.) Recognizing this fact, some intellectuals of
the Right have characterized liberalism as exhausting the premodern "moral capital" that long sustained it,[27] leaving American institutions awash in a sea of egoism. In fact, the customary
behavior of conservatives themselves reinforces this perception;
they are part of the problem they identify. As Victor Ferkiss[28]
has noted, conservative literature contains "much fervent rhetoric about tradition, but what is embraced is the liberal capitalist tradition." Conservatives, he continues, "accept the
fundamental liberal premises of an intrinsically necessary social
struggle and of the ethical primacy of growth and change." To
them, "[e]conomic growth through technological innovation
is the supreme good of humanity." This emphasis on productivity and growth is assisted by the way the liberal half of the
conservative synthesis—limited government and economic
laissez-faire—frequently works to the tangible benefit of large
business enterprises whose activities often so thoroughly distort
the free market.[29] If any verification for these propositions is
required, one need only consider the Reagan administration's
first year, with its pro-business economic and regulatory policies and its subordination of the Moral Majority agenda.

Thus, its electoral successes notwithstanding, contemporary
American conservatism is often a fit subject for ridicule. Still,
some of the problems to which conservative intellectuals have
addressed themselves do merit attention. In particular, the contention that the liberal individualist movement tends to destroy

the moral capital necessary for limited government to be viable is clearly in line with the arguments presented in this chapter. It suggests that unless new ordering structures have replaced the old, liberal individualism's inherent inadequacies will surface. The overall demise of the inferior statuses would seem to provide a partial test for these arguments. These statuses were linked in various ways to forms of moral capital which, it was asserted, played a vital stabilizing role when direct political controls were relatively weak. Although in some cases their departure is hardly to be mourned, it was accompanied by a corresponding decline in the importance of such traditional restraints as those imposed by family, church, and local community.[30] If liberal individualism were what it often purports to be—a system of values not requiring illiberal admixtures in order to be viable—these changes should have led toward a libertarian order where individuals are independent, self-defining units scornful of constricting group affiliations and capable of ordering their affairs with little govermental assistance. Generally, this has not happened. Instead, American life has come to be substantially dominated by large groups, a pervasive governmental presence, and a variety of new status relationships differing from their feudal predecessors mainly in their indeterminancy. No sooner, it seems, were ostensibly self-reliant Americans released from traditional status ties than they fell subject to a new status system based on the large organization and the interventionist state. This system imposes all sorts of restraints on the individual and for this reason tends to vindicate the arguments advanced here.

What remains to be seen is how these controls came to exist and why they took the form that they did. For the status-freedom relationships typifying the traditional statuses, the liberal and illiberal components of the relationship were connected mainly through time and place. That is, the status elements were largely of premodern origin, and the post-1600 freedom aspects were generally independent of and conceptually opposed to these. But after significantly diminishing the influence of traditional forms of authority, liberal individualism would seem to have been left without a major competitor. From where, then, did the new system of restraints emerge? Any

answer to this question will almost inevitably lead to the conclusion that liberal ideals, rather than being overcome by outside forces, were in fact implicated in their own partial demise.
To see how this came to be, it is necessary to examine the links
between the liberal individualist advance and the rise of the
modern organization,[31] the locus of the status relationships at
issue here.[32]

There is no dearth of theories purporting to account for the
advent of modern bureaucracy.[33] Only three of these, each
linked in its own way to the liberal individualist advance, will
be considered here. First, the large group can be seen as a logical outgrowth of the laissez-faire mentality. Combination with
other individuals to effect collective purposes promises significant competitive advantages and increased power over those
who do not do so.[34] Here the link to liberal individualist ideas
is explicit. Second, the corporation can be seen as reflecting
the distinctly modern post-seventeenth-century urge toward
the domination and exploitation of nature.[35] On this view of
its development, the size and internal differentiation of the corporation are necessary so that it may fulfill its productive purposes as effectively as possible. Indicative here is the technological determinism of J. K. Galbraith,[36] who asserts that the
imperatives of techological advance dictate ever-larger organizations because only such entities can handle the increased com-
plexities of planning, development, manufacture, demand
creation, and distribution such advances bring in their train. In
this case, the link to liberal individualism is less obvious but
every bit as intimate because modern technology and the manipulative attitude it embodies are commonly viewed as derivative
from the egoistic postmedieval orientation.[37] Finally, there is
the communitarian explanation for the rise of the organization,
which basically sees it as a response to the anomie brought
about by the decline of traditional social structures and the
need for some alternative form of community.[38] Here, the rise
of the modern group is not expressive of liberal postures.
Rather it is a response to them, a response based on drives denied expression by liberal tendencies but not extinguished
thereby. Since this explanation is far less familiar than its competitors, it will receive extended attention here.

Perhaps the earliest statement of this general position is the corporation theory contained in Hegel's *Philosophy of Right*.[39] Hegel purported to display the development of freedom in a dialectical, though not historical, fashion, beginning with the simple egoistic liberalism embodied in legal institutions such as property, contract, tort, and crime and culminating in the status-based liberty found in the modern state. As with much of Hegel's philosophy, the *Philosophy of Right* presupposed the destruction of prior organic communities and the onset of modern individualism. Thus, it was an attempt to fulfill communitarian aspirations within this liberal context by incorporating the isolated individual within a new, distinctly modern, social and political whole.[40] Thus although the structure of the book is not historical, the modern state that Hegel describes and celebrates at its conclusion seems to have been intended as a model for the emergent historical epoch.[41]

The persuasiveness of Hegel's account depends on one's estimate of his general philosophy, and no attempt to expatiate on this extraordinarily difficult subject will be made here. Instead our concern is to describe the treatment of the corporation presented in the *Philosophy of Right*. Hegel's definition of the term *corporation* is not completely clear, although it does seem to include business activities, and the term probably should be given an expansive meaning. As conceived by Hegel, the corporation develops out of the laissez-faire of the dialectical stage he calls "civil society." Civil society is typified by the prevalence of "selfish ends,"[42] which are satisfied and organized through something like Adam Smith's "invisible hand," as well as by the external "umpire" state of classical liberalism, with its general, universalistic rules. The type of rationality possessed by the consciousness dominating civil society manifests itself in an endless specialization of the means of manufacture: that is, in a division of labor. Also, "[t]he infinitely complex, criss-cross, movements of reciprocal production and exchange, and the equally infinite multiplicity of means therein employed, become crystallized" into social classes (agriculture, business, and government-bureaucratic).[43] But in its egoistic self-aggrandizement, civil society "destroys itself and its substantive concept in this process of gratification"; it "affords a spectacle of extravagance and want as well as of the physical and ethical degeneration common to them both."[44] In particular (the influence on Marx is evident), it promotes the destruction of the family and the creation of a proletarian rabble.[45] All of this creates a need for unity between the external political state and the isolated individual. The first means by which this occurs is the police, a concept seemingly equivalent to what is now called the police power. This involves the punishment of crime, some regulation of trade, public education, the care of dependent families, and public relief. The need for union also seems to be what gives rise to the corporation, which Hegel terms "the second ethical root of the state"[46] (the family being the first) and which "come[s] on the scene like a second family for its members."[47] Thus, it is through the corporation that the isolated individual achieves purpose and identity:

> . . . the Corporation member needs no external marks beyond his own membership as evidence of his skill and his regular income and subsistence, i.e. as evidence that he is a somebody. It is also recognized that he belongs to a whole which is itself an organ of the entire society, and that he is actively concerned in promoting the comparatively disinterested end of this whole. Thus, he commands the respect due to one in his social position.[48]

It is roughly at this point that Hegel makes a transition to the state, of which all the subsidiary groups discussed are organic members.

Lest Hegel's corporation theory be thought a peculiarity, it should be noted that his ideas have recurred again and again in the 160 years following publication of the *Philosophy of Right*. Such explanations differ from Hegel's account, though, in being less concerned with the genesis of the organization than with the forces impelling individuals to identify with it.[49] Uniting them are human efforts "to find in large-scale organizations the . . . status and security . . . formerly gained in the primary associations of family, neighborhood and church."[50] To Sheldon Wolin, this was a common thread linking a variety of diverse thinkers—for example, nineteenth-century French

authoritarian conservatives like de Maistre and de Bonald,
sociologists such as Emile Durkheim, philosophical idealists
like Bradley, a congeries of nineteenth-century radicals and
anarchists, exponents of enlightened capitalism, such as Adolf
Berle, and modern theorists of organizational life like Elton
Mayo.[51] As Wolin puts it:

> The idea of community and the idea of organization did
> not develop as two separate and parallel strands during
> the nineteenth and twentieth centuries. What is interest-
> ing, and at times poignant, is the way that they converge.
> The nostalgia for the vanished warmth of the simple com-
> munity and the obsession with the possibilities of large-
> scale organization are frequently piled on top of each
> other. As the century wore on and men were sobered by
> the impracticality of recapturing the shared warmth of a
> close communion, they stubbornly refused to surrender
> the hope of community. Instead, they insisted on imput-
> ing its values to the stark and forbidding structures of
> giant corporations.[52]

Much in the same vein is Daniel Bell, for whom the rise of the
business corporation, the university, the government agency,
or the large hospital, "each with its hierarchy and status system," satisfies the need for "a group which could provide a
sense of kindredness and common purpose for its members"
in order "for *anomie* to be resolved."[53] To elaborate:

> To the extent that the traditional sources of social sup-
> port (the small town, church and family) have crumbled
> in society, new kinds of organizations, particularly the
> corporation, have taken their place; and these inevitably
> become the arenas in which the demands for security,
> justice and esteem are made. To think of the business
> corporation, then, simply as an economic instrument is to
> fail totally to understand the meaning of the social
> changes of the last century.[54]

For all this, though, it is questionable how well modern organizations have fulfilled the assimilationist tasks assigned them

by so many thinkers. In the early 1950s, for instance, Nisbet argued that because of their "rational impersonality," modern organizations generally do not satisfy continuing needs for "spiritual belief and social status" and thus do not "answer adequately the contemporary quest for community." In fact, he continued, this organizational impersonality spills over into society at large, becoming "the moral background of vague and impotent reactions against technology and science, and of aggressive states of mind against the culture as a whole."[55] Events since the time Nisbet penned these rather prophetic words testify to his insight. To the extent that his assertions are accurate, the communitarian argument takes on a different aspect. Modern organizations may represent a conscious or unconscious striving for lost forms of community, but due to the nature of the modern situation they inevitably reflect, they fail to satisfy such strivings fully.

The existence of organizational statuses supports the general argument that liberal individualism requires restraints. Unlike the traditional statuses, however, the restraints seem to be derivative from the liberal individualist advance because each of the three proffered explanations for the rise of modern bureaucracy was rooted in a different aspect of this phenomenon. Which alternative best explains the rise of the institutionalized group and the status systems it spawned? To answer this question definitively would require an explicit view on the nature of historical causation, and this book offers no such view. Still, some comparison of each alternative's power to explain events is possible.

All three explanations clearly account for the existence of organized groups. For quite different reasons, the second and third of them (the "Galbraithian" and the "communitarian") virtually require that organizational statuses exist. At least for non-Hegelians, however, the communitarian argument seems fairly implausible as an explanation for the *creation* of the organization. It is difficult to regard, for instance, IBM as solely rooted in drives for community. The communitarian account, though, does explain why individuals seek organizational affiliations, as does the first argument (the "power over others" hypothesis). (This question, of course, is not wholly separable from the inquiry why the organization came to exist in the first place.) In addition, each account is probably consistent with the prevalence of liberal positive freedom values within the organization. This is, after all, increasingly the sort of water within which large groups now swim, and certain structural features of intraorganizational life seem to compel it.[56] To the extent that it is seen as Hegelian in origin and inspiration, though, the communitarian position is less consistent with the prevalence of liberal freedom because the capacity envisioned by Hegel's version of positive liberty was fairly determinate in nature. The communitarian explanation, however, is superior to its opponents in at least one respect: it can account for the disaffection with organizational life so noticeable in the 1960s and early 1970s. The other two approaches seem to presuppose an egoistic, manipulative, materialistic view of human nature. If this were the whole story, rejection of the organization would seem very unlikely unless it did not afford the individual competitive advantages or failed to deliver the goods in productive terms. But disaffection with the modern organization is quite consistent with the communitarian approach.

The ascendancy of modern bureaucracy is best viewed as resulting from the interplay of the three explanations offered, that is, it is attributable to some combination of the drives for individual advance, for material abundance, and for community. Explaining this ascendancy has revealed a contradiction permeating organizational life, one generated by the liberal individualist movement. Desires for personal advance and material productivity are fairly direct expressions of the liberal attitude, while the quest for community is basically illiberal in nature. Denied the expression it once found in traditional status structures, this drive fastened upon the organized group as a substitute. Yet since the dominant consciousness is increasingly individualist-rationalist-manipulative, the stuff of which this new community is made—modern bureaucracy, its impersonal forms, and the indeterminate capacities it fosters—sometimes fails to satisfy the individual and provokes personal disaffection. Thus the liberal individualist movement seems to express itself in an increasingly egoistic and manipulative posture, on the one hand, and a reversion from the bureaucratic consequences of this, on the other.

With these observations in mind, we are perhaps in a better position to understand the status-freedom relationships found within large modern institutions. To the extent that communitarian forces are operative, the organizational fusion of status and positive liberty is readily explicable. On this view of institutional affiliation, individuals are virtually bereft of substance outside the group, and group statuses to a large extent are constitutive of personal identity. The various therapeutic controls assisting this identification, on the other hand, represent liberal individualism's manipulative aspect. No doubt adding to their effectiveness is the fact that many people— stripped of substance by the erosion of group ties and the self-dissociation the liberal individualist advance tends to produce[57] — are not equipped to resist such conditioning. For the various reasons discussed here and in chapter 3, the prevalence of liberal notions of capacity within the organization[58] is hardly surprising. Indeed, it is difficult to see how things could be otherwise. This may promote a certain amount of communitarian disaffection, but therapeutic controls seem capable of filling the breach for the time being.

More difficult to explain on the assumptions used here, though, is the sort of disaffection represented by increased demands for rights within the organization. This is almost certainly not a reaffirmation of traditional rugged individualism, if for no other reason than that it does not embody a rejection of group life as such. To some extent, no doubt, it is an outgrowth of the softer individualism[59] which seems to be one of liberalism's current manifestations. While dependent on the organization, people of this sort also appear resentful of its controls, at least when these take overtly authoritarian forms. However, in their desire for a humanized work place, exponents of employee rights often seem less hostile to group dominance when it assumes a therapeutic guise.[60] Since controls of this sort seem at least as pernicious from a libertarian standpoint as directly coercive checks, the relative lack of resistance to them may seem surprising. This is less inexplicable, however, if the employee rights phenomenon is seen as a manifestation of communitarian disaffection. Since the universe of discourse is increasingly liberal in substance, communitarian drives often are not recognized for what they are. For the same reason, the fail-

ure to satisfy these drives will often be verbalized in liberal
terms: for example, as procedural arbitrariness or the denial of
certain rights.[61] It is the individual's dependence on the organization and her or his tendency to acquiesce in therapeutic controls, though, that suggest that such protests are frequently not
what they seem.

Some attempt at summarization may be useful here. Just as
the rise of the organization admits of no single-factor explanation, the individual's identification with it cannot be described
in simple terms. Indeed, the picture of organizational affiliation
just suggested is inordinately complex and contradictory. Central to that discussion are certain tendencies inherent in liberal
individualism and the contradictions these generate. In a pure
or unmixed form, liberal individualism expresses drives toward
individual competitiveness and material productivity through
manipulation of nature, both of which usually strengthen the
hold of the organization. And the demise of prior status restrictions and the self-dissociation also created by the liberal advance tend to dilute personal capacity and to make the individual an easy mark for organizational conditioning. This conditioning, of course, generally expresses the manipulative orientation characterizing the liberal outlook. Also pushing the individual toward affiliation with the group are communitarian drives
left unsatisfied by the advance of liberal individualism. But the
organizational "community," shaped as it is by the liberal ethos,
often proves inadequate to its assimilationist task. Because of
this ethos, though, such disaffection often finds expression
in liberal rhetoric not expressive of its real genesis.

The Paradoxical Reverse Statuses

From time to time, it has been suggested that liberal individualism tended to self-destruct when isolated and emphasized
to the exclusion of other values. Nowhere, perhaps, is this more
true than in the case of the reverse statuses.[62] The highly emotional debate on reverse discrimination has often obscured one
fairly obvious fact: that both its proponents and its detractors
can lay claim to arguments with an undisputed liberal pedigree.
Thus, while the reverse statuses clearly revive ascriptive cate-
gorizations the liberal individualist advance was thought to have
eliminated, they are just as clearly rooted in that advance. To

say this is to say that attempts to maximize liberal values can produce quite illiberal consequences. For our purposes, the principal significance of the reverse statuses is the way they demonstrate liberal individualism's tendencies toward self-contradiction. They are less useful for advancing the basic argument that liberal individualism requires restraints.

Opponents of reverse discrimination have a thoroughly liberal case to make. In their view, such discrimination violates interrelated liberal ideals like equal opportunity,[63] equality before the law, and formal racial neutrality. What undermines their argument is the realization that a regime of formal ascriptive neutrality is only formal. It permits innumerable instances where past discrimination causes diminished present capacity, thus making the competitive struggle unequal from its inception. The familiar metaphor of the race in which certain competitors are burdened with shackles or weights is entirely apt here. Worse yet, the inequalities such an inherently unequal competition produces may perpetuate themselves over time in a sort of vicious cycle.

The various systems of reverse racial preferment can be viewed as a response to this problem—a response animated by the thoroughly liberal desire to make equal opportunity before an equal starting line genuinely equal. To some extent, such preferment can correct for denials of capacity resulting from past discrimination. Although this is more conjectural, it may also increase the capacity of minority groups over the long haul. This, it is sometimes claimed, may eventually make reverse discrimination unnecessary. Thus, reverse racial preferment creates a new status-freedom relationship: a fusion of status and liberal positive freedom goals. In addition, by restricting the negative freedom of certain majority members, the reverse statuses may indirectly vindicate the argument that liberal individualism requires restraints for its promise to be equally enjoyed by all. In this, it is roughly comparable to the countless governmental restrictions protecting weaker parties against the depredations of the powerful.[64]

Such considerations, one assumes, were of little comfort to Alan Bakke or Brian Weber, and there is no denying that programs of minority preferment do an injustice to relatively innocent whites. Such programs obviously constitute racial dis-

crimination. Although discrimination of this sort may be the
best of a bad bargain, its odiousness is hardly reduced by
calling it "benign" or saying that it is not "invidious" or does
not "stigmatize."[65] In addition, critics contend, minority
preferences revive discredited ascriptive criteria of selection,
create a system of group rights, and thus undermine the idea
that individuals should be treated as individuals. In short, they
assert, reverse racial preferences are thoroughly illiberal. If
the reverse statuses are examined in a vacuum, this is all quite
true. Such reasoning, though, ignores their thoroughly liberal
purposes. This reinforces the general point urged here: that
aggressive attempts to advance liberal ideals can produce
quite illiberal results. The whole conundrum almost tempts
one to consider the merits of Hegelian logic, for which
"finite characterizations or formulae supersede themselves,
and pass into their opposites."[66]
a world where disparities in capacity abound, however, can cause
liberal individualism to self-destruct in a quite different and al-
together more profound fashion. Past racial discrimination is
not the only source of diminished capacity, and racial minorities are not the only groups so deprived. This poses an obvious
question: why limit the pursuit of equalized life chances to
racial minorities, and why make racial quotas the only means
for advancing this end? After all, it might be argued, individuals deserve their socioeconomic position, their family socialization, and their innate abilities no more than they deserve
their racial characteristics. Fred Hirsch has made this point quite
effectively:

> . . . Which disabilities are to be removed? The early and
> fully bourgeois concept of equality of opportunity singled
> out ascriptive disabilities of birth—hereditary distinc-
> tions of status and role. But the other visible hereditary
> advantage, of wealth, soon appeared equally stark, as an
> arbitrary handicap to those who had little or none of it.
>   In contemporary times, research has made clear that
> further advantages are transmitted by parents in intelli-
> gence and family environment: neither in the cradle nor
> at the school gate do different children have an equal

start in life. And then what of other differences in inherited or environmentally influenced characteristics which in individual cases may be of decisive importance for economic achievement—differences in health, in capacity for self-control and discipline, in physical strength? Can a competition that takes no account of these differences in initial capacities—as distinct from the use made of these capacities—be regarded as giving equal opportunity? Finally, if we could find a way of testing this utilization of personal capacity, or effort, what of capacity for effort itself? Is inherited lethargy a lesser handicap than inherited physical weakness?[67]

Thus, a truly equal opportunity based on genuinely equal capacity would seem to require, among other things, the elimination of inherited financial advantages, standardized patterns of socialization (for example, elimination of the family), equal education, and ultimately even genetic engineering. But standardized capacities in a standardized environment should produce fairly standardized people after the competitive race ceases. As Hirsch says: "once the concept of economic opportunity is taken seriously, it expands without natural barrier toward equality of outcome."[68] Maintaining such a system of equal competition would require intrusive centralized controls making the positive state look timid indeed. Plainly such measures, though motivated by the desire to make liberal ideals meaningful, are hardly consonant with their usual formulation. Viewed in this light, reverse racial preferment appears to be a rather moderate approach—actually, a compromise between unsatisfactory extremes.

From a liberal perspective at least, the problems generated by reverse discrimination admit of no pleasing resolution. This is not to deny that some policies are preferable to others,[69] only that any available course of action[70] will entail severe costs. This is also not to preclude the possibility that an authoritative resolution of the problem will eventually emerge. For instance, an emergent era of economic stagnation may well doom minority preferences in the long run. So far, however, the Supreme Court and the federal judiciary still seem deter-

mined to compel and to uphold quota-like measures. But if
cases like *Fullilove* v. *Klutznick*[71] are any indication, the basis
for continuing to do so may shift. What could emerge is a movement away from the nurturing purposes which have usually
dominated this area to a quite different approach: legitimizing
reverse racial preferment only as a concession to minority
political power.[72] That is, the question whether to uphold
or deny minority preferences may increasingly come to depend
upon the outcome of a thoroughly egoistic group struggle.[73]
The ability of such measures to survive in a climate of this sort
obviously is uncertain. Whatever the ultimate result, the nurturing aspect of liberal positive freedom is likely to disappear,
suggesting that the continued advance of liberal individualism
eventually may destroy liberal positive freedom's constructive
aspects.[74]

Notes

1. R. Nisbet, The Quest for Community 4 (Oxford paperback ed.
1969). Nisbet is hardly an unqualified admirer of the developments he
describes.

2. *Id.*

3. A. MacIntyre, Against the Self-Images of the Age 282-83 (Notre
Dame paperback ed. 1978).

4. Dworkin, *Three Concepts of Liberalism*, New Republic, April 14,
1979, at 41, 48.

5. What would seem to be required for the choices of a determinate
self to be completely open is the absence of any relation between choices
and antecedent mental states. A certain determinate state, that is, could
not in any way shape, limit, or influence the subsequent choice. The plausibility of such a view is obviously not very great, and acceptance of it
might compel the belief that human behavior is perfectly random, a possibility discussed below.

6. F. H. Bradley, Ethical Studies 56 (2d Oxford paperback ed. 1962).

7. Suggestive here is Hegel, Phenomenolgy of Mind 599-614, especially 604-5 (Harper Torchbook ed., J. B. Baillie tr.) *See also* F. Bergmann,
On Being Free 52 (paperback ed. 1977).

8. *See, e.g.*, M. Oakeshott, Experience and Its Modes 29-33 (1933).

9. *See, e.g.*, F. Capra, The Turning Point: Science, Society and the
Rising Culture ch. 3 (1982).

10. Hegel's Philosophy of Right §5 (Remark) (T. M. Knox tr.).

11. F. H. Bradley, *supra* note 5, at 11. *See also* F. Bergmann, *supra* note 6, at 17-19.

12. F. Bergmann, *supra* note 6, at 42.

13. *Id.* at 41.

14. The discussion that follows is derived from D. Yankelovich, New Rules 49-59 (1981). The people described are real, but pseudonyms are used.

15. These statuses also present a fusion of status position and the authoritarian version of positive freedom.

16. *See, e.g.*, the text accompanying note 46 in chapter 3.

17. *E.g.*, D. Bell, The Cultural Contradictions of Capitalism 275 (1976); I. Kristol, Two Cheers for Capitalism 4 (1978).

18. *E.g.*, D. Bell, *supra* note 17, at 55-61.

19. I. Kristol, *supra* note 17, at 139. *See also id.* 84-89.

20. *See* D. Riesman, The Lonely Crowd 13-17, 24-25, 40-44, 57-60, 66-70, 87-96, 109-25, 159-60 (abridged paperback ed. 1961).

21. R. Nisbet, *supra* note 1, at 237.

22. F. Hirsch, Social Limits to Growth, 142-43 (1976) (emphasis in original). When Hirsch states that the "obligations of custom and status" were abandoned in the nineteenth century, presumably he is not speaking in absolute terms and instead is comparing that century to the vastly more status-laden and stratified medieval order. For the "fortunate legacy" quotation, *see id.* at 143.

23. I. Kristol, *supra* note 17, at 166.

24. That is, when blacks were not being sold and shipped to other localities and when Indian tribes were not being destroyed and/or relocated.

25. Frequently, the reverse is true of contemporary liberals urging positive government and tending to be relatively permissive on life-style issues. However, the disenchantment with affirmative government characterizing the late 1970s and early 1980s, as well as a growing "life-style liberalism" on the part of some conservatives, have blurred these lines a bit.

26. *See, e.g.*, F. Meyer (ed.), What Is Conservatism? (1964), which explicitly presents the problem and attempts (probably unsuccessfully) to resolve it. On the diversity of conservative viewpoints, *see, e.g.*, G. Nash, The Conservative Intellectual Tradition in America Since 1945 (1976).

27. *E.g.*, Burnham, *Notes on Morality, Authority, Power*, 22 Nat'l Rev. 1283, 1284-85 (Dec. 1, 1970). This idea is usually associated with the English historian Christopher Dawson.

28. The quotations that follow are from V. Ferkiss, The Future of Technological Civilization 64, 66 (1974).

29. This is not to say that conservatives in power are unwilling to employ government when this is advantageous to business interests. As

Theodore Lowi has suggested, the main difference between contemporary liberals and conservatives may lie not in their attitudes toward the state but in the groups they represent. T. Lowi, The End of Liberalism 46-49, 51 (2d ed. 1979).

30. On this, *see generally* R. Nisbet, *supra* note 1.

31. The discussion that follows focuses mainly, though not solely, on the large corporation.

32. Although little explicit attention will be devoted to this matter, the discussion that follows goes some way toward explaining the rise of positive government as well.

33. For a compendium of explanations for the rise of the corporation, *see* A. S. Miller, The Modern Corporate State 57-85 (1976).

34. *Cf.* W. Friedmann, Law in a Changing Society 293 (2d Penguin ed. 1972) (discussing the inevitable tendency toward concentration in unregulated laissez-faire).

35. *E.g.*, S. Wolin, Politics and Vision 364, 377-80 (1960).

36. *See, e.g.*, J. K. Galbraith, The New Industrial State ch. 2 (2d rev. ed. 1971).

37. *See, e.g.*, V. Ferkiss, *supra* note 28, at 1-60. *See also* W. Leiss, The Domination of Nature (1972). This is discussed in more detail in chapter 6.

38. *See, e.g.*, S. Wolin, *supra* note 35, at 366-68, 393-403, 407-10.

39. *See generally* Hegel's Philosophy of Right § §142-246 (T. M. Knox tr.). In the discussion following, citation will be made only to direct quotations.

40. *See, e.g.*, C. Taylor, Hegel 427, 449-61 (paperback ed. 1975).

41. *See, e.g.*, *id.* at 426-27.

42. Philosophy of Right, *supra* note 39, §183.

43. *Id.* § §201-02.

44. *Id.* §185.

45. *See id.* § §238, 243-45.

46. *Id.* §255.

47. *Id.* § 252.

48. *Id.* §253.

49. These two questions, however, are not completely separable.

50. R. Nisbet, *supra* note 1, at 49.

51. *See* S. Wolin, *supra* note 35, at 366-68, 393-403, 407-10.

52. *Id* at 366.

53. D. Bell, The Coming of Post-Industrial Society 288 (paperback ed. 1973).

54. *Id.* at 289.

55. R. Nisbet, *supra* note 1, at 71-72.

56. *See* the discussion in the last section of chapter 3.

57. The term *self-dissociation* refers to the discussion of liberal individualism in extremis contained in the opening section of this chapter.

58. Here, the reference is to those approximations of liberal positive freedom discussed in the first section of this chapter and not to liberal individualism in its randomized or self-destructive forms.

59. *See, e.g.*, the quotation accompanying note 193 in chapter 3.

60. As noted in chapter 3, it seems that the drive for employee rights and the use of therapeutic controls have gone more or less hand in hand.

61. Of course, such claims are often quite valid on their own terms and also meaningful to the individual as denials of negative liberty.

62. For some elaboration of the points made below and some appropriate citations, *see* chapter 4. *See also* Phillips, *Neutrality and Purposiveness in the Application of Strict Scrutiny to Racial Classifications* (to be published in the TEMPLE LAW QUARTERLY).

63. This was not expressly made an aspect of liberal individualism when it was defined above, but it plainly is a thoroughly liberal idea, one typifying liberalism in its classical and its twentieth-century forms.

64. This comparison cannot be pushed too far. There are obvious differences between, say, the legislation challenged in *Lochner* v. *New York* (discussed in chapter 3) and the *Bakke* quota, but both do involve restrictions on individuals or groups possessing competitive advantages, this being done to protect weaker parties.

65. This use of the word *benign* generally focuses on the motives of decision makers and not on the purposes discrimination might advance or its tangible distributional effects. But a white person denied an opportunity because of a racial quota is not likely to derive much comfort from the assertion that the discrimination from which she or he suffered was not motivated by racial hostility or by a perception that whites are not the moral equals of blacks.

66. Hegel's Logic § 81 (Oxford ed., Wm. Wallace tr. 1975).

67. F. Hirsch, *supra* note 22, at 162-63 n.2.

68. *Id.*

69. Assuming that this is of any concern at all, I tend to favor existing schemes of reverse racial preferment.

70. Opponents of reverse discrimination sensitive to the problems discussed here occasionally urge racially neutral compensatory programs of all sorts, such as remedial training, special education in basic skills, and even enterprise zones. Generally, though, the measures suggested fail to equal the massiveness of the problem. A societal commitment truly adequate to this problem is extremely unlikely.

71. 448 U.S. 448 (1980). *See* the discussion of this case in chapter 4.

72. *See id.* at 541-42 (Stevens, J., dissenting) (PWEA quota motivated by minority legislators' demand for "piece of the action").

73. Perhaps Chief Justice Burger's *Fullilove* opinion, with its extreme deference to Congress, can be explained in this light. *See id.* at 490-92 (Burger, C. J.).

74. This suggestion is based on the earlier argument that liberal freedom in its extreme forms tends to destroy all internal capacities and rationally culminates in something like suicide.

CHAPTER 6

The Future

Attempts to predict the future are fraught with difficulties. The many such efforts in recent years, and the wildly divergent conclusions they often reach, amply testify to this. Still, the analysis presented here is not without its implications for the years ahead. The principal actor in that account is the ongoing advance of liberal individualism. Due to its indeterminacy, liberal freedom always requires restraints of some sort in order to be socially viable. A corollary of this proposition, it would seem, is that as liberal individualism erodes inner restraints, the need for external controls increases correspondingly. The intensity of these, moreover, should vary directly with the absence of characterological checks. Thus, if liberal ideas continue their movement into the personal sphere, the need for restrictive external checks could become paramount in coming decades. To say this is to do little more than to reinvoke hackneyed, if valid, cliches like "anarchy breeds tyranny," generalizations that do not tell us what form the future system of control will take. A multitude of fairly concrete social factors will probably be decisive in resolving this question. Before considering such practical questions, though, it will be useful to bolster the assertion that extreme individualism promotes despotic rule. The vehicles for doing so are the otherwise-divergent accounts contained in Thomas Hobbes's *Leviathan* and Book VIII of Plato's *Republic*.

Hobbes and Plato on Freedom and Statism

The Leviathan

Thomas Hobbes, Wolfgang Friedmann tells us, "is individualist, utilitarian and absolutist. . . . From his political and legal
theory emerges modern man, self-centered, individualistic,
materialistic, irreligious, in pursuit of organized power."[1] The
oppressive statism of Hobbes's *Leviathan* is a consequence of
these traits.

> This individualism is the thoroughly modern element in
> Hobbes and the respect in which he caught most clearly
> the note of the coming age. . . . The absolute power of the
> sovereign . . . was really the necessary complement of his
> individualism. Except as there is a tangible superior to
> whom men render obedience and who can, if necessary,
> enforce obedience, there are only individual human be-
> ings, each actuated by his private interests. There is no
> middle ground between humanity as a sand-heap of sepa-
> rate organisms and the state as an outside power holding
> them precariously together by the sanctions with which
> it supplements individual motives.[2]

Understanding why this is so requires some discussion of the
Leviathan. Before undertaking this task, though, it is necessary
to establish Hobbes's credentials as a liberal. This, in turn, requires some elaboration of the liberal individualist posture.

Hobbes as a Liberal

In this book, liberal individualism has been defined in a fairly
simple fashion: as concerned with maximizing the self's unfettered ability to choose. This underlies both negative freedom
and the liberal variant of positive freedom. Liberalism so defined is also bound up with a syndrome of attitudes characterizing the modern, roughly post-1600, era. As its preoccupation
with the self and its choices might suggest, liberalism regards
the individual as the fundamental unit of society and groups
as aggregations of individuals whose purposes do not transcend
those of their constituent human parts.[3] Also, both negative

freedom and liberal positive freedom are value free in the sense that they do not identify freedom with any particular determinate action. They deny the traditional sort of teleology that sees human behavior as tending toward virtuous ends. As Roberto Mangabeira Unger has concluded, "liberalism must be . . . uncompromisingly hostile to the classic idea of objective good."[4] Underlying this hostility is a sharp dualism between reason, which discovers universal truths of a merely descriptive nature, and desire.[5] The assertions of reason are valid and objective; those of desire are subjective and arbitrary.[6] The drive for liberal freedom perhaps excluded,[7] this would seem to entail a fairly complete moral relativism. But every historical movement needs some ethical impetus, and liberalism, in addition to its concern with freedom, has tended to embrace what Unger calls a "morality of desire." This morality, he says, "defines the good as the satisfaction of desire, the reaching of the goals to which our appetites and aversions incline us."[8] As the terms *appetites* and *aversions* suggest, liberalism tends to emphasize least-common-denominator values like liberty, equality, physical security, material plenty, and a range of other concerns that might broadly be termed hedonistic or utilitarian. From liberalism's egoism, hedonism, and tendency to objectify the surrounding world, finally, there emerges a manipulative, exploitive posture toward nature, a posture quite evident in the successes of modern technology.[9]

To a considerable degree, Hobbes's *Leviathan*[10] displays these various elements of the liberal syndrome.[11] Indeed, with the possible exception of Machiavelli, Hobbes is the first thoroughly modern political philosopher.[12] Although Hobbes may not be a thoroughgoing materialist,[13] he does root human sensation and thought in the action of external objects or bodies. But human knowledge as he conceives it is not concerned with their nature. Instead, he states that such knowledge is basically of two sorts: of fact (sense data) and of consequences (causal relations among the names people attach to recurring categories of sensual fact). The latter sort of knowledge he regards as science. Not regarded as valid human knowledge and not part of scientific inquiry due to the diversity of human opinion they display are value words such as justice. To Hobbes, good and evil are rooted in personal desire and aversion. There is nothing in its nature inherently so and no common rule on ethical matters outside an organized society with a recognized rule giver. It does appear, however, that ethical conclusions of a sort can be reached by looking to drives that are widely, perhaps universally, shared by people. Chief among these is the desire for peace. The passions inclining people toward peace include the fear of death and the desire for "commodious living."[14] The other customary moral virtues are good not because of their inherent qualities but because, or to the extent that, they promote peace. Another consequence of the desire for peace is "a perpetual and restless desire of power after power, that ceaseth only in death."[15] This desire is not, as the popular picture of Hobbes would have it, the result of some innate lust for power or the insatiable character of human desires. Rather, "the cause of this, is not always that a man hopes for a more intensive delight, than he has already attained to; or that he cannot be content with a moderate power: but because he cannot assure the power and means to live well, which he hath present, without the acquisition of more."[16]

Hobbes's views on liberty and equality are also thoroughly liberal. He defines liberty solely in negative terms and explicitly disavows any positive conception of freedom. In fact, this liberty is consistent with "necessity" or determinism.[17] Turning to liberty as a value, Hobbes seems to regard it as a virtual absolute in the absence of organized social life. For instance, it is a law of nature that in the presocial state every one has a right to everything, including another's body. The justification of this apparent "ought" is not clear, but like Hobbes's valuation of peace, it seems to represent widespread human tendencies springing from the natural condition of man.[18] As for equality, Hobbes asserts that all men are relatively equal both in physical strength and in qualities of mind, in the process disavowing the Aristotelian idea that some men are by nature superior to others. Hobbes, however, is obviously not an egalitarian in the sense that he values equality of condition.

A manipulative or exploitive posture toward nature does not figure prominently in the *Leviathan*, but it is suggested at various points. It follows from Hobbes's conception of man as a desiring creature and from his conception of science. To Hobbes,

"regulated" thought is controlled by desire.[19] Science is a prime
example of such thought, and it helps determine the means
through which desire can be satisfied. It establishes reliable
causal relations among names referring to sense data, which in
turn relate to external bodies. Thus, it seems to follow that
regulated thought is concerned with the control of physical
nature for the satisfaction of desire.

The Genesis of the Leviathan

The natural condition of man, according to Hobbes, is not a
product of social life; rather Hobbes's natural man is the primary, irreducible fact of his political philosophy. Given his
view of man's natural condition, Hobbes's task was to explain
why people do live in societies and to justify the political
authority that societies exhibit. His device for accomplishing
this is the well-known state of nature, which elaborates the
implications of man's natural condition. Hobbes is equivocal
on the question whether this state ever actually existed, and
it should be taken as an analytical device.[20] That is, it should
be seen as an answer to the question why political authority
of a certain sort should exist given Hobbes's radically individualistic premises.

The plight of man in the state of nature is not the product
of innate human depravity or savagery but rather is a rational
consequence of human egoism and the lack of an authoritative
power to constrain it. Individuals in this state want to live and
to live commodiously. They also want to maximize the power
to ensure satisfaction of these desires. At least in a climate of
material scarcity, these drives will be a source of conflict. Other
factors exacerbate this conflict. First, most people are relatively
equal in physical power and mental attainments. This would
seem to preclude a permanent takeover by a natural superior.
Also, physical equality leads to "equality in the hope of attain-
ing our ends."[21] Moreover, rational consideration of this fact
compels preemptive attacks on possible competitors. Second,
at this point Hobbes introduces a new psychological element:
that of pride or glory. This involves the manifested opinion of
one person for another and causes disputes arising from "signs
of contempt, or undervaluing."[22] All of this leads to Hobbes's

contention that man's natural state is a "war of every one against every one":[23] that is, a state where violence is a permanent possiblity though not always an actual fact. Hobbes's conclusion cannot be avoided by asserting that some local strongman will impose long-term order because of the equality premise. Also, his conclusion cannot be overcome by asserting natural human cooperativeness without a detailed refutation of his psychology and, quite possibly, a denial of the liberalism he represents. Finally, a policy of live and let live could prevent the war of all against all only if it were universalized, and numerous reasons have been adduced to argue that this is very unlikely. In any event, it would be irrational for any individual to act on the assumption that others will show self-restraint.

The consequence of this state of war is that the various benefits of civilization are rendered extremely precarious: life in the state of nature is "solitary, poor, nasty, brutish, and short."[24] But man's desire for peace, coupled with his reason, provide a solution to the dilemma. The outlines of such a solution are provided by Hobbes's laws of nature. These are not moral commands existing apart from natural human propensities but instead are founded on human desire and endeavor. While always binding in some abstract sense, they are not practically obligatory without the presence of some external power sufficient to secure their enforcement. They can be summed up in a negative formulation of the Golden Rule: "Do not that to another, which thou wouldest not have done to thyself."[25] The most important laws of nature are the following: (1) to endeavor peace whenever possible but to use all the advantages of war when peace is not possible; (2) to lay down the right to all things and to be content with as much liberty against others as one would allow other men against oneself; (3) to perform all covenants made (which Hobbes calls justice). These laws provide the basis for Hobbes's commonwealth. Since peace is its end and since the laws of nature are impotent without some external force to back them up, the commonwealth must be based on a covenant by which individuals confer their collective power to a sovereign able to govern them with near impunity. The creation of a commonwealth can be by "acquisition" (a "covenant" resulting from conquest) or by "institution" (an actual agreement). In either case, the powers of the sovereign are the same.

The powers of the Hobbesian sovereign are extensive. Hobbes's picture of man's natural propensities and his picture of life in the state of nature virtually compel this. In particular, Hobbes sees man as lacking any natural sense of community, social solidarity, or duty. To him, "a social body has no existence except through its constituted authorities."[26] This means that social checks like status relationships do not bind man in his natural state and, one assumes, are not very significant within the social compact either. As a result, external sovereign command must take on virtually the whole burden of ordering. In addition, since the sovereign shares the self-interested traits of his subjects, it is practically useless to expect him to limit his power. If the subjects attempt to retain certain rights against the sovereign, they are compelled either to relinquish them when challenged or else face the war they entered the covenant to escape. And even winning the new war poses the same problems anew: either a new ruler will emerge, or the winners will soon be fighting among themselves, thus necessitating a new compact. Perhaps these considerations explain Hobbes's statement that "whosoever thinking sovereign power too great, will seek to make it less, must subject himself to the power, that can limit it; that is to say, to a greater."[27]

Hobbes nevertheless remains a thoroughgoing liberal. The *Leviathan* is merely necessary. It is based on individual self-interest, not "higher" claims like divine right or the various rationales for twentieth-century totalitarianism. For instance, he recognizes the negative liberty of the subject in the silence of the laws. Also, he admits that the exercise of sovereign power may be accompanied by abuses and justifies these only as less bad than the alternatives. In fact, if the sovereign fails to maintain order, he forfeits any practical, and perhaps moral, claim to obedience.

Book VIII of the Republic

Evidently the *Leviathan* supports my general argument that liberal individualism requires restraints if it is to be viable. It also bolsters the claim that as liberal freedom assumes extreme forms, compensatory controls must become more oppressive. Specifically, since to Hobbes internal checks on the pursuit of self-interest are absent by hypothesis, the needed restrictions

on this must be external to the individual and must be quite
severe. But while Hobbes's picture of life in the state of nature
looks like a concretization of the randomization argument,[28]
he clearly does not contemplate the more pronounced sorts of
self-liberation. Hobbes sees freedom in negative terms only; this
freedom is consistent with determinism; and his natural man is
governed by fairly basic drives from which he apparently cannot
free himself. This is not true, however, of the account presented
in Book VIII (and the beginning of Book IX) of Plato's *Republic*.
Self-liberation assumes extreme forms there, and this leads to
tyranny not through rational calculation but by setting loose
depraved tendencies lurking within all men. Because it is not
based on rational self-interest, this tyranny may be more vicious
and arbitrary than that envisioned by Hobbes.

In Books VIII and IX of the *Republic*,[29] Plato sets out a four-
stage process of decline beginning with the perfection of his
ideal city and then proceeding downward through timocracy
(the rule of the strong and warlike), oligarchy (the rule of the
wealthy), and democracy (the rule of the many), to tyranny
(the arbitrary rule of the most vicious and depraved). In this
process, the correspondence between personal character and a
particular form of government is continually stressed, each
type of state displaying a characteristic individual type. We pick
up the story after the transition from oligarchy to democracy,
in which, Plato says, all share in citizenship, and public offices
are usually assigned by lot.

Plato's democratic state is liberal individualism in extremis,
or perhaps in caricature. This is evident in democratic man, who
"establishes and maintains all his pleasures on a footing of equality . . . and so lives turning over the guardhouse of his soul to
each as it happens along until it is sated, as if it had drawn the
lot for that office, and then in turn to another, disdaining none
but fostering them all equally."[30] Here, the tendency toward
liberal randomization is quite apparent:

> And does he not, said I, also live out his life in this fashion,
> day by day, indulging the appetite of the day, now wine-
> bibbing and abandoning himself to the lascivious pleasing
> of the flute and again drinking only water and dieting, and
> at one time exercising his body, and sometimes idling and

neglecting all things, and at another time seeming to occupy himself with philosophy. And frequently he goes in for politics and bounces up and says and does whatever enters his head. And if military men excite his emulation, thither he rushes, and if moneyed men, to that he turns, and there is no order or compulsion in his existence, but he calls this life of his the life of pleasure and freedom and happiness and cleaves to it to the end.[31]

The basic principle of the democratic polity is liberty. This manifests itself in a variety of ways, among them the maximization of unfettered personal choice, near-complete freedom of speech, a great diversity of human character types, and an atmosphere in which political leadership is obtained by those professing the greatest love for the people. Moreover, Plato contends that this liberty expresses itself in a drive to remove all status differentiations. The democratic state, we are told, is notable for "assigning a kind of equality indiscriminately to equals and unequals alike."[32] This is manifested in the decline of parental authority, the equality of aliens and citizens, the reluctance to restrain criminals, the loss of authority by teachers, the imitation of the young by the old (and vice-versa), the equality of slaves and citizens, the equality of men and women, and, metaphorically, even the equality of man and beast. This generalized decline in traditional forms of social authority has its counterpart in the political sphere, expressing itself in hostility to public authority, especially when it attempts to infringe upon democratic liberties.

Plato's contempt for liberal ideas derives from his views of the good life and the good society. But here he argues that such attitudes, when carried to an extreme, necessarily lead to tyranny, the arbitrary and repressive rule of the worst man. This transition is a sort of dialectical reversal: "any excess is wont to bring about a corresponding reaction to the opposite in the seasons, in plants, in animal bodies, and most especially in political societies."[33] The general theme underlying this transition is the tendency for the spirit of liberty to move from the external to the internal sphere. This effects man's liberation from all personal restraints, including those internal checks that prevent the exploitation of others.

Plato begins his discussion of the transition by asserting that there exist within all men "a terrible, fierce, and lawless brood of desires,"[34] most of which are suppressed and which find expression mainly in dreams. When the son of the democratic man comes under the influence of "seducers" who inflame such desires within him, the influence of his democratic parents (who compromised with such drives) is not sufficient to prevent their takeover. As a result, the son comes to live a life of complete licentiousness. But this requires money, and after borrowing on his estate becomes impossible, the son may appropriate the wealth of his parents or even kill them. Then he might turn to other crimes, including murder, to support his lawless drives. Such drives are present to the highest degree in the tyrant himself, but they are also widely disseminated throughout society before the transition from democracy to tyranny. This general situation provides a backdrop for Plato's account of the specific path by which the tyrant comes to rule.

According to Plato, the democratic state comes to possess three distinct classes. First, there are the politically active "drones" who dominate public life. The drones first arose during the decline of oligarchy and basically were a dispossessed pauper class. They came in two varieties: the "stingless," consumeristic parasites who eventually degenerated into beggars, and those "armed with stings," who became criminals. Presumably the latter are our main concern here. Second, there are certain "capitalist" semioligarchs who are more or less productive, or at least amass wealth. Third are the people generally, who work at a wide range of normal occupations. The drone politicians attempt to expropriate the wealth of the capitalists; the capitalists resist; and, after propagandistic efforts, the people are induced to appoint one man as their protector against the capitalists. It seems, however, that the politically active drones possess the tyrannical nature to a considerable degree and that the protector is "that one of them who has the greatest and mightiest tyrant in his own soul."[35] Although the protector may at first appear benign, he soon sets out on a tyrannical course. First to be eliminated are his capitalist foes. If, as is likely, there is an assassination attempt on the protector, he will ask the people for a corps of bodyguards, and these in time will come to comprise drones and ex-slaves for hire. In order to keep the populace unified and to consolidate his domestic power, the protector may be compelled to engage in foreign wars. If the few remaining virtuous citizens oppose this course of events, they will be eliminated. Finally, the protector will begin to appropriate the wealth of the populace at large, and if the people resist him, they will be suppressed, thus bringing into existence a full-fledged tyranny.

The Dilemmas of Industrial Society and the Coming Need for Control

This account of Plato and Hobbes is only suggestive. Enlisting great names to bolster an argument can carry one only so far. Also, neither thinker's argument is impregnable. Plato's account, in particular, is loose and almost allegorical. For Hobbes, whose rigorously logical pursuit of his premises' implications is often praised, the premises themselves are vulnerable. This is particularly true of his view of human psychology and his asocial natural man.[36] A rather different view of man's natural condition helped lead another social contract theorist, John Locke, to postulate a less repressive social order than the Hobbesian *Leviathan*.[37] Also, widespread material abundance could negate some, but not all, of the conflicts Hobbes associates with the state of nature.

Nevertheless it would require a quite facile optimism to deny the relevance of Hobbes's and Plato's accounts. In order to bolster the argument that accelerating liberal individualism will provoke increased controls, attention will now turn to certain relatively tangible problems increasingly besetting industrialized nations like the United States. Many of these are related to, or provoked by, the reigning liberal orientation, and they are likely to make the need for control an increasing preoccupation of coming decades. The reasoning supporting this conclusion is essentially Hobbesian. Much of the argument made here, though heard with decreasing frequency in the Reaganite 1980s, is quite familiar. It differs from standard accounts of this sort only in adding the worst fears of the Right to those of the Left. It depends to some degree on energy, raw materials, environmental, and foreign policy predictions that are quite controversial. In-

deed, it is possible to find equally credentialed experts on either
side of almost every assertion made here. Thus, I make no attempt to prove these assertions, and the discussion of them will
be fairly brief. The problems discussed should be viewed as a set
of more or less probable constraints combining with liberal
individualist drives to make intensified controls fairly probable
in the future. Although these constraints interact, they need not
all be effective in order for severe social restrictions to be necessary.

By now it has become a commonplace that one of the main
reasons for the relative absence of distributional struggles in
America's Golden Age,[38] the 1945-1970 period, was the rapid
growth of its economy.[39] This rising tide lifted all boats, affording most individuals better material living standards in absolute
terms and diluting redistributionist impulses. This material pre-
condition for stability, however, may be difficult to maintain
in coming decades.[40] Diminished reserves of energy and raw
materials may make economic growth far more difficult than
previously. Even if, as some economists contend, the supply of
such commodities is determined by price, the higher prices
needed to maintain supply would themselves place constraints
on growth. Environmental concerns are now less discussed than
in the 1970s, but changes in fashion do not disprove the environ-
mentalist case. The ability of the environment to absorb and
sustain industrial activity may place some ultimate limit on eco-
monic growth.[41] In the short run, efforts to reduce adverse environmental impacts undeniably increase costs of manufacture
and absorb resources that otherwise could be used for consumption items. Difficulties of this sort have already had a negative
impact on the American economy, and it is not difficult to
project their intensification in years ahead.

The extent to which such material problems will inhibit economic growth is not clear, but it is evident that they will pose
a significant constraint on the ability to satisfy material wants.
This reflects a more general dilemma: that there is some inherent limit on the planet's ability to support exponential growth.[42]
Underlying the problems referred to is modern technology and
the manipulative, exploitive attitude it expresses,[43] a posture
characterizing modern liberalism from its beginnings. Reflecting

on this fact, some observers have asserted that these emergent problems reflect an inevitable self-contradiction contained within liberal premises, self-aggrandizement through exploitation of the material world eventually coming up against the finitude of that world.[44] It is often asserted that the technology creating these difficulties will also provide their cure, but faith in the technological fix is only that—an act of faith.

If such surmises are at all accurate, a stagnating collective per-capita product is likely to cause increased social struggle.[45] Hobbes's war of all against all was rooted in material scarcity to a considerable extent. The pervasiveness and intensity of this conflict, as well as the forms it will take, are open to conjecture, but the overall tendency is difficult to escape. In such a context, the need for control is obvious. "Who says scarcity," Arthur Selwyn Miller contends, " says authoritarianism."[46] Control could result from something like Hobbesian rational calculation, in which case aggressive governmental action would be collectively demanded to end disorder and to impose some minimally acceptable distribution of goods and services, or it could arise through a process not unlike that producing Plato's "protector," as populist demagogues take the side of "the people" against capitalist "oligarchs."

So far, the discussion has proceeded without reference to the international arena, a context in which Hobbes's generalizations about the state of nature assume their greatest relevance. In all likelihood, international conflicts and threats will exacerbate statist tendencies. The fate of the domestic economy is now inextricably linked with events occurring outside America's borders.[47] Such events could easily add to the United States's economic difficulties, thus intensifying the pressures toward control. The effect of international developments on access to energy and raw materials is well known. Military efforts to protect these sources will probably require greater defense spending, which will divert resources from other sectors. Also, the tremendous population increases and overall economic problems faced by less developed nations[48] have created pressures for some sort of international wealth redistribution, and these pressures will probably increase in the future. American acquiescence to these pressures should increase domestic economic problems.

If, as is more likely, redistributionist claims are resisted, increased
defense efforts may be required to make such resistance effective
or to protect American economic interests abroad. This, again,
could only exacerbate internal economic difficulties, as resources otherwise devoted to consumption are directed toward
nonconsumable military hardware instead. Worse yet, the
tactics employed by less developed nations attempting to force
redistribution, could provoke additional controls in another,
quite different, fashion. Robert Heilbroner, for instance, has
discussed the possibility of terrorist-based nuclear intimidation
directed against American cities using so-called suitcase bombs.[49]
A wide range of lesser terrorist actions is quite possible also. In
all likelihood, the measures employed to protect against such
tactics would have to be quite intrusive and repressive. As this
suggests, not all the external pressures tending toward increased domestic control are of a directly economic nature.
Foremost among these noneconomic threats is the ever-continuing
struggle with the U.S.S.R. and its satellites. Even if this preceived
threat is not genuine,[50] the willingness of policy makers to act as
if it is will drain resources otherwise deployable for different uses.
This is especially likely if Russian armaments and influence
continue to grow as they have over the past twenty years. Tak-
en together, these international developments could convert the
United States into a siege state with increased militarization,
extensive political controls, and a diminished consumer output.
Even this, though, would merely bring America into line with
what seems to be a worldwide trend toward militarily based
statist forms of rule, whether of the Left or the Right. Finally, if
conservative and neoconservative fears of eventual subordination
to Russian designs become the reality, domestic controls should
be quite restrictive indeed.

Possibly, however, one could recognize most of these constraints yet reject their seeming statist implications. Why, it
might be urged, cannot Americans summon the social and political will to confront such challenges and overcome them without the need for draconian controls? As an abstract proposition,
this argument may possess considerable weight, but there are
many reasons to doubt that such a response will be forthcoming.
Certain inveterate American mental habits make it unlikely. Miller, for instance, has effectively argued that "Micawberism" (the

belief that "something will turn up"), "reductionism" (exces-
sive specialization and the inability to take a holistic view), and
"incrementalism" (reactive, piecemeal policy making) inhibit
both the ability to see emerging threats for what they are and
the capacity for timely and coherent response to them.[51] What
is more, the liberal individualist advance itself makes such a response unlikely. In fact, it is difficult to imagine a syndrome of
values less suited to a time of social challenge. Lester Thurow
has recently argued that although solutions to America's eco-
monic woes are not lacking, these solutions inevitably will require that strategically situated groups make sacrifices.[52] Promoting the willingness to do so is difficult in a climate where
all have become accustomed to ever-increasing abundance and
where most, influenced by corporate stimuli to consume, demand more of the same in the future. More fundamentally, a
system of ideas stressing self-interest can provide no convincing
reasons for individuals and groups to subordinate their concerns
to the public good. What it dictates instead is that others bear
the necessary burdens.[53] Such reasoning might encourage a
majority to impose the needed sacrifices on various minorities,[54]
but in a widely representative political system this will not be
easy. Nor is this difficulty likely to be overcome by strong leadership, since its existence implies a willingness to be led, and
there is little reason to think that contemporary Americans
possess any such disposition.[55] Ultimately, as with the Hobbesian social compact, there may be little choice but to submit to
some form of stringent coercion. The point made here, though,
is that this eventuality could conceivably be precluded by the
acceptance of lesser restraints now, and that the prevalence of
individualistic attitudes makes this quite improbable.

The continuing advance of liberal ideas of freedom could
make effective societal response even less likely. It is hard to see
how extreme cases of individual self-dissociation could give rise
to any kind of coherent behavior at all, and it is not obvious
how their qualified real-life exemplars, people like Mark and
Abby Williams, would be able to summon any sustained commitment to purposes transcending the self. Such types are far
more likely to abandon already-tenuous ties to future generations,[56] ties that are utterly irrational from a thoroughly individualistic perspective. When directly confronted by the threats

already described, they may well choose to maximize gratifica-
tions while there still is time, "finish[ing] . . . life in an orgy of
self-indulgence that knows no bounds."[57] Also possible[58] is "a
state of utter existential despair, or relapse into a suicidal solip-
sism"[59] in which the destruction of civilization might seem entirely fitting.[60] Again, though, such tendencies most likely will
only delay the coming era of control and will help ensure that it
will assume quite repressive forms when it does arrive.

All of these considerations suggest the desirability of different
moral conceptions; what is doubtful is their emergence in the
near future. Predictions that liberal individualism's contradictions will generate new values and new social forms abound.[61]
Although the details inevitably vary and any composite picture
does an injustice to individual writers, something like the following scenario often emerges: the future should and will be
dominated by relatively small, decentralized participatory communities populated by people with a spiritualized, holistic view
of humanity and nature and possessed of a humanized technology in harmony with true human needs and the requirements of
ecological balance. Whatever its desirability,[62] though, the likelihood of such a consummation remains in considerable doubt.
One of the reasons is that it ignores certain fairly permanent
features of human nature. As Miller puts it:

> Others perceive a second Protestant Reformation, one in
> which an ethic of conservation will replace the age-old
> ethic of domination of nature. That, however, surely is a
> dream; it is based upon a faith that human nature not
> only can change but is changing. We can hope, as hope
> we should, that such a transformation will occur. And
> we can work, as work we should, toward its fulfillment.
> But it would be folly to think that it will come without
> effort—or, indeed, will come at all. Man is a predator,
> not only against nature itself, but against himself.[63]

Miller also contends that "[i]f change comes, it must be with
utmost rapidity."[64] There is virtually no reason to expect this
to occur. A thorough shift in orientation not unlike that accom-

panying the demise of feudalism could require centuries. Moreover, the argument that the rapid pace of technological change
somehow provokes rapid changes in values ignores the fact that
technological change occurs within a certain form of consciousness and thus provides no analogy to shifts in consciousness itself.[65] Further, there is no guarantee that some new respirituali-
zation, even if it occurs swiftly, will take benign forms. Irrationalist, tribalist, nativist, nationalist, racist, even fascist possibilities cannot be excluded. The famed 1960s counterculture, for
instance, was not free from irrationalist tendencies, although
in the end its liberal propensities won out. The collapse of the
counterculture merely reinforces the general point already made:
that a sweeping change in values is highly unlikely in the short
run. Certainly our dwindling contingent of radicals is incapable
of forging a new and better order, if for no other reason than
that they are imbued with liberal ideas[66] and thus are insuffi-
ciently radical.

For the foreseeable future, then we seem to be left with the
possibilities offered by the prevailing liberal individualist paradigm. This is not to deny the existence of various illiberal, anti-
individualistic tendencies in contemporary society. Such tendencies are indisputably there, and they have figured prominently in this book, particularly in its discussion of the organizational milieu. The manifest inability of liberal individualism
to satisfy such drives makes it likely that they will intensify in
the future. What is very improbable, though, is that they will
coalesce into a coherent force capable of effecting radical social change. In fact, it is likely that such drives will reinforce
the overriding tendency toward statist control. For example,
extreme nationalism arguably has served as a surrogate for
drives of an essentially communitarian, or even religious, nature, and may once more occupy this role in the future. Worship
of the state and the presidency expresses similar impulses and
could once again assume some of its former potency. (The once-
vital phenomenon of Kennedyism is instructive here.) While the
Moral Majority seems more like a disaffected traditionalist
minority than the threat perceived by some liberals, the forces
it represents are real enough and will not disappear for the
foreseeable future. But although factors of this sort may help

cement political authority and provide some willingness to
sacrifice for larger ends,[67] it is still individualist drives that are
likely to predominate. Illiberal eruptions no doubt will continue
to fill the social stage but only against the backdrop of a pervasive liberalism. They will not deflect, and probably will assist,
the overall tendency for liberal individualism to generate statism.

Possible Forms of Control

The discussion so far has proceeded as if the continued advance of liberal individualism will generate an out-and-out
statism in which the formal political machinery will assume the
principal controlling role. Actually, though, the argument is
theoretically consistent with various systems of ordering. But
any future control structure will have to emerge from the current social and political setting, and this obviously limits the
range of available alternatives. It is unlikely, for instance, that
traditional status relationships will assume anything like their
former role in American society.[68] Because of the comparative
absence of strongly internalized personal controls today, it is
likely that external restraints will predominate in the future.[69]
Chief among these is the political state—the various arms and
organs of formal government. As Miller has demonstrated, there
is abundant historical precedent for the coercive use of governmental power in times of emergency.[70]

The exact forms that sovereign power will take in the future
are somewhat conjectural; these will depend mainly on the particular threats actually confronted. Almost certainly, the role
of the federal government will expand, both absolutely and relative to the states, because almost all of these challenges will require a consistent, coordinated national response. Within the
federal government, it is likely that the executive—the presidency and the agencies—will come to predominate over Congress
and the courts.[71] This will reflect the need for coherent and
unified policies directed at problems whose resolution may exceed the capacity of bodies representing a wide array of interests or devoted to the protection of discrete minorities. Almost
certainly the national government will be forced toward a greater role in economic planning.[72] Extensive regulation of wages
and prices is another likely possiblity if the effort to satisfy

competing groups in a time of relative scarcity leads to extreme inflation.[73] If energy and raw materials shortages become extreme and political pressures make higher prices unpopular, widespread rationing may be undertaken. Government assistance to vital industries, including loans to failing firms, could become even more prevalent than today.[74] Such assistance may include greater controls on labor and may be assisted by the nationalization of some industries. If scarcity causes mass unemployment, this could be attacked by vast government work projects. Turning away from economic matters, greater intrusiveness of law enforcement agencies is possible if domestic discord becomes too intense, terrorist activities mount, or foreign threats loom too near. Whether the various life-style freedoms, such as the use of various drugs or sexual permissiveness generally, will be seriously restricted is less clear. In all likelihood, these will be permitted so long as the interests of the state are not directly threatened.[75] They are, after all, manifestations of the prevailing liberal individualist ethos.[76] They may also help limit restiveness in a time of discontent by siphoning off energies otherwise deployed in asocial directions.[77] Finally, unless foreign or domestic threats become intolerable, freedom of speech will probably be preserved, if for no other reason than its centrality to the interests of large media organizations.

Although the power of the formal governmental organs will almost certainly increase in response to emergent crises, this is hardly the whole story. This power very likely will be exercised with considerable deference to large private groups. In fact, such groups should expand their already significant role in the process of social ordering.[78] William Scott and David Hart argue that, since "[s]uccessful change depends upon the durability of some essential institution within the society," "[t]he fate of a society during a revolutionary period is most often guided by its most enduring institution."[79] In contemporary America, they conclude, this institution is the modern organization, "if for no other reason than that it has the inertia of material success going for it."[80] Given the linkage between large-scale organization and the effective deployment of technology,[81] this inertial endurance is likely to continue. Only with difficulty can one envision a short-run cataclysm sufficient

to destroy giant institutional structures like IBM or Gulf Oil,
and even a revolutionary regime should want to utilize their
abilities.

Thus, it seems that in the future there will be two significant
sources of order: the formal government and the large institutionalized group. Because governmental policy will be influenced by the needs of such groups, there will be substantial
interlocks between the public and the private spheres. As a result, the future is likely to be marked by strong tendencies
toward the corporate state paradigm. That is, society increasingly will be susceptible to characterization as an organized
totality in which the distinction between the public and the
private is blurred. In effect, the Hegelian definition of the state
as a sort of organism embracing the formal political machinery
and major social groups[82] will more and more become an accomplished fact. Within this social whole, corporations are
likely to have pride of place.[83] As Heilbroner has described his
most likely near-term future, for instance:

> . . . certainly the purpose behind the imposition of state
> regulation and control is to maintain that inertial core of
> institutions and privileges central to a business civilization.
> The prerogatives of many enterprises may have to be cur-
> tailed under a system of national planning, but the busi-
> ness framework, with its profit-generating capability, will
> be protected as long as it is possible to do so. I would sug-
> gest that the emerging economic structure of the near-
> term future will therefore be characterized by large, bu-
> reaucratic corporations, organized into a viable whole by
> a planning agency that attempts to reconcile the drive for
> business profits with the evident need to curtail activity
> in some areas and to encourage it in others. As part of this
> coordination of private and public activity, the planning
> agency will also seek to avoid disasters, either at the
> macro or micro level, that threaten the stability of the
> business system as a whole. Thus . . . the drift into plan-
> ning, as with previous enlargements of government pres-
> ence, represents an effort to adapt the system of private
> property and market privilege to new dangers and chal-
> lenges that might otherwise disrupt it fatally.[84]

To some extent, these developments may be consistent with an apparent reassertion of classical liberal fundamentals. That is, the formal organs of government may be quite activist where corporate interests are at stake yet quite unintrusive in areas where corporations assume significant ordering roles. This tendency, like the corporate state hypothesis, has obvious counterparts in the present and recent past. This conjunction of laissez-faire doctrine with group power has sometimes typified American constitutional law, and despite the recent talk about the Burger Court's judicial restraint, it was quite active in this respect throughout the 1970s. Commercial advertising, for instance, now receives a qualified form of First Amendment protection.[85] Also, corporate political speech unrelated to the business and affairs of the corporation is entitled to full First Amendment protection,[86] although the scope of this emergent group right is perhaps not completely clear. In addition, new life has been breathed into the contract clause,[87] and in one case[88] it has been employed in a blatantly pro-business fashion. These doctrines, and others, are part of what Professor Laurence Tribe has described as "the Court's growing solicitude for the interests of corporate capitalism."[89] Finally, there has also been a generalized tendency to restrict the reach of the state action doctrine.[90] Because this narrows the range of situations where constitutional guarantees will be applied, it could be of some assistance to large groups in the control of their employees.

Status and Freedom in the Future Corporatist Order

In the coming era of control, the principal ordering function performed by the large group will be to direct individuals whose lives may increasingly come to lack any other focus. As a result, the emergent social order might be likened to an organism[91] in which large institutions are the metaphorical organs and individuals the cells of these organs. This obviously suggests that the individual's identification with his or her organizational status will increase in years ahead, but this identification may not be easily accomplished.

Clearly negative freedom will be less evident in the future. The formal institutions of government will be forced to impose more external restrictions, and it should be increasingly difficult to assume the traditional entrepreneurial role in a

corporatist order. Also, dropping out of that order usually will
not be feasible in a time of economic stagnation. Thus, the individual will be under considerable pressure to affiliate with
some group. Within the organizational milieu, external restrictions like surveillance may become more prevalent than is true
today. Both inside and outside the organization, though, the
various life-style freedoms could continue and even increase,
although these may be largely control devices in practical
effect.

As I have argued, a fusion of organizational status and positive freedom better describes organizational life than does the
opposition between status and negative liberty. At first, it
might seem that the continued advance of liberal individualism
would make this generalization less valid in the future. First,
increased self-liberation could create considerable hostility
toward intensified external controls and thus make their opposition with negative freedom a matter of quite pressing personal
concern.[92] Second, the onward march of liberal freedom might
well undermine the individual's attachment to the organization
because extreme forms of personal self-dissociation[93] could
erode even the capacity for identification with organizational
purposes.

In all likelihood, though, the tendency toward a merger of
individual identity and the demands of an organizational status
will intensify with the passage of time. Understanding why this
will probably be so requires a brief recapitulation of the forces
leading individuals toward identification with the group. Although these are practically complementary, they are also somewhat contradictory. First, there are straightforward drives for
individual advance, success, and so forth; these should increase
in years ahead as the organization becomes the only safe outlet
for such aims. But such reasons for affiliation with the organization are quite consistent with resentment of the restraints it
will impose. Second, there is a tendency toward dilution of the
capacities needed to make resistance to organizational blandish-
ments possible. The continuation of this trend might make organizational conditioning even more effective. On the other hand,
since the ability of organizational conditioning to "take" seems
to require the maintenance of some settled traits, continued

self-dissociation might undermine this conditioning. A real-life approximation of the thoroughly randomized individual, for instance, will hardly be much of an organization man. Third, communitarian drives attract individuals toward the organizational milieu. The modern organization, though, is probably not an adequate surrogate for lost forms of community, and drives of this sort may assume increasingly unstable irrationalist and illiberal forms so long as liberal freedom continues its advance. "A free society," Irving Kristol asserts, "gives birth in massive numbers to 'free spirits,' emptied of moral substance but still driven by primordial moral aspirations. Such people are capable of the most irrational actions."[94]

In such a context, the need for intensified organizational controls will be quite pressing. External checks like surveillance will probably increase. Also therapeutic controls of an indirect, cooptive nature—T groups, participatory management, sensitivity training, and so forth—no doubt will be more widely and intensively employed. Both within and without the organization, various life-style freedoms may serve to tranquilize dissent and divert antisocial impulses. Miller has likened such techniques to the soma pills employed in Aldous Huxley's *Brave New World*,[95] and Scott and Hart speak of "bliss-trip drugs" for the masses in a similar context.[96] But neither external nor therapeutic controls may suffice, and it is possible that more aggressive and intrusive technologically based forms of conditioning may be necessary. Such methods have not yet found wide application, but they seem feasible in theory. Skinnerian methods of conditioning using rewards and punishments to reinforce desired behavior are one possibility.[97] Others include electrical and chemical stimulation of the brain (ESB and neuropsychopharmacology). Scott and Hart envision these as possibilities for enhancing elite performance in a future they see as quite demanding and stressful.[98] In their view, such techniques will be employed only to enhance executive decision making, aggressiveness, and creativity, but they might well assist adaptation to the organization as well. If this is so, it is difficult to see why their use would be limited merely to enhancing performance in the abstract. Methods of this sort, if effective and widely used, provide a fascinating solution to the personal problems

extreme liberal individualism creates. The manipulative attitude
technology expresses has been part of the liberal outlook from
its beginnings. As this outlook generates more and more pronounced forms of self-dissociation, technology itself might
come to save the day by invading the human psyche to impose
a sort of harmony.

By way of conclusion, it might be appropriate to examine the
suggested organizational future in light on the constructs used
throughout this book. Negative freedom will be of less and less
significance, both because it will be subject to increasing external limitations and, though this is more conjectural, because
more effective organizational controls will make its absence an
infrequent cause for complaint. The fusion of organizational
status and something resembling liberal positive freedom typifying modern organizational life will no doubt continue, but
the significance of this is questionable. Enough has been said
already to cast doubt on the whole notion of human omnipo-
tentiality. To the extent that autonomous self-direction is an
attainable goal, it is not likely to find realization in an institutional milieu where openness and permissiveness are to some
extent tools of control. Moreover, it is difficult to square the
use of potentially potent conditioning agents like ESB and
neuropsychopharmacology with any idea of human autonomy.

The latter set of techniques, in fact, is more consistent with
the fusion of status and authoritarian positive freedom. This
would probably not involve Platonic-Aristotelian ideas of virtue, or traditional ascriptive classifications, because organizations generally would not appear to require these. But the
Hegelian fusion of status, duty, and personal capacity—the
adjustment of individual inclination to the performance of socially significant work—would seem to be an obvious aim of
future organizational conditioners. With such possibilities in
mind, Miller states that "[f]reedom is becoming Hegelian—one
is free to do what he ought to do."[99] This would no doubt provoke a demurrer from Hegel himself were he to return to life.
To him, freedom was a condition in which certain innate human potentialities found their proper institutional object and
was not a product of technological conditioning operating upon
a blank slate. On the other hand, both possibilities might ap-

pear the same to the individual, and the behavioral consequences of each might seem indistinguishable to the observer.
Hegel, one supposes, would respond that there are right and
wrong kinds of identification and that the technologically conditioned individual would thus neither feel his essence realized
nor be properly realized in reality. Obviously, the appropriate
characterization of technological conditioning raises fairly basic
philosophical problems, problems this book makes no attempt
to resolve. In all likelihood, though, the corporatist order of
the future will be less free than its predecessors, no matter what
meaning one gives the word freedom.

A Postscript

The picture of the future I have sketched may seem rather
grim, but, all things considered, it is fairly optimistic. There
was no mention, for instance, of the ever-present threat of full-
scale nuclear war. In addition, such distinctly possible occur-
rences as a total economic collapse or widespread environmental degradation did not receive serious attention. The anarchic,
destructive potential of liberal individualism in extremis was
brushed aside by assuming the minimum of will and creativity
needed for some viable social order. Our likely corporatist future is hardly a cause for rejoicing, but while there is no great
reason for optimism on this score, it conceivably possesses a
modicum of long-term survival value. This order, though, does
seem quite deficient when viewed alongside the liberal ideals
of which America is the historical exemplar. But despite their
undoubted virtues, these ideals are quite problematical in vacuo,
and it is largely due to a one-sided emphasis on this syndrome
of ideas that we now face a series of quite exacting challenges.
The 300-odd year march of the sovereign self and its detached,
egoistic, manipulative posture toward man and nature seems to
be reaching its limits. It is the predominance of this form of
consciousness that now so radically limits us.

Notes

1. W. Friedmann, Legal Theory 122 (5th ed. 1967).
2. G. Sabine, A History of Political Theory 475 (3d ed. 1961).

3. *E.g.*, R. M. Unger, Knowledge and Politics 81-83 (1975).
4. *Id.* at 77.
5. *See, e.g., id.* at 38-41.
6. *See, e.g., id.* at 42-46, 51-55, 76-81, 119-21.
7. If liberalism tends to be value free, why is it characterized by an intense preoccupation with liberty? One possible reason is that liberal freedom is a consequence of a generalized relativism, the absence of reasons for constraining the self becoming a positive demand that the self be unconstrained. In this regard, *cf.* J. Stone, Human Law and Human Justice 233-34, 237, 247 (1965) (discussing the way the legal philosophers Gustav Radbruch and Hans Kelsen saw individual rights, tolerance, democracy, and so forth as arising from a relativistic position).
8. R. M. Unger, *supra* note 3, at 47.
9. *See, e.g.*, V. Ferkiss, The Future of Technological Civilization 22-30 (1974).
10. The following account is derived from the first 21 chapters of the Leviathan. Only direct quotations will receive citations. These are to the 1962 Collier paperback edited by Michael Oakeshott.
11. On Hobbes as a liberal, *see, e.g.*, V. Ferkiss, *supra* note 9, at 23-24; R. M. Unger, *supra* note 3, at 37-40, 46-49, 53, 64-71, 76, 80, and accompanying notes.
12. *E.g.*, L. Strauss, The Political Philosophy of Hobbes xv-xvi (Phoenix paperback ed., E. Sinclair tr. 1963) (preface to the American edition).
13. *Compare, e.g.*, G. Sabine, *supra* note 2, at 457-61, with M. Oakeshott, Hobbes on Civil Association 15-26 (1975).
14. Leviathan, *supra* note 10, at 102 (ch. 13).
15. *Id.* at 80 (ch. 11).
16. *Id.* (ch. 11).
17. *Id.* at 160 (ch. 21).
18. *Cf.* M. Oakeshott, *supra* note 13, at 32-33.
19. Leviathan, *supra* note 10, at 29 (ch. 3).
20. G. Sabine, *supra* note 2, at 464.
21. Leviathan, *supra* note 10, at 98-99 (ch. 13).
22. *Id.* at 99-100 (ch. 13).
23. *Id.* at 100 (ch. 13).
24. *Id.* (ch. 13).
25. *Id.* at 122 (ch. 15).
26. G. Sabine, *supra* note 2, at 470.
27. Leviathan, *supra* note 10, at 157 (ch. 20).
28. *See* the text accompanying note 11 in chapter 5.
29. The following discussion is from sections 544c to 580a of the translation of the Republic by Paul Shorey contained in E. Hamilton &

H. Cairns (eds.), Plato: The Collected Dialogues (1961). Citations are to
direct quotations only.

    30. *Id.* 561b. *See also id.* 572c-d.

    31. *Id.* 561d-e.

    32. *Id.* 558c.

    33. *Id.* 563e-564a.

    34. *Id.* 572b.

    35. *Id.* 575c.

    36. Robert Nisbet has suggested that the natural man so dear to the
hearts of social contract theorists was in reality derived from concrete
character types typifying the seventeenth and eighteenth centuries. *See*
R. Nisbet, The Quest for Community 225-26 (Oxford paperback ed.
1969).

    37. *See* Locke, Second Treatise of Civil Government chs. 2-3, 7-19.

    38. A. S. Miller, Democratic Dictatorship, The Emergent Constitution
of Control 31 (1981).

    39. *E.g.,* Kristol, *The Worst Is Yet to Come,* Wall Street Journal, Nov.
26, 1979 (editorial page).

    40. *See, e.g.,* V. Ferkiss, *supra* note 9, ch. 5. *See generally* R. Heilbroner,
An Inquiry into the Human Prospect (paperback ed. 1974).

    41. *See, e.g.,* R. Heilbroner, *supra* note 40, at 46-55 (stressing especially
the atmosphere's limited capacity to absorb heat without long-term climac-
tic changes).

    42. This limit might be avoided by positing an infinite universe open to
human exploitation, but the relevance of this assertion to the problems
discussed here is limited, even if it is accurate.

    43. *E.g.,* R. Heilbroner, *supra* note 40, at 56-57.

    44. *See, e.g.,* V. Ferkiss, *supra* note 9, at 57-58.

    45. *See, e.g.,* R. Heilbroner, *supra* note 40, at 82-95.

    46. A. S. Miller, *supra* note 38, at 226.

    47. *See, e.g.,* Kristol, *supra* note 39.

    48. *See, e.g.,* R. Heilbroner, *supra* note 40, at 32-40.

    49. *Id.* at 42-45.

    50. I generally regard this threat as genuine, but acceptance of the
argument made here does not depend on this assumption. All that is required for this is that the threat *might* be genuine (thus creating another
more or less probable constraint); that relevant decision makers will perceive it as genuine and will act accordingly; or that they will adopt this
line for domestic political reasons of all sorts and act accordingly.

    51. *See* A. S. Miller, *supra* note 38, at 162-66.

    52. *See* L. Thurow, The Zero-Sum Society (1980).

    53. *Cf.* M. Olsen, The Logic of Collective Action (1965).

54. Something of this sort may be the practical effect of Reagan economic policies in 1981-1982.

55. *See* A. Hacker, The End of the American Era 217 (1970).

56. *See, e.g.*, R. Heilbroner, *supra* note 40, at 114-16.

57. *Id.* at 119.

58. *See* the text accompanying notes 5, 9, and 10 in chapter 5.

59. R. Heilbroner, *supra* note 40, at 119.

60. *See id.* at 142-43.

61. A good example is W. Harmon, *The Coming Transformation*, Futurist (April 1977), at 106.

62. There are also some reasons to question its internal consistency and viability. For example, what happens if decentralized communities decide upon pollution, racial discrimination, or the sole exploitation of valuable local resources? How will traditional liberal values be reconciled with the new spiritualism and emphasis on the community? How will such communities defend themselves in an age when technologically sophisticated weaponry is often decisive? To some extent, these problems might be avoided by positing a worldwide consensus on the new values, but this is just the problem.

63. A. S. Miller, *supra* note 38, at 227.

64. *Id.*

65. Perhaps technological advance will make possible the widespread inculcation of appropriate values. But to the extent that liberalism is open to all values, this creates an obvious problem: which values are to be chosen? As the beginning of chapter 5 suggests, it is not obvious that liberalism can provide a definitive answer, although some new philosophy presumably could. Also, it could be argued that an extreme embrace of technology will give rise to a new consciousness through some sort of dialectical reversal in which a one-sided form of consciousness reverts to its opposite. This argument, though, would have to be founded on something like Hegelian or Marxist premises.

66. This generalization, I think, would include any contemporary Marxists.

67. That is, it may partially, but only partially, resolve the problem posed *supra* at note 55 and accompanying text.

68. *See, e.g.*, A. Hacker, *supra* note 55, at 208-17 on the demise of the traditional restraints created by community, church, family, and so forth.

69. These may include external techniques effecting significant internal changes.

70. *See* A. S. Miller, *supra* note 38, chs. 5-6.

71. *See id.* at 113. *See also id.* ch. 8.

72. *See, e.g.*, R. Heilbroner, Business Civilization in Decline 32-38 (paperback ed. 1976).

73. *Cf.* D. Bell, The Cultural Contradictions of Capitalism 239-43 (1976).

74. *E.g.*, R. Heilbroner, *supra* note 72, at 33.

75. *E.g.*, A. S. Miller, *Constitutional Law: Crisis Government Becomes the Norm*, 39 Ohio St. L. J. 736, 748-49 (1978).

76. To some extent, too, they assist in stimulating individuals to consume, as the briefest examination of network television suggests.

77. *E.g.*, A. S. Miller, *supra* note 38, at 177-78.

78. This is described in the next section.

79. W. Scott & D. Hart, Organizational America 210 (paperback ed. 1979).

80. *Id.*

81. *See* notes 31-33 and accompanying text in chapter 5.

82. *See* Z. Pelczynski (ed.), Hegel's Political Philosophy: Problems and Perspectives 1-29, esp. 13-14 (Cambridge paperback ed. 1971). *See also* A. S. Miller, *supra* note 38, at 54-69.

83. There are other possibilities, though the rise of Reaganism makes them seem less likely than previously. One is dominance by what the neoconservatives call the "New Class"—that liberal amalgamation of academics, media people, regulatory personnel, intellectuals, and so forth. Here, power would be more likely to reside in formally public bodies, with corporate interests somewhat subdued and quality-of-life concerns somewhat in the ascendancy. Also, organized labor might forge an alliance with the New Class or instead might become a junior partner in a corporate-dominated future.

84. R. Heilbroner, *supra* note 72, at 35-36. As the title of Heilbroner's book suggests, though, the long-run trend may be away from business dominance, with corporatist tendencies only a passing phase on the road to a genuine statism.

85. The most recent example is *In re* R.____ M. J.____, 50 U.S.L.W. 4185 (1982). Some "commercial speech" cases, though, could fairly be regarded as breaking up state-sanctioned schemes of price maintenance and allowing price competition by freeing channels of consumer information. *See, e.g.*, Va. State Bd. of Pharmacy v. Va. Consumer Council, 425 U.S. 748 (1976).

86. *See* First Nat'l Bank of Boston v. Bellotti, 435 U.S. 765 (1978); Consolidated Edison Co. v. Pub. Serv. Comm'n, 447 U.S. 530 (1980).

87. On this, *see* notes 31-58 and accompanying text in chapter 3. On the revival, *see, e.g.*, Schwartz, *Old Wine in New Bottles? The Renaissance of the Contract Clause*, 1979 Sup. Ct. Rev. 95.

88. Allied Structural Steel Co. v. Spannaus, 438 U.S. 234 (1978) (striking down state legislation protecting the pension rights of discharged employees because it impaired the contract obligations created by a pre-

existing private pension plan). *See* L. Tribe, American Constitutional Law 45-50 (1979 Supp.).

89. L. Tribe, *supra* note 88, at 50. *See also id.* at 56.

90. On this, *see* notes 89-112 and accompanying text in chapter 3. The key case here is Jackson v. Metropolitan Edison Co., 419 U.S. 345 (1974).

91. Miller uses the mechanical metaphor of the computer, in which people are tiny parts. A. S. Miller, *supra* note 38, at 175.

92. It should be clear that the relative presence or absence of negative freedom may have little to do with the question of concern in chapter 3: whether its presence or absence is a living reality for most people. Obviously, for instance, some people in totalitarian regimes can come to love their chains. On the other hand, even slight restrictions could come to seem extremely burdensome in a highly individualistic climate.

93. Here, I am referring to the text accompanying notes 6, 10, and 11 in chapter 5.

94. I. Kristol, Two Cheers for Capitalism 268 (1978).

95. A. S. Miller, *supra* note 38, at 7, 20, 177-78.

96. W. Scott & D. Hart, *supra* note 79, at 181.

97. *Id.* at 192.

98. *See id.* ch. 8.

99. A. S. Miller, *supra* note 38, at 180.

Bibliography

Avineri, Shlomo. *Hegel's Theory of the Modern State.* Cambridge: At the Press, 1972.

Bell, Daniel. *The Coming of Post-Industrial Society.* New York: Basic Books, 1973.

———. *The Cultural Contradictions of Capitalism.* New York: Basic Books, 1976.

Bentley, Arthur. *The Process of Government.* 1908. Reprint. Evanston: Principia Press of Illinois, 1935.

Bergmann, Frithjof. *On Being Free.* Notre Dame: University of Notre Dame Press, 1977.

Bergold, Laurel. "The Changing Legal Status of American Women." *Current History* 40 (1976): 206.

Berle, Adolf A. "Constitutional Limitations on Corporate Activity—Protection of Personal Rights from Invasion through Economic Power." *University of Pennsylvania Law Review* 100 (1952): 933.

Berlin, Isaiah. *Four Essays on Liberty.* London: Oxford University Press, 1969.

Bierstedt, Robert. *The Social Order.* 4th ed. New York: McGraw-Hill, 1974.

Brown, J. A. C. *The Social Psychology of Industry: Human Relations in the Factory.* Baltimore: Penguin Books, 1954.

Bosanquet, Bernard. *The Philosophical Theory of the State.* 4th ed. 1923. Reprint. London: Macmillan, 1925.

Bradley, Francis Herbert. *Ethical Studies.* 2d ed. 1927. Reprint. London: Oxford University Press, 1962.

Burnham, James. *Suicide of the West.* New York: John Day, 1964.

———. *The Managerial Revolution.* 1941. Reprint. Bloomington: Indiana University Press, 1960.

———. "Notes on Morality, Authority, Power." *National Review* 22
     (1970): 1283.
Capra, Fritjof. *The Turning Point.* New York: Simon and Schuster, 1982.
Conant, Michael. *The Constitution and Capitalism.* St. Paul, Minn.: West, 1974.
Corwin, Edward S. *Liberty against Government.* 1948. Reprint. Westport,
     Conn.: Greenwood Press, 1978.
Crozier, Michel J.; Huntington, Samuel P.; and Watanuk, Toji. *The Crisis
     of Democracy,* New York: New York University Press, 1975.
Dorsen, Norman; Bender, Paul; and Neuborne, Burt. *Emerson, Haber and
     Dorsen's Political and Civil Rights in the United States,* vol. 1.
     Boston: Little, Brown, 1976.
Dworkin, Ronald. "Three Concepts of Liberalism." *New Republic,*
     April 14, 1979.
Ehrlich, Eugen. *Fundamental Principles of the Sociology of Law.* New
     York: Russell & Russell, 1962.
Elliot, Ward E. Y. *The Rise of Guardian Democracy: The Supreme
     Court's Role in Voting Rights Disputes, 1845-1969.* Cambridge:
     Harvard University Press, 1974.
Ely, John Hart. "The Constitutionality of Reverse Racial Discrimination."
     University of Chicago Law Review 41 (1974): 723.
Engdahl, David. *Constitutional Power: Federal and State.* St. Paul, Minn.:
     West, 1978.
Ewing, David. *Freedom inside the Organization: Bringing Civil Liberties
     to the Workplace.* New York: McGraw-Hill, 1977.
Ferkiss, Victor. *The Future of Technological Civilization.* New York:
     George Braziller, 1974.
Friedmann, Wolfgang. *Law in a Changing Society.* 2d ed. Harmondsworth,
     Middlesex: Penguin Books, 1972.
———. *Legal Theory.* 5th ed. London: Stevens & Sons, 1967.
Galbraith, John Kenneth. *The New Industrial State.* 2d ed. Boston:
     Houghton Mifflin, 1971.
———. *Economics and the Public Purpose.* Boston: Houghton-Mifflin,
     1973.
Glazer, Nathan. *Affirmative Discrimination: Ethnic Inequality and
     Public Policy.* New York: Basic Books, 1975.
Goodwin, Richard. *The American Condition.* Garden City, N.Y.: Double-
     day, 1974.
Green, Thomas Hill. *Lectures on the Principles of Political Obligation.*
     1882. Reprint. Ann Arbor: University of Michigan Press, 1967.
———. *Prolegomena to Ethics.* Edited by A. C. Bradley. New York:
     Thomas Y. Crowell Co., Apollo Edition, 1969.
———. *Works of Thomas Hill Green.* Edited by R. L. Nettleship. London:
     Longmans, Green & Co., 1900.

Gunther, Gerald. *Cases and Materials on Constitutional Law.* 10th ed. Mineola, N.Y.: Foundation Press, 1980.

Hacker, Andrew. *The End of the American Era.* New York: Atheneum, 1970.

Hafen, Bruce. "Children's Liberation and the New Egalitarianism: Some Reservations about Abandoning Youth to their 'Rights'." *Brigham Young University Law Review* (1979): 605.

Hale, Robert. "The Supreme Court and the Contract Clause." *Harvard Law Review* 57 (1944): 512, 621, 852.

Harmon, Willis. "The Coming Transformation." *Futurist* (April 1977): 106.

Hartz, Louis. *The Liberal Tradition in America.* New York: Harcourt, Brace, 1955.

Hegel, Georg W. F. *Hegel's Philosophy of Right.* 1821. Reprint. London: Oxford University Press, 1973.

Heilbroner, Robert. *An Inquiry into the Human Prospect.* New York: W. W. Norton, 1974.

———. *Beyond Boom and Crash.* New York: W. W. Norton, 1978.

———. *Business Civilization in Decline.* New York: W. W. Norton, 1976.

Hirsch, Fred. *Social Limits to Growth.* Cambridge: Harvard University Press, 1976.

Hobbes, Thomas. *Leviathan.* Translated by Michael Oakeshott. New York: Macmillan, Collier Books, 1962.

Hobhouse, L. T. *Liberalism.* 1911. Reprint. London: Oxford University Press, 1979.

Horwitz, Morton. "The Jurisprudence of *Brown* and the Dilemmas of Liberalism." *Harvard Civil Rights—Civil Liberties Law Review* 7 (1979): 599.

Karst, Kenneth. "Foreword: Equal Citizenship under the Fourteenth Amendment." *Harvard Law Review* 91 (1977): 1.

Kristol, Irving. *On the Democratic Idea in America.* New York: Harper and Row, 1972.

———. *Two Cheers for Capitalism.* New York: Basic Books, 1978.

Krutch, Joseph Wood. *Human Nature and the Human Condition.* New York: Random House, 1959.

———. *The Modern Temper.* New York: Harcourt, Brace, 1929.

Kurland, Philip. "Ruminations on the Quality of Equality." *Brigham Young University Law Review* (1979): 1.

Lasch, Christopher. *Haven in a Heartless World: The Family Besieged.* New York: Basic Books, 1977.

———. *The Culture of Narcissism.* New York: W. W. Norton, 1978.

Leiss, William. *The Domination of Nature.* Boston: Beacon Press, 1974.

Lekachman, Robert. *Greed Is Not Enough: Reaganomics.* New York:

Pantheon Books, 1982.

Linton, Ralph. *The Study of Man*. New York: D. Appleton-Century Co., 1936.

Locke, John. *Two Treatises of Government*. Edited by Thomas I. Cook. New York: Hafner, 1947.

Lowi, Theodore. *The End of Liberalism: The Second Republic of the United States*. 2d ed. New York: W. W. Norton, 1979.

Maccoby, Michael. *The Gamesman*. New York: Simon and Schuster, 1976.

MacIntyre, Alasdair. *After Virtue*. Notre Dame: Notre Dame University Press, 1981.

———, ed. *Hegel: A Collection of Critical Essays*. Notre Dame: Notre Dame University Press, 1976.

Maine, Sir Henry. *Ancient Law*. 1861. Reprint. Boston: Beacon Press, 1963.

Mason, Alpheus T. *The Supreme Court from Taft to Warren*. Rev. ed. Baton Rouge: Louisiana State University Press, 1968.

Matson, Floyd W. *The Broken Image: Man, Science and Society*. New York: George Braziller, 1964.

Mayo, Elton. *The Social Problems of an Industrial Civilization*. Boston: Division of Research, Graduate School of Business Administration, Harvard University, 1945.

Michels, Robert. *Political Parties*. Translated by Eden and Cedar Paul. Glencoe, Ill.: Free Press, 1958.

Miller, Arthur S. "Constitutional Law: Crisis Government Becomes the Norm." *Ohio State Law Journal* 39 (1978): 736.

———. *Democratic Dictatorship: The Emergent Constitution of Control*. Westport, Conn.: Greenwood Press, 1981.

———. "A Modest Proposal for Helping to Tame the Corporate Beast." *Hofstra Law Review* 8 (1979): 79.

———. *The Modern Corporate State: Private Governments and the American Constitution*. Westport, Conn.: Greenwood Press, 1976.

———. "On Politics, Democracy and the First Amendment: A Commentary on *First National Bank of Boston v. Bellotti*." *Washington and Lee Law Review* 38: (1981): 21.

———. "Reason of State and the Emergent Constitution of Control." *Minnesota Law Review* 64 (1980): 585.

———. *The Supreme Court and American Capitalism*. New York: Free Press, 1968.

———. "Toward 'Constitutionalizing' the Corporation: A Speculative Essay." *West Virginia Law Review* 80 (1978): 187.

———. "Toward a Concept of Constitutional Duty." *Supreme Court Review* (1968): 199.

Muller, Herbert J. *Issues of Freedom: Paradoxes and Promises*. New

York: Harper and Brothers, 1960.

Nisbet, Robert A. *The Quest for Community*. New York: Oxford University Press, 1953.

Oakeshott, Michael. *Hobbes on Civil Association*. Berkeley: University of California Press, 1975.

Olson, Mancur. *The Logic of Collective Action: Public Goods and the Theory of Groups*. Rev. ed. New York: Schocken Books, 1971.

Parsons, Talcott. *Essays in Sociological Theory*. Rev. ed. Glencoe, Ill.: Free Press, 1954.

Pelcyznski, Z. A., ed. *Hegel's Political Philosophy: Problems and Perspectives*. Cambridge: At the Press, 1971.

Perry, Michael. "Modern Equal Protection: A Conceptualization and Appraisal." *Columbia Law Review* 79 (1979): 1023.

Phillips, Michael J. "The Life and Times of the Contract Clause." *American Business Law Journal* 20 (1982): 139.

——. "Neutrality and Purposiveness in the Application of Strict Scrutiny to Racial Classifications." *Temple Law Quarterly*, in press.

——. "Status and Freedom in American Constitutional Law." *Emory Law Journal* 29 (1980): 3.

——. "Thomas Hill Green, Positive Freedom and the United States Supreme Court." *Emory Law Journal* 25 (1976): 63.

Pirsig, Robert M. *Zen and the Art of Motorcycle Maintenance*. New York: William Morrow, 1974.

Plant, Raymond. *Hegel*. Bloomington: Indiana University Press, 1975.

Plato. *The Republic*. In Edith Hamilton and Huntington Cairns, eds. *Plato: The Collected Dialogues*. Princeton: Princeton University Press, 1961.

Ratner, David. "Corporations and the Constitution." *University of San Francisco Law Review* 15 (1980-81): 11.

Riesman, David. *The Lonely Crowd*. Abridged ed. New Haven: Yale University Press, 1961.

Rifkin, Jeremy. *The Emergin Order: God in the Age of Scarcity*. New York: G. P. Putnam's Sons, 1979.

Roberts, Barry S. "Toward a General Theory of Commercial Speech and the First Amendment." *Ohio State Law Journal* 40 (1979): 115.

Sabine, George. *A History of Political Theory*. 3d ed. New York: Holt, Rinehart and Winston, 1961.

Schumacher, E. F. *A Guide for the Perplexed*. New York: Harper and Row, 1977.

——. *Small Is Beautiful: Economics as if People Mattered*. New York: Harper and Row, 1975.

Schwartz, Bernard. *A Commentary on the Constitution of the United States*. New York: Macmillan, 1963.

———. *The American Heritage History of the Law in America*. New York: American Heritage Publishing Co., 1974.

———. "Old Wine in Old Bottles? The Renaissance of the Contract Clause." *Supreme Court Review* (1979): 95.

Scott, William C., and Hart, David K. *Organizational America*. Boston: Houghton Mifflin, 1979.

Shklar, Judith. *Freedom and Independence: A Study of the Political Ideas of Hegel's Phenomenology of Mind*. Cambridge: At the Press, 1976.

Stone, Julius. *Human Law and Human Justice*. Stanford: Stanford University Press, 1965.

———. *Social Dimensions of Law and Justice*. Stanford: Stanford University Press, 1966.

Strauss, Leo. *The Political Philosophy of Hobbes*. Translated by Elsa Sinclair. Chicago: University of Chicago Press, Phoenix Books, 1952.

Taylor, Charles. *Hegel and Modern Society*. Cambridge: Cambridge University Press, 1979.

Thorson, Thomas Landon. *The Logic of Democracy*. New York: Holt, Rinehart and Winston, 1962.

Thurow, Lester. *The Zero-Sum Society: Distribution and the Possibilities for Economic Change*. New York: Basic Books, 1980.

Tribe, Laurence. *American Constitutional Law*. Mineola, N.Y.: Foundation Press, 1978.

Trubeck, David. "Toward a Social Theory of Law: An Essay on the Study of Law and Development." *Yale Law Journal* 82 (1972): 1.

Unger, Roberto M. *Knowledge and Politics*. New York: Free Press, 1975.

———. *Law in Modern Society: Toward a Criticism of Social Theory*. New York: Free Press, 1976.

Van Alstyne, William. "Rites of Passage: Race, the Supreme Court and the Constitution." *University of Chicago Law Review* 46 (1979): 775.

Whyte, William. *The Organization Man*. New York: Simon and Schuster, 1956.

Wilson, Colin. *The Outsider*. Boston: Houghton Mifflin, 1956.

Wolin, Sheldon. *Politics and Vision: Continuity and Innovation in Western Political Thought*. Boston: Little, Brown, 1960.

Wright, Charles Alan. "The Constitution on the Campus." *Vanderbilt Law Review* 22 (1969): 1027.

Yankelovich, Daniel. *New Rules: Searching for Self-Fulfillment in a World Turned Upside Down*. New York: Random House, 1981.

Index

Achieved status: defined, 8; as including organizational statuses, 92-94; and negative freedom generally, 9, 19-20; and positive freedom generally, 13, 69-70. *See also* Government employees; Homosexuals; Military personnel; Prisoners; Tribal Indians

Aliens: constitutional status of, 47-50; and equal protection, 48, 122-23. *See also* Orientals

Analytical positivism. *See* Legal positivism

Ascribed status: and authoritarian positive freedom generally, 10, 103-4; defined, 8; and negative freedom generally, 8-9, 19-20; in organizations, 103-4. *See also* Aliens; Blacks; Children; Homosexuals; Illegitimates; Mental patients; Orientals; Reverse statuses; Tribal Indians; Women

Ascriptive status. *See* Ascribed status

Authoritarian positive freedom: and ascribed status, 10, 103-4; and blacks, 31-32; and children, 24-25, 28-29, 30; defined, 5-6; and organizational status, 103-4, 206-7; and status generally, 9-12; and tribal Indians, 40-41; and women, 21-22

Baker v. *Carr,* 142

Bell, Daniel, 170

Bentley, Arthur, 71

Bergmann, Frithjof, 158-59

Black, Hugo, 44

Blackmun, Harry, 41, 129-30

Blacks: discrimination favoring, 35-36, 124, 127-45; equal protection and discrimination against, 35, 51, 122-23; general constitutional status of, 30-36; social significance of traditional status, 164

Bosanquet, Bernard, 41, 104; conception of the state,

203-4, 206; incompleteness
of, 154-55; and organiza-
tional statuses, 98-100; relation to liberal positive freedom, 156; and reverse
statuses, 121, 131-32, 134,
136, 138-39, 145; and school
integration, 140-41
Nisbet, Robert 19, 153-54, 162,
171

Oakeshott, Michael, 142
Ogden v. *Saunders,* 77
One man-one vote, 142-45
Organization. *See* Group
Organizational statuses; clash
with negative freedom, 98-
100; "communitarian" ex-
planation for, 167-74; as
facilitating organizational
control, 94-98, 203-7; as
fused with liberal positive
freedom, 98-109; future relation to freedom, 206-7;
genesis in liberal individualism, 164-74; as statuses
generally, 92-94
Orientals, constitutional status
of, 42-45, 122-23. *See also*
Aliens
Other-direction, 105-6

Parsons, Talcott, 8
Pitney, Mahlon, 80-81
Plato, 5, 28, 103, 195; on
genesis of tyranny, 189-93.
Works: *Republic,* 189-93
Plessy v. *Ferguson,* 33-34,
35
Police power, 77-78, 83-84, 169;
defined, 112 n.52
Positive freedom, 4-5. *See also*
Authoritarian positive free-

dom; Liberal positive
freedom
Positive state, 70-71, 72, 73;
and constitutional doctrine,
78, 81-82, 82-84, 86-87; as
undermining rule of law,
89-90
Positivism. *See* Legal positivism
Powell, Lewis, 127-30
Prisoners, constitutional status
of, 50-52, 164
Procedural due process, 79
Professional schools, 134-35
Proportional representation.
See Reverse statuses, and
proportional representation
Public function doctrine. *See*
State action, public function doctrine
Public-private blurring, 71-73;
as evidenced by state action
doctrine, 84-88; future
growth of, 202

Rational basis test. *See* Equal
protection, rational basis
test
Reagan, Ronald, 165
*Regents of the University of
California* v. *Bakke,* 126-30,
132-35, 136, 140
Rehnquist, William, 20, 50-51,
52-53, 54-55, 130
Religion, 198-99; social sig-
nificance of, 162-64
Reverse discrimination. *See*
statuses
Reverse racial preferences.
See Reverse statuses
Reverse statuses: in employ-
ment, 135-38; and equal pro-
tection, 123-35; and group

About the Author

MICHAEL J. PHILLIPS is Associate Professor of Business
Law at Indiana University's School of Business. He holds a
J.D. degree from Columbia University, an LL.M. and an
S.J.D. from the National Law Center at George Washington
University.

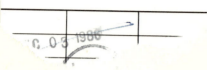

Date Due